Reading just the first paragraph in Ann Spangler's exquisitely written book carried my mind into a cozy, candlelit scene, sitting at the feet of a master storyteller. Her colorful descriptions and dancing phrasing served to paint moving pictures in my imagination. I could "see" the Bible stories in a way that illuminated them as never before. Clearly, *Less Than Perfect* is a pleasure to read and a must for anyone desiring to know the men and women of the Scriptures more intimately and see more of ourselves through them.

SUSAN GREGORY, bestselling author,
The Daniel Fast

As children we enjoyed our storybook Bibles, with brightly colored illustrations and sanitized stories about our flannelgraph heroes. In *Less Than Perfect*, Ann Spangler invites us to take a grown-up look at biblical characters and meditate on how God used them despite their lack of storybook perfection. I especially enjoyed her vibrant tale-telling and many cultural insights. Each chapter is sprinkled with nuggets from the ancient world that shed new light on the lives of biblical characters in the world that they knew.

LOIS TVERBERG, author, *Reading
the Bible with Rabbi Jesus*

Ann Spangler's latest book *Less Than Perfect* is a moving tribute to the fact that God uses broken people who are often seen as failures to others. These are beautifully written stories that will touch the deepest part of your heart and inspire a fresh faith in Jesus Christ and his grace.

JIM CYMBALA, Senior Pastor,
The Brooklyn Tabernacle

D0424765

Ann Spangler has a gift of making the Bible come alive. Her beautiful storytelling combined with historical insights give us powerful lessons we can apply to our own less-than-perfect lives.

Ann Spangler makes Bible people feel like close cousins—if not like us ourselves. Taking us by the hand, she guides us through these ancient lives with a contemporary lens that's candid, courageous, inspiring, and insightful. With Ann Spangler, such Bible voyages are always remarkable journeys. Don't miss this one!

In her vividly but faithfully imagined vignettes of thirty biblical characters, Ann Spangler unerringly gets to the heart of the matter: God always works with deeply flawed people, and he often works in spite of them. Ann's rich portraits capture the strangeness of each character's times and yet the familiarity of their situations. These stories—of Adam and Eve and their varied offspring—warn and encourage us both: after all, we too are sons of Adam and daughters of Eve, and these stories are our stories. They remind us of what runs in our blood and of the One whose blood can redeem it all.

Those who think the Bible is full of perfect people have never really read the Bible at all. In these less-than-perfect people we find more than we expect. Thank you, Ann, for helping us use our imagination to feed our souls. Ann reminds us that there is only one kind of person—broken. As she invites us to run our fingers over the jagged edges of these biblical lives, we are reminded of our own complexity and our own great need of God's patience. Ann is a master storyteller! She makes the people of Scripture as vibrant as those we meet in a novel or in daily life. No one-dimensional saints here! Only desperate people—whether they know it or not—in need of God.

DERON SPOO, pastor, First Baptist Tulsa;
author, *The Good Book: 40 Chapters*
That Reveal the Bible's Biggest Ideas

Ann Spangler's knowledge and understanding of ancient history, laws, and cultures allow her to weave informative commentary between the pages of Scripture. Through detailed descriptions of scenes and emotions, the stories and characters come alive, giving the reader a front-row seat as the drama unfolds. The author's creative retelling of Bible stories reminds us again how God used flawed and less than perfect people in his ultimate plan for redemption.

CRYSTAL BOWMAN, bestselling, award-winning
author of more than 100 books for children,
including *Our Daily Bread for Kids, Devotions*
for Beginning Readers, and *M is for Manger*

OTHER BOOKS BY ANN SPANGLER

Finding the Peace God Promises

He's Been Faithful (Carol Cymbala with Ann Spangler)

*I Am with You: Daily Meditations on
Knowing and Experiencing God*

Men of the Bible (coauthored with Robert Wolgemuth)

The Names of God: 52 Bible Studies for Individuals and Groups

The Names of God Bible (general editor)

The One-Year Devotions for Women

Praying the Names of God

Praying the Names of Jesus

The Rescue (Jim Cymbala with Ann Spangler)

She Who Laughs, Lasts!

Sitting at the Feet of Rabbi Jesus
(coauthored with Lois Tverberg)

The Tender Words of God

Women of the Bible (coauthored with Jean Syswerda)

LESS THAN PERFECT

Broken Men and Women of the Bible
and What We Can Learn from Them

ANN SPANGLER

ZONDERVAN

Less Than Perfect
Copyright © 2018 by Ann Spangler

Requests for information should be addressed to:
Zondervan, *3900 Sparks Dr. SE, Grand Rapids, Michigan 49546*

ISBN 978-0-310-34172-7 (softcover)
ISBN 978-0-310-35542-7 (audio)
ISBN 978-0-310-34173-4 (ebook)

Published in association with Yates & Yates, www.yates2.com.

Art direction: Curt Diepenhorst
Interior design: Denise Froehlich
Editorial: Sandra Vander Zicht, Robert Hudson

First printing May 2018 / Printed in the United States of America

CONTENTS

INTRODUCTION

Before one word of the Bible was ever written down, its stories and instructions were spoken aloud. Though modern cultures rely heavily on the writings they produce, many ancient cultures shared and recorded their stories and faithfully handed them down by telling them from one generation to the next.

Certainly that must have been how many of the stories included in this book were first told and retold and then passed from generation to generation, perhaps around a campfire under starry skies. When the sun went down and their work was done, people shared a meal and told stories about their nation and tribe, entertaining each other with memories of colorful characters and events—real people whom their parents, grandparents, and great grandparents had known.

Some unsavory stories, like the ones about Amnon or about Samson's wicked girlfriend, Delilah, may have been reserved for later, to be told only after the children went to bed. The stories remained remarkably accurate because of the way they were reported, and these and other stories eventually made their way into the Bible we read today.

From their earliest years, children would have considered the stories of people like Sarah, Jacob, and Judah, as part of their family history. These characters were like elderly aunts and uncles who happened to be the first shoots on their family tree.

Unlike other holy books, the Bible never whitewashes its characters. That's part of what makes it so believable. We sense that the people who populate its pages are real human beings with many of the same vulnerabilities and problems that trouble our world. If the Bible were merely a puff piece, surely several of these stories would never have made their way into its pages.

For all our attempts to introduce children to the Bible, Scripture is essentially a book for adults. That means we need to get beyond the Sunday School versions of these stories. In *Less Than Perfect* I've done my best to reimagine them in a way that will bring them to life in today's world. Though fictional techniques are used to tease out certain elements in the story, I have tried to tread lightly in order to keep them as close to the biblical text as possible. Because the stories occurred in a world that's distant from ours in both time and culture, I have woven in background information to act as a bridge between the past and the present. My goal is to make it as easy as possible for you to walk across that bridge so you can read these stories and understand them in much the same way as those who heard them thousands of years ago would have.

The phrase *less than perfect* may seem like a vast understatement when it comes to some of the people whose stories are featured, characters like Herod the Great or his wicked granddaughter Herodias, for instance. Can even their lives instruct us? For those who believe Scripture to be the inspired Word of God, these and other stories are in the Bible for a reason. In retelling them, I will try to uncover what we can learn about God, ourselves, and the less than perfect world in which we live.

Many years ago, the Russian writer Alexander Solzhenitsyn, astutely remarked: "If only there were evil people somewhere, insidiously committing evil deeds, and it were necessary only to separate them from the rest of us and destroy them. But the line dividing good and evil cuts through the heart of every human being. And who is willing to destroy a piece of his own heart"[1]

The Bible illustrates the truth of this. In its first few pages we see Adam and Eve living happily in the garden paradise God had created for them. But after only a few paragraphs they begin to lean toward darkness, listening to lies that will plunge them into a broken world of their own making. Consequent themes of deception, alienation, and violence thread their way through all the stories that follow. Even David, one of the Bible's greatest heroes, who is called "a man after God's own heart," has a shadow side that causes tremendous pain to those around him.

Instead of cluttering the stories with citations to track each and every quotation from the Bible, I've tried to streamline things by including information to help you find where each story appears in Scripture. In some cases, the story cannot be fully explored without visiting a variety of places in the Bible where the character appears and then reappears. To increase your grasp of Scripture, each story is capped with a brief section, entitled "The Times." This is where you will find a little more information about the historical and cultural context in which it unfolded. For those who want to delve even deeper, the last section of each chapter, entitled "The Takeaway," includes questions for discussion and reflection designed for individual or group Bible study.

Whether you read the Bible straight through or trace it from the underside—by reading about some of its most broken men and women—I hope you will realize that it is and always has been the world's greatest storybook. The more familiar you become with its stories, the more you will begin to recognize the creative hand beneath them all until one day it will dawn on you that there is only one great story being told, and that is the story of how God saves us by entering into our broken world and becoming one of us.

CHAPTER 1

THE STORY OF ADAM

How Eating the Wrong Thing
Wrecked Everything

For dust you are and to dust you will return.

GENESIS 3:19

On a day before days were made, God begins to do something so stupendous and surprising that no one could have imagined it, assuming there had been anyone around to witness it. He is speaking the universe into being, creating the heavens and the earth. Out of chaos he will carve a world.

So day after day his all-powerful word penetrates the empty darkness, filling it with all manner of beautiful things—earth and sky, mountains and meadows, and great billowing waves that splash and crash into each other as though applauding what God is doing.

Above and beyond the earth float galaxies, too many to count. Like great, swirling bonfires, they set the universe alight, filling it with wonder.

There is music in the heavens above and in the sea below, for the largest of God's creatures sing songs in the watery deep while the smaller ones flit back and forth across the sky, trilling their joy.

Let there be . . . Let there be is all God says, and there are flowers and forests, rivers and streams, and all kinds of wild and wonderful beasts. A noisy world, it overflows with the sounds of bellowing, bleating, braying, chirruping, chortling, hooting, howling, quacking, snorting, and squealing.

But the most wonderful thing of all springs up from the earth itself. For God, who has looked over everything he has made and called it good, bends down in a final burst of energy and scoops up a fistful of dust. But what can he do with dust?

He can make something bold and brave and smart and strong. Something curious and clever, fearless and free. Something that will become Someone. After God forms the dust into a shape he can love, he breathes into its nostrils, and man becomes a living being.

This new creature—an amalgam of dirt and divine possibility, is called *adam*, meaning "of the earth." And so it is that God creates human beings in his image; in the image of God he creates them; male and female he creates them.

By the time the first man arrive on the scene, the Lord God has already planted a garden in the east, in Eden, a special place in which the greatest of his creatures can dwell. It is a paradise, filled with all kinds of trees—ones pleasing to the eye and good for food. Everywhere you look there are winding paths, clear blue pools, and trees laden with fruit. In the middle of this magnificent garden stand two mysterious trees, the tree of life and the tree of the knowledge of good and evil.

God explains that there is just one thing he must not do. "You are free to eat from any tree in the garden," God affirms. "But you must not eat from the tree of the knowledge of good and evil, for when you eat from it you will certainly die" (Genesis 2:16).

Though the Lord begins by emphasizing human freedom to eat from every other tree in the garden, it will not be long before people begin to think of God as a divine killjoy, as though by denying them one thing, he has denied them everything.

Now the Lord God had already formed the creatures of the sea, the birds in the sky, and the animals that dwell on the earth. Bringing each before the man, he waits to see what he will name them. One by one the man pronounces their names: "jackass," "pig," "lion," "cow," "fish," "cat," "hawk," "gazelle," "goat," "fox," "horse," "vulture," "sheep," "elephant," "ape," "camel," "eagle"—the names go on and on. When finally he has named each animal, it

In the ancient world, the act of naming often indicated the assigning of a function or the decreeing of a destiny. As such it was considered an act of authority. ■

———

Lois Tverberg comments that "when God 'operates' on Adam, he takes out *tzela echad*—literally one side of him. The translation of *tzela* as 'rib' occurs only here— everywhere else it refers to one 'side' of something, like when poles were inserted in each of the two sides of the ark in Exodus 37:3."[1] ■

is clear that none of them, no matter how magnificent, talented, beautiful, shapely, or smart they are, is a match for the man himself.

"It isn't good for the man to be alone," God remarks, and then says: "I will make a helper suitable for him." Causing him to fall into a deep sleep, God splits the man and creates a brand new person.

When Adam wakes and sees the stunning companion God has brought him, he is ecstatic, so thrilled in fact that he utters his very first sentence: "This is now bone of my bones and flesh of my flesh; she shall be called 'woman,' for she was taken out of man." Because Adam understands that part of him has gone missing, he wants to have her all to himself.

From then on Adam and Eve, for that is what he will call her, are inseparable. Two innocents in paradise, they are content to explore the length and breadth of their garden home, dangling their feet in its cool refreshing streams as they feast on peaches, pears, pomegranates, figs, dates, melons, almonds, olives, honey, and more. Completing each other, they feel whole and happy. Despite their nakedness, they feel no shame.

One day, while they are strolling in the garden close to the tree of the knowledge of good and evil, they encounter a creature that

Adam had already named, *nahas,* a word whose root means "shiny" and "enchanting." Indeed the serpent is charming, but it is also sly and full of malice.

Wasting no time, it begins a subtle assault. Addressing the woman, the serpent asks, "Did God really say, 'You must not eat from any tree in the garden'?"

While Eve considers how to answer his question, Adam stands passively by. "We may eat fruit from the trees in the garden, but God did say, 'You must not eat fruit from the tree that is in the middle of the garden, and you must not touch it, or you will die.'"

Delighted that the women is willing to converse with him, the cunning creature responds with a flat-out lie topped off with a twisted promise: "You will not certainly die. For God knows that when you eat from it your eyes will be opened, and you will be like God, knowing good and evil."

Interesting that the first lie is a nasty bit of slander about God. Rather than rushing to the Lord's defense or refusing to listen at all, Adam and his wife let the serpent's words slip into their hearts, where they cast a shadow over everything they know about God.

By now they are standing in front of the forbidden tree with fruit so luscious that it begs to be eaten, at least that's what Eve thinks. Emboldened by her conversation with the snake, she reaches out her hand, twists off a piece, and bites into its firm, sweet flesh. Reaching for another, she hands it to Adam, who takes a bite.

Before the two can finish, they feel a tightening in their chests as their hearts harden and constrict. What had once seemed natural and innocent—their frequent and ardent lovemaking—suddenly appears as something beastly and foul. Indeed their eyes have been opened, just as the serpent had promised. But instead of perceiving the good, they see only wrong. Trying to hide from each other, they cover their nakedness with leaves from the fig tree.

Suddenly they hear a sound like the rushing wind. As Adam crouches behind a tree, he hears the Lord calling, "Where are you?"

"I heard you in the garden," Adam says, "and I was afraid because I was naked; so I hid."

"Who told you that you were naked?" God thunders. "Have you eaten from the tree of which I commanded you not to eat?"

"The woman whom you gave me, she gave me some fruit, and I ate." Even to Adam the response sounds cowardly. But he will not take it back.

Turning to Eve, God asks, "What have you done?"

Like Adam, she shifts the blame, saying, "The serpent deceived me, and I ate."

Turning to the serpent God says:

> Because you have done this,
>   you are cursed more than all cattle,
> and more than every beast of the field;
>   on your belly you shall go,
> and you shall eat dust
>   all the days of your life.
> And I will put enmity
>   between you and the woman,
> and between your seed and her Seed;
>   he shall bruise your head,
>   and you shall bruise His heel.

To Adam, God says: "Because you have heeded the voice of

your wife, and have eaten from the tree of which I commanded you, saying, 'You shall not eat of it':

> Cursed is the ground for your sake;
>> in toil you shall eat of it
>> all the days of your life.
> Both thorns and thistles it shall bring forth for you,
>> and you shall eat the herb of the field.
> In the sweat of your face you shall eat bread
>> till you return to the ground,
>> for out of it you were taken;
> for dust you are,
>> and to dust you shall return.

That's how the very first human beings—created from the dust of the ground and the breath of God—fell from their lofty place. Instead of ruling the earth with ease, they learn that the earth will rule them. Rather than remaining a lush garden paradise, it will resist their labor from morning 'til night until finally it swallows them whole. No matter how much sweat they expend, nothing will prevent them from returning to their beginnings, to the ground from which they came.

After clothing them in garments of skin, God says, "The man has now become like one of us, knowing good and evil. He must not be allowed to reach out his hand and take also from the tree of life and eat, and live forever." To prevent Adam and his wife from eating the fruit, which would make them immortal and doom them to a never-ending life of sin, he banishes them from Eden, stationing cherubim and a flaming sword to guard the way to the tree of life.

Fortunately God still loves everything and everyone he has made. In the midst of pronouncing judgment, he promises the woman that one from among her offspring will someday crush the serpent's head.

Even after hearing the grievous sentence that God has rendered for sin, Adam expresses his hope for the world's future by naming his wife Eve, because "she will become the mother of all the living."

After innumerable years and too many sorrows to count, a daughter of Eve whose name is Mary, will give birth to a son. He will be a new Adam, rescuing the world from its sin.

THE TIMES

Adam's story took place before recorded time.
His story is told in Genesis 1–4.

The Hebrew title for the book of Genesis is *Bereshith*, which is also the first word of the Bible. English translations render it "In the beginning." Though the first two chapters of Genesis paint creation as a world of perfect beauty and harmony, the peace that characterized God's world was quickly shattered when Eve and then Adam disobeyed God.

According to Genesis 1:27, "God created mankind [*adam*] in his own image, in the image of God he created them; male and female he created them." In the first three chapters of Genesis the Hebrew word *adam* can be translated "man," "mankind," "human," or "human being," though English translations often translate it as a proper name. Technically, "Adam" does not appear as a proper name until Genesis 4:25.

It is interesting to note that when Jesus was asked about divorce, he responded by recalling the creation account: "Haven't you read . . . that at the beginning the Creator 'made them male and female,' and said, 'For this reason a man will leave his father and mother and be united to his wife, and the two will become one flesh'? So they are no longer two, but one flesh. Therefore what God has joined together, let no one separate" (Matthew 19:4–6). As Lois Tverberg has pointed out, even before the time of Jesus, Jewish sages believed that "in marriage, a man and woman are reunited back together into one complete person because somehow they were originally made together in the first place."[2]

When Adam disobeyed God, he lost not only his home but also

the intimate relationship he had always enjoyed with his Creator. Additionally, his work of caring for creation would become not a joy and a delight, but something bruising and painful because the earth would resist him at every turn. Though the first man was formed from both lower and higher elements—the dust of the ground and the breath of God (Genesis 2:7)—it would be the lower elements that would prevail. In the end he would die and be consigned to the dust.

With the first sin came brokenness, conflict, pain, disease, suffering, sorrow, and death. It created a division within the human heart, alienating us from God, others, and even ourselves. It would take a new Adam to heal the breach that sin created.

THE TAKEAWAY

1. Take a moment to paint a picture in your mind of what life was like before and after Adam disobeyed God. What do you see?

2. Sin entered the world through the eyes and ears of a man and woman. Describe times in your own life when you failed to listen to God.

3. Notice that the first lie in the history of the world was about God's character. Note too that Jesus called the devil "a liar and the father of lies" (John 8:44). What lies about God have you been tempted to believe?

4. To some extent, the story of the first human beings tells us not only about what happened once but also about what always happens. How does this account of the world's beginnings provide insight into our world today? How does it provide insight into your own struggles?

CHAPTER 2

THE STORY OF EVE

The Lie That Broke God's Beautiful World

The heart is deceitful above all things, and
desperately wicked: who can know it?

JEREMIAH 17:9

Bzzt, bzzt. She swats the flies away, but they keep on coming, too many to count. She has grown used to the constant annoyance, just one of many. Their favorite spot is around her eyes, where they gather to suck the tears away before she has time to shed them.

Still, Eve is a splendid creature, the most beautiful woman in the world, her husband says, enjoying his little joke. She has big honey-brown eyes, smooth skin, and thick, dark hair that flows like a river down her back.

Eve has a memory, but it is not long. It swirls about her now, filled with images sharp and bright and shadows deep and long.

She knows what it is like to walk in God's garden, in paths that wind through green meadows and lead to still waters. When she is hungry, she merely reaches out a hand to pick the food that grows in lush abundance.

She recalls what it is like to feel every sense satisfied, every need cared for. To walk with God in the cool of the day. To know the immensity of his love. He tells her she is made in his image. That she and her husband are to rule over the fish of the sea and the birds of the air and over the whole, wide world he has made. They are to be fruitful and multiply so they can care for his great creation.

God speaks to them of how he separated light from darkness and fashioned two great lights—the greater light to govern the day and the lesser light to govern the night. He tells of his delight in placing the stars on their track in the sky. To Eve they look like tiny pricks of brilliant light seeping through the canopy of night.

She listens in wonder as he speaks of how he made a home for her and Adam in the east of Eden, a garden paradise in which all kinds of trees grow—trees pleasing to the eye and good for food. In the middle of the garden grow the tree of life and the tree of knowledge of good and evil.

She remembers, too, what Adam has told her. How God shaped him out of the dust of the ground. He can still recall the hot, sweet breath of God waking his soul to life. He loves to tell about the day God paraded the animals in front of him—alligators, baboons, gazelles, skinks, parrots, crows, cheetahs, curlews, monkeys, macaws, pythons, bullfrogs, trumpeter swans, yaks, flying foxes, hummingbirds, egrets, and great, strutting peacocks. God and Adam laughed long and hard as the most preposterous of his creatures passed by. The best part was that Adam got to name them all.

Adam never tires of reminding her that among the most marvelous of the creatures God had made, none was found to be his match. So the Lord God caused him to fall into a deep slumber; and while he was sleeping, he had fashioned a woman from his side.

God's delight was evident when he presented her to Adam and heard him exclaim,

> This is now bone of my bones
>   and flesh of my flesh;
> she shall be called "woman,"
>   for she was taken out of man.

This is Eve's favorite part of the story. She loves to hear Adam tell the tale—how stunned he was to meet her. Her breath, he says, smelled like the fragrance of apples and her breasts were like clusters of fruit. Her mouth was the finest wine.

Eve and Adam. Adam and Eve. The two complete each other. She smiles as she recalls their life together in Eden.

She remembers, too, what she did not know at first—that there could be a place less perfect, a life less loving, a future less bright. That sin could lurk at your door, waiting for a chance to beat you down and shatter you into a thousand jagged pieces, each one a thorn and a barb. Deceit, blame, want, shame, and terrible grief— all these and worse she has known.

She returns to her memories of what once was. She thinks of all the plants in paradise and of the luscious fruit they bore. The trees were the most delightful. Stately palms, gnarled olive trees, tremendous oaks, and fig trees perfect for playing a hiding game with Adam. But she especially loved the ones that grew in the center of the garden. One of them had bright, green leaves lit up with tiny lights that danced inside. The other had deep, purple leaves shot through with veins of red.

Why, she wondered, had God told them they were free to eat from any tree in the garden except from the tree of knowledge of good and evil, warning them that death would surely follow if they did? What exactly was this death he spoke of?

One day, while Eve was thinking such thoughts, and while she and Adam were walking together in the center of the garden, a creature appeared. Not just any creature but one craftier than all the wild animals God had made. The serpent spoke in beguiling tones: "Did God really say, 'You must not eat from any tree in the garden'?" Why, he asked, would a good God deny them anything? Weren't she and Adam the crown of his creation?

For the first time, it dawned on Eve that God might be withholding something she needed to know. But she feared such thoughts, and so she merely said, "We may eat fruit from the trees in the garden, but God did say, 'You must not eat fruit from the tree that is in the middle of the garden, and you must not touch it, or you will die.'"

"You will not surely die," the serpent told her. "For God knows that when you eat of it your eyes will be opened, and you will be like God, knowing good and evil."

To know what is good in every situation. To see the end from the beginning and everything in between. To be able to achieve a goal with flawless precision and absolute certainty, surely this was wisdom. Why would God want to keep this gift of power from her?

She turned to Adam as though to find an answer to her silent question, but he said nothing. They were near the tree now. Plucking a piece of fruit, she held it in her hand, delighting in the firmness of its flesh. She took a bite and then handed another piece of fruit to Adam, who ate it without the slightest protest.

Suddenly their eyes were opened, and they could see the wrong in each other's hearts. Ashamed of their nakedness, they sewed leaves from a fig tree to cover themselves.

Then Eve and Adam heard a sound they feared. God himself was walking in the garden. So they hid. "Where are you?" God called.

But who can hide from God?

"I heard you in the garden," said Adam, "and I was afraid because I was naked; so I hid."

Then God, who already knew the answer to his question, inquired of Adam, "Who told you that you were naked? Have you eaten from the tree that I commanded you not to eat from?"

Struggling to explain, Eve's husband spit out the truth, but not the whole truth. He began with an insinuation, blaming God for what he had done. Hadn't God given him the woman? Then he bent the consequences in Eve's direction, saying "The woman *you* put here with me—she gave me some fruit from the tree, and I ate it."

Then God turned to Eve and said, "What is this you have done?"

The question pierced her like a knife, cutting her heart in two. But she spoke evasively, just as Adam had, refusing to bear the blame. "The serpent deceived me," she said, "and I ate."

And then she cowered, her arms above her head as though to ward off blows.

But God merely turned toward the serpent, and said,

> Because you have done this,
> Cursed are you above all the livestock
>   and all the wild animals!
> You will crawl on your belly
>   and you will eat dust
>   all the days of your life.
> And I will put enmity
>   between you and the woman,
>   and between your offspring and hers;
> he will crush your head,
>   and you will strike his heel.

But that was not the end of it.

Then God turned to the woman and said,

> I will make your pains in childbearing very severe;
>   with painful labor you will give birth to children.
> Your desire will be for your husband,
>   and he will rule over you.

God's words struck like lightning in a sudden storm, flashing across the sky with startling clarity, showing them everything they had lost. The future loomed bleak and harsh before them.

As for God, he was grieved by what had happened, how the man and woman he had loved into being had failed to love him in return. He could not let Adam and Eve remain in the garden he had created just for them. For if they reached out their hand and ate from the tree of life, they would live forever and there would be no possibility of becoming other than what they were now, broken and bent by sin. So God banished them and placed on the east side of the garden of Eden cherubim and a flaming sword flashing back and forth to guard the way to the tree of life.

But it was not completely dark. Though Eve and her husband had swallowed the biggest lie of all, God had something more in mind for them than punishment.

Adam named his wife Eve, because she would become the mother of all the living. With great anguish, she gave birth to several sons and daughters. Her eldest son became a murderer and her second son his victim. As for Adam, he labored from morning until evening to gather enough food to keep his family alive.

And as for God?

Fortunately for Eve and for Adam and for all the children who would become their descendants, God had seen the end from the beginning with everything in between. In his great love, and with absolute certainty, he had set a plan in motion that would provide a way for his children to come home to him.

THE TIMES

Eve's story took place before recorded time.
Her story is told in Genesis 1–4.

According to the worldview that prevailed among Israel's neighbors in the ancient Near East, the primary role of human beings was to serve the needs of the gods. They were to do the menial work the divine beings were tired of doing, especially the work of providing food for themselves.

By contrast, Genesis presents God as the one who not only creates the first human beings but who provides food for them by fashioning a garden paradise for them to live in. The garden Genesis describes isn't merely a flower garden or a garden filled with vegetables, but something like a landscaped park with paths, pools, fruit-bearing plants and trees, and life-giving water flowing through it. It was a magnificent garden, the kind that might have adjoined a temple or a palace. The implication in Genesis is that the garden home of Adam and Eve adjoined God's residence in Eden.[1]

Genesis also makes it clear that men and women, unlike the rest of the living beings God made, were created in God's image. That the gods planted images of themselves on earth would not have been a novel idea. Surrounding peoples believed that these images, which took the shape of idols, monuments, or even kings, were actual images of divinity, containing the god's essence, which enabled them to do the god's work on earth.

But Genesis presents only one God, and he is the Creator of everything. Instead of treating Adam and Eve as his slaves, God begins by lovingly providing for their needs and then treating them as his royal image bearers, telling them to "be fruitful and increase in number; fill the earth and subdue it. Rule over the fish in the sea and the birds in the sky and over every living creature that moves on the ground" (Genesis 1:28).

Living in our broken world, it is hard to imagine all that Adam and Eve lost by giving into temptation and transgressing God's clear command. Unable to reclaim their lost innocence, they were filled with shame, distressed by desires that leaned toward darkness rather than light.

THE TAKEAWAY

1. Why do you think God planted Adam and Eve in a garden paradise? What did it say about his expectations for how the first humans were to tend his world, as expressed in Genesis 1:28?

2. In Eden, Eve must have had the perfect relationship with her husband. What do you think that first marriage was like in the beginning?

3. Have you ever disobeyed God because you didn't understand or agree with one of his commandments? What was the result?

4. In what ways would you say the image of God is most broken in people today? How do you think God wants to restore his image in us?

CHAPTER 3

THE STORY OF CAIN

Wounded Pride Leads to Murder

Am I my brother's keeper?

GENESIS 4:9

Cain senses something stalking him wherever he goes. Even in the fields where he is happiest, tilling the ground and gathering the harvest, he feels a menacing presence.

Since he can't name the thing, he brushes it off as fancy. Tries to disregard it.

A brawny man, with dark, curly hair grown to shoulder length, he is the pride of his mother, the undeniable evidence of her creative power. For on the day her baby was born, she exclaimed, "God created a man, and now so have I!"[1] Out of travail and great pain, from deep within her flesh, Eve had succeeded in bringing forth a son.

It falls to Cain, then, as the first man born of woman, to set the stage for all of history, to reveal what lies hidden in the human heart—its furies and passions, its jealousy and shame.

From his parents Cain has heard stories of the splendid garden in Eden and of what it was like to walk with God in the cool of the day, never wanting for anything. This sounds to him more like tale than truth. Yet he knows there is a God. How else to explain the rising sun, the passing seasons, and the gifts that sprout from the soil?

A man whose soul is anchored in the land, Cain becomes a farmer while his younger brother Abel becomes a herder.

At harvest time he brings an offering of crops in order to secure God's blessing. Abel brings an offering too—the fat portions of the best animals in his flock.

Since God's vision can penetrate everything, even the darkest corners of the human heart, he accepts Abel's offering but withholds his favor from Cain. Perhaps he wants to test this firstborn son of Adam, allowing space to see what is in his heart. But Cain is a man who cannot stand waiting, especially when he is clearly in the right. After all, he is the firstborn, the best and the brightest. Why has God not accepted his offering? Why should little brother Abel be given what rightfully belongs to him?

In the midst of Cain's jealous thoughts, God speaks to him. "Why are you angry? Why is your face downcast? If you do what is right, will you not be accepted? But if you do not do what is right, sin is crouching at your door; it desires to have you, but you must rule over it."

If Cain will calm down long enough to listen, he will realize that God is like a father trying to guide his child. Like a good son, he will heed the warning about the lurking, sinister power of sin, whose presence he has already sensed.

Some commentators see Genesis 4:7 as a reference to a Mesopotamian demon who lingers around doorways.[2] ▪

But Cain is too angry to accept correction. He wants only to shake a fist at God and rail at life's unfairness. Why should he, superior in every way to his younger brother, be rejected?

Because rising anger, like rushing water, always seeks a path, Cain hatches a plan to lure his gullible brother out into the open fields, into the wild where no one will see or hear Abel's pleas for mercy. And then he strikes him down.

Abel's cry of bloody murder immediately ascends to God.

"Where is your brother Abel?" the Lord asks Cain.

"I don't know. Am I my brother's keeper?"

"What have you done?"

Cain cringes, lowering his head and covering his ears, but the question reverberates, forcing him to face what he has done.

Like his mother snatching fruit from a forbidden tree, Cain

has plucked the life of his brother out of the land of the living. Like her, and like his father too, he has fallen into sin by trying to make himself like God.

"Listen! Your brother's blood cries out to me from the ground," God declares. "Now you are under a curse and driven from the ground, which opened its mouth to receive your brother's blood from your hand. When you work the ground, it will no longer yield its crops for you. You will be a restless wanderer on the earth."

Because he spilled his brother's blood, there will be no refreshing rain to revive Cain's fields.

"My punishment is more than I can bear," he wails. "Today you are driving me from the land, and I will be hidden from your presence; I will be a restless wanderer on the earth, and whoever finds me will kill me."

"Not so," the Lord replies. "Anyone who kills Cain will suffer vengeance seven times over." Then he places a mysterious mark on Cain so that anyone who sees it will not kill him.

So Cain, the first man born of a woman, leaves his family and goes to live in the land of Nod, east of Eden. The last we see of him he is busy fathering a son and founding the world's first city.

Literally, *the land of Nod* translates to "the land of wandering." ■

Eve and Adam lose both of their sons—one to murder and the other to exile. Comforting each other in the midst of their sorrow, they make love again, and God blesses them with another son, whom Eve names Seth. This time, there is no boasting about her wonderful creative powers, but only gratitude. For God has graciously given her a son to replace the one who was killed by his brother.

As time passes, God gives Adam and Eve more children and human beings begin to multiply and fill the earth. But the more they proliferate, the worse things get. Before long, God begins to regret that he has ever made them. Perceiving that the human heart is occupied with evil all the time, the Lord's own heart is filled with pain. Determined to deal with the violence and corruption that have spread across the land, he lets his eyes roam back and forth across the earth to see if he can find at least one good man.

They come to rest on Noah, a righteous man who springs, not from the line of Cain but from the line of Seth. By helping Noah and his family survive the devastating flood to come, God will show his mercy once again.

THE TIMES

Cain's story took place before recorded time.
His story is drawn from Genesis 4–5

The first few chapters of Genesis set the stage for how human life will unfold on earth. The vision it creates is both raw and real. By killing his brother, Cain unleashes a cycle of violence and victimization that will characterize human life throughout history. One has only to watch the evening news to understand how the world God so lovingly created descended into conflict and chaos.

The New Testament speaks of "the way of Cain," connecting it moments later to "clouds without rain, blown along by the wind" or "wandering stars, for whom blackest darkness has been reserved forever" (Jude 1:11–13).

Fortunately for all of us there is an opposite way, a way of faith that leads toward God and away from a self-centered life. The writer of Hebrews says, "By faith Abel brought God a better offering than Cain did. By faith he was commended as righteous, when God spoke well of his offerings. And by faith Abel still speaks, even though he is dead" (Hebrews 11:4).

The instinct to present gifts to God would have been a natural one. By making an offering to God, both brothers would have been expressing their understanding that blessings come from his hand. While Abel gave God the best he had, the text simply says that Cain offered "some of the fruits of the land." Perhaps Cain held back the best part of the harvest for himself. Maybe he offered something merely to get something in return. Whatever the case, God read his heart and rejected his gift.

The New Testament connects Abel's faith with the quality of

his offering. Perhaps Abel had the faith to believe not only that God was powerful but also that God was good and that he could be trusted. By contrast, Cain appeared to trust only in himself and in his assessment of what was right and wrong. By doing so he became a wandering star, for whom black darkness was forever reserved.

THE TAKEAWAY

1. It is easy to distance ourselves from Cain, assuming that he was merely a bad man whose story has nothing to do with ours. But what if the Bible offers Cain as a model of what can happen to human beings apart from God? If that is true, what might be the implications for your life and relationships with others?

2. God asks Cain several questions: "Why are you angry?" "Why are you disappointed?" "If you do well, won't you be accepted? (Genesis 4:6). Why do you think God approaches Cain by asking questions instead of immediately calling out his sin? What insights might God's approach to Cain suggest about how he approaches us when we sin? How can we remain sensitive to God's voice when we face temptation?

3. Cain's story speaks to us of how sin can wreak havoc in a family for generations. As you consider your own family history, what sins or failures from previous generations still have an impact on you or members of your family?

CHAPTER 4

THE STORY OF SARAH

How a Ninety-Year-Old Gets Pregnant and Sets Tongues Wagging

The One enthroned in heaven laughs; the
Lord scoffs at them.

PSALM 2:4

Older than dirt. That is Sarah. Her skin hangs like sackcloth, wrinkled and rough. Yet hers is a face that still makes men look, so beautiful it once charmed kings.

You might think her a fool for all the nonstop laughter. Her body shakes with it. But she is no fool, only a woman who can't stop marveling at what God has done. Though her husband is more than a hundred years old and she not far behind, she's pregnant with his child. Who wouldn't find that funny? Two old sticks kindling a fire!

But then it comes—yet another jab of pain snaking down her leg. Ow! The added weight is hard to bear, and loose joints make her wonder whether she will topple over. Though the baby is so ripe she can hardly bend, she never complains. How could she since the Almighty has answered her prayers?

Sarah laughs again, this time because her baby is kicking. He's like a little rabbit whose feet thump softly against her belly. It won't be long before I hold him in my arms, she thinks.

But how does she know it will be a son?

Sitting in a quiet corner of her tent, Sarah thinks back, remembering all the hurtful things that once were whispered behind her back. She remembers the bitterness she felt every time she heard other women cluck-clucking because God had not blessed her with children. Surely, they would say, Sarah must have done something exceedingly wicked for God to have closed her womb.

Her Egyptian maid Hagar had always been the first to throw a stone. She claimed God had cursed Sarah because she had been unfaithful to Abraham when the two had traveled to Egypt. But what Hagar never added was that Abraham had asked Sarah to tell a lie to save his skin. The couple had fled the parched deserts of the Negev for the lush land of Egypt. Where better to escape a famine than in that place of rich abundance created by the Nile River's frequent flooding? In Egypt there were plenty of cucumbers, melons, garlic, and fresh fish to eat. But there was also a price to be paid. There always was.

Fearing what lay ahead, Abraham had urged Sarah to tell the Egyptians she was his sister lest they decide to murder him in order to have her. And so she recited the lie—but not quite a lie, because Abraham was her half-brother.

God changed Sarai's name to Sarah and Abram's name to Abraham in Genesis 17 to signify their special relationship with him. For the sake of simplicity I have chosen to render her name as "Sarah" throughout the story. ▣

Geologists and archaeologists have discovered evidence of a three-hundred-year drought cycle that took place at the end of the third millennium and the beginning of the second millennium BC, dovetailing with one of the periods in which Abraham and Sarah were thought to have lived.[1] ▣

As Abraham had feared, word of her beauty spread quickly until Pharaoh declared that he must have her for his own. After showering Sarah's "brother" with gifts of sheep, cattle, donkeys, camels, menservants, and maidservants—of which Hagar was one—clueless Pharaoh had added Sarah to his harem.

Before visiting Pharaoh's bedchamber, Sarah needed to look the part—to be transformed into an Egyptian beauty. Fortunately, that took time. Anointed with perfume made from precious oils and a crush of fragrant flowers, her face had been painted white, its worry lines erased by a potion of cypress kernels, frankincense, wax, and milk. Her dark, curly hair had been covered with a black woolen wig whose braided tresses fell straight to her shoulders. She wore bracelets, rings, and a large necklace made out of gold.

Gazing at herself in a mirror of burnished bronze, Sarah had wondered about the woman who looked back at her with so much sadness in her eyes. She had saved her husband's life, but what would happen now? Would Abraham return home without her? How could she bear to part with him, living out her life as a captive in Pharaoh's harem?

Then something amazing happened. A plague descended. Swift and terrible, it ravished Pharaoh's household, leaving only Sarah untouched. The stench of stomachs emptied in a hurry soon flooded the harem and every corner of Pharaoh's house. When he finally rose from his sickbed, Pharaoh summoned Abraham. "What have you done to me?" he accused. "Why didn't you tell me Sarah was your wife? You pretended she was your sister. Now your God has cursed me. Take her and go!"

So Sarah and Abraham had been hurried out of Egypt and loaded down with all the gifts Pharaoh had given. One of these was Hagar, an Egyptian maiden who was destined to become Sarah's maid.

Whenever Hagar recounts the tale, she leaves out the part about God standing up for Sarah, choosing instead to speculate on what it must have been like for her mistress to have become part of Pharaoh's harem.

Sarah knows about her handmaid's tendency to gossip, forever telling half-truths to cast her mistress in a bad light. Why, she wonders, did she ever allow Abraham to sleep with Hagar? At the time, it had seemed reasonable to invoke the custom of letting another woman provide an heir when she could not. She had hoped it would ease the shame of her own barrenness.

Meek and eager to please, Hagar had gone willingly to Abraham's bed. How could Sarah have known that the moment the young woman's belly started to swell with life, she would grow fat with self-importance, behaving as though she, and not Sarah, were the favored wife?

So Sarah had begun to despise her young maid, making her life a misery. To escape Sarah's abuse the young woman had fled into the wilderness. When that happened, the older woman had felt a momentary twinge of guilt. But then Hagar had come stumbling back with foolish tales of an angel who had appeared to her and persuaded her to return.

Despite constant strife, Sarah had grown old in the knowledge that her place was secure in Abraham's heart. Then something happened that made her think she was first in God's heart too. As her belly began to swell, so too did her hope. Even so, it was impossible to ignore the wagging tongues of neighbors and friends along with all their endless questions.

How could a ninety-year-old woman survive the birth of a child, they had asked. Even if she did, how could her shriveled-up breasts produce enough milk? But she knew exactly what the people were saying. She also knew the promise God had made, first in a dream to Abraham and then last year in broad daylight when he visited them both at their tent near the great trees of Mamre.

That was when the laughter began. Her husband had been sitting at the entrance of his tent in the middle of the day when suddenly he saw three strangers approaching. A generous man, Abraham begged them to linger and enjoy his hospitality. Ducking quickly inside the tent to ask Sarah to prepare some bread, he instructed a servant to slaughter the best calf from his herd.

The moment Sarah completed her task, she began to feel ill.

Holding her hand to her stomach, she remembered the long forgotten pain she had experienced whenever her monthly flow began. But that had stopped years ago. Minutes passed until she was certain. She must stay in the tent until her days of uncleanness had passed. Whispering the news to Abraham, she explained why she would miss the meal that was about to begin.

She could see the shock on his face, the worry in his eyes. What woman's disease had she contracted? Would she be able to survive it?

Ever the gracious host, Abraham brought curds and milk and the roasted calf, setting the feast before his guests.

As they spoke, one of them asked, "Where is your wife, Sarah?"

Surely they were wondering why she wasn't at the meal.

"There in the tent," Abraham replied, invoking a euphemism to explain that, like all menstruating women, she was secluded in her tent.

Then one of them said, "I will surely return to you about this time next year, and Sarah your wife will have a son." At once, Abraham realized that this was no ordinary stranger. God himself had spoken.

Eighty-nine-year-old Sarah had been listening to the conversation from the entrance to the tent. Hearing the stranger's outlandish promise, she began to laugh, exclaiming

Though the biblical text (Genesis 18:1–15) never explicitly states that Sarah's period started again, some scholars point out that there is no evidence that men and women ate separately in the ancient world. That custom seems to have developed later. So Abraham's guests may have noted the irregularity and inquired about it. When he replied that his wife was "in the tent," Abraham may have been employing a polite euphemism, indicating that she was menstruating and unable to join them. For this to have been the case, she would have needed to begin menstruating just after baking the bread because bread baking would have been forbidden to menstruating women.[2]

to herself, "After I am worn out and my husband is old, will I now
have this pleasure?"

"Why did Sarah laugh?" the Lord asked Abraham. "Is anything
too hard for the LORD? I will return to you at the appointed time
next year, and Sarah will have a son."

Afraid, Sarah replied, "I did not laugh."

Speaking directly to Sarah this time, God said, "Ah, but you
did laugh."

And laugh she did and laugh she would until the day her son
Isaac—whose name means "laughter"—is finally born. She and
Abraham laugh together. The joy rises up strong and wild, and
even were she to try, she cannot push it down. "God has brought me
laughter," she says, "and everyone who hears about this will laugh
with me. Who would have said to Abraham that Sarah would nurse
children? Yet I have borne him a son in his old age."

And so it is that in her old age Sarah comes to understand
that God has a sense of humor. Despite every shred of trouble and
every evil circumstance, she knows that in the end he will prevail,
laughing all his enemies to scorn.

But Sarah still has enemies. And they are close at hand.

Years go by. Now Isaac is three, and he has just been weaned.
Since death sweeps away so many babies, his good health is reason
to celebrate. Despite the feast that Abraham throws to mark the
strength of his youngest son, Sarah is worried. So she presses him:
"Get rid of that slave woman and her son," she tells her husband,
"for that woman's son will never share in the inheritance with my
son Isaac."

But Abraham's heart is breaking because he loves both sons.
How can he deny one to favor the other?

To Sarah's great relief, the Lord appears to Abraham and weighs in on her side, instructing her husband to "do whatever Sarah says." So Abraham sends Hagar and Ishmael packing, straight into the wilderness.

But instead of meeting their deaths, as one might expect, they encounter a messenger from God. Because of an angel and a well of water and the Lord's protecting hand, Ishmael grows up and, as the Scripture says, turns into "a wild donkey of a man."

Sarah only knows that she is thankful to be rid of him and Hagar. Finally she can die a happy woman. Of course, she doesn't know that her husband will one day take their son on a three-day journey into the wilderness and then up a mountain to be sacrificed. Abraham will make an altar, place Isaac on it, and then raise his knife to slaughter him.

When Sarah is gathered to her ancestors at the age of 127, she can imagine neither the glories nor the troubles that lay ahead for the descendants of the two sons of Abraham—the Arabs, who are Ishmael's descendants, and the Jews, who come from Isaac's line.

Had she been able to peer even further into the future, to the time when another beloved son would ascend the very same mountain on which Abraham was told by God to slay his son—she would have come to know the deepest truth of all. No matter how wickedness multiplies or troubles mount up, God will indeed have the last word, laughing his enemies to scorn.

THE TIMES

Sarah may have lived around 2156–2029 BC.
Her story is told in Genesis 12:1–20; 16:1–8; 17:1–22; 18:1–15;
21:1–13. She is also mentioned in Galatians 4:22–31.

During the lifetime of Abraham and Sarah, the surrounding peoples worshiped an array of gods. Gradually, the concept of a more personal god emerged, with people expressing special devotion to a particular god who would become their special protector and provider. This may have been how Abraham and Sarah first viewed God when they heard him promise to give them many descendants.

Devotion to the family deity would have passed from generation to generation, but other gods would also have been worshiped. Only in Israel would the God of Abraham and Sarah come to be known as the God of the whole nation.

Because the ancient world had so little understanding of what caused diseases and disorders, superstitions abounded, causing additional shame to those who suffered from sickness or physical ailments.

Sarah's grief at being unable to bear children would have been made sharply worse because her barrenness would have been seen as a sign of divine judgment. Surely she had done something to make God angry, and he was exacting punishment by withholding children.

Though ancient peoples would have perceived a connection between menstruation and the timing of a pregnancy, they would not have grasped the biological reality that a human being is created only when a female egg is fertilized by male sperm. They believed that life was created when a man planted his seed into a woman's womb. The woman was seen as a receptacle or incubator in which the seed could grow. If a couple failed to conceive after the man had done his duty, or if the child miscarried, the wife was invariably blamed.

Sarah's barrenness must have put tremendous pressure on her marriage. She couldn't have known that her inability to bear children earlier in life had nothing to do with her sin but everything to do with God's plan to bring about a new people—children of the promise—of whom Abraham would be father and Sarah would be mother. Her pregnancy must have brought a profound sense of vindication and relief.

Four thousand years after her death, Sarah's story lives on. Scripture states that she was buried in the Cave of Machpelah in what is known today as the Tomb of the Patriarchs, along with other key figures whose stories are told in the book of Genesis— Abraham, Isaac, Jacob, Rebekah, and Leah. Located in the West Bank city of Hebron, the site traditionally ascribed to the tomb can still be visited today. It is not far from where Sarah would have sat in her tent, laughing out loud when she first heard God's outrageous promise to give her and Abraham a son.

THE TAKEAWAY

1. Like many biblical characters, and many real people, Sarah is not an entirely virtuous person. Comment on the bad aspects of her character as revealed in the story. Which do you relate to most?
2. Sarah was sixty-five when God promised he would make Abraham (and by inference Sarah) into a great nation. But

Isaac wasn't born until twenty-five years later. Why do you think God spoke the promise so far in advance?

3. By suggesting that Abraham sleep with her maid to produce an heir, Sarah was merely following the customs of the time. She was also trying to make God's promise come true. Have you ever tried to force God's hand? What were the results?

4. Do you believe God has promised you something? How would you characterize your experience as you waited, and perhaps still wait, for the promise to be fulfilled?

CHAPTER 5

THE STORY OF JACOB AND ESAU

A Con Artist Gets Scammed

As it is written, Jacob have I loved, but Esau have I hated.

ROMANS 9:13

Looking up at the ink-black sky, his head resting on a stone, Jacob can think of nothing but his troubles. The events of the past day, indeed of his past life, weigh heavily, dragging him into a swirl of anxiety from which he cannot escape. He feels a growing ache, as loneliness and fear descend. The problem, he knows, began a long time ago, before he was even born.

How is it that he, Jacob, the clever son of Isaac and Rebekah, has arrived in Bethel, a place in the middle of no place? Before he drifts off to sleep, Jacob conjures the past, hoping it will make sense of the present and open a path to the future. But his memories do nothing but keep him awake.

He thinks back many years, beginning with the circumstances surrounding his birth.

Though married for twenty years, the brilliant, beautiful Rebekah lacks the one thing she longs for—a child. Observing her sorrow, Isaac prays and God graciously opens her womb.

As her belly swells with life, Rebekah feels an inner agitation as if a struggle is taking place inside her. Troubled by what this may mean, she inquires of the Lord and hears this:

> Two nations are in your womb,
>> and two peoples from within you will be separated;
> one people will be stronger than the other,
>> and the older will serve the younger.

A few months later two babies are born in such quick succession it seems like they are chasing each other into the world. With the youngest grasping the heel of the eldest, they are tiny wrestlers locked in combat.

The first boy looks like a miniature man, with arms and legs that are already covered in hair. Rebekah and Isaac name this lusty boy Esau, meaning "red," because he is as red and rough as the earth itself.

They name their second boy Jacob, meaning "he grasps the heel."

As their mother watches them grow, she remembers what God has said, that her children would give birth to two nations, one of which would rule the other.

Like water and oil, the two refuse to blend. As time passes, Esau becomes a hunter who is happiest in the open fields while his brother Jacob is content to stay at home, dwelling among the tents.

Because their father loves the taste of wild game, he favors his manly son Esau, while his wife favors her clever son Jacob.

One day, while Jacob is busy cooking up a pot of red-lentil stew, Esau comes in from the fields. "I'm dying of hunger," he says. "Let me have some of that red stew."

"First sell me your birthright," Jacob says.

"Look, I am about to die!" Esau retorts. "What good is a birthright to me?"

As Esau dips bread into the stew, shoveling great wads of it into his mouth, Jacob marvels at his good fortune. Because of his brother's ungovernable appetite, he has secured the rights of the firstborn son. Now he and not Esau will inherit a double portion of his father's wealth.

So it is that one day Isaac, who by now is both feeble and blind, summons Esau, saying, "My son, I am an old man with little time

The firstborn son customarily inherited twice as much as his brothers. While this may sound like a good deal, he would have had the additional responsibility of serving as head of the family, which could entail, among other things, providing for the care of his mother and any unwed sisters. ∎

left to enjoy life. Take your quiver and bow and go out to the open country to hunt some wild game for me. Then prepare the food in just the way I like it, and I will give you my blessing before I die."

Through this ritual of meal and blessing, Isaac is planning to promote Esau. Eager to obtain his father's blessing, Esau grabs his bow and leaves.

Realizing what is about to take place, Rebekah quickly intervenes.

Instructing Jacob, she says, "My son, listen to me and do exactly what I tell you. Bring two of the best young goats from the flock. I'll prepare them just the way your father likes. Then you can bring the food to him so that he may give you his blessing before he dies."[1]

"But Mother, "Jacob objects, "Esau is hairy while my skin is smooth. What if Father touches me? He will think I am deceiving him, and that will bring down a curse and not a blessing!"

"Let the curse fall on me," Rebekah answers. "Just do as I say."

While his mother is busy cooking, Jacob dresses up in Esau's clothing. To complete the ruse, Rebekah covers the smooth skin on his neck and hands with pieces of animal hide.

When the meal is ready, Jacob carries it to Isaac, saying, "Father, I have done just as you told me. Please sit up and eat some of my game, so that you may give me your blessing."

But Isaac is not quite as feeble-minded as he looks. "How did you find it so quickly, my son?"

"The LORD your God gave me success."

Isaac beckons his son to come closer. Touching his hands and then his neck, he declares, "The voice is the voice of Jacob, but the hands are the hands of Esau. Are you really my son Esau?"

"Yes, Father, I am your firstborn son Esau," Jacob lies.

As his appetite surpasses the last of his lingering doubts, Isaac eats the meal and then announces a blessing over his son.

> Ah, the smell of my son
> > is like the smell of a field
> > that the LORD has blessed.
> May God give you heaven's dew
> > and earth's richness—
> > an abundance of grain and new wine.
> May nations serve you
> > and peoples bow down to you.
> Be lord over your brothers,
> > and may the sons of your mother bow down to you.
> May those who curse you be cursed
> > and those who bless you be blessed.

The moment Jacob leaves, Esau returns from the hunt. After preparing a dish of wild game, he places it in front of his father and then asks for his blessing.

"Who are you?" Isaac cries out.

"I am Esau, your firstborn son," he exclaims.

Shocked because he realizes that God himself has made the choice between his sons, Isaac replies, "Who was it, then, that hunted game and brought it to me? I finished eating just before you came, and then I blessed him—and indeed he will be blessed!"

"Bless me—me too, my father!" Esau wails.

But Isaac will not oppose God, not even for the sake of his

favorite son. "Your brother," he says, "came deceitfully and took your blessing."

"Isn't he rightly named Jacob?" Esau cries. "This is the second time he has taken advantage of me. First he took my birthright, and now he's taken my blessing! Haven't you reserved any blessing for me, my father?"

"I have made him lord over you and have made all his relatives his servants, and I have sustained him with grain and new wine. So what can I possibly do for you, my son?"

"Do you have only one blessing, my father? Bless me too, my father!"

As Esau weeps, his father, declares,

> Your dwelling will be
> > away from the earth's richness,
> > away from the dew of heaven above.
> You will live by the sword
> > and you will serve your brother.
> But when you grow restless,
> > you will throw his yoke
> > from off your neck.

Enraged by his brother's duplicity, Esau vows to kill him as soon as their father dies.

Hearing this, Rebekah urges Jacob to flee. "Your brother is consoling himself with thoughts of murdering you," she tells him. "Flee to Haran, to the home of my brother Laban. Stay there for a while until Esau's wrath subsides. I will send word as soon as it's safe for you to return. Why should I lose you both in one day?"

With his father's blessing, Jacob hurries north in search of his Uncle Laban. The first night he sleeps beneath the stars in Bethel. Lying on the ground with his head resting on a stone, he recalls the events of the past in a vain attempt to make sense of the present. Finally, when he can remember no more, he drifts off to sleep.

As Jacob dreams, this is what he sees— the Lord God Almighty standing at the top of a great stairway, stretching from heaven to earth. On it, angels descend and ascend as they carry out their missions on earth.

"I am the LORD, the God of your father Abraham and the God of Isaac," the voice says. "I will give you and your descendants the land on which you are lying. Your descendants will be like the dust of the earth, and you will spread out to the west and to the east, to the north and to the south. All peoples on earth will be blessed through you and your offspring. I am with you and will watch over you wherever you go, and I will bring you back to this land. I will not leave you until I have done what I have promised you."

When Jacob wakes up, his anxiety has vanished. He no longer thinks about running away but only about God's promise to be with him wherever he goes. "Surely," he thinks, "the LORD is in this place, and I was not aware of it. This is none other than the house of God—the gate of heaven."

Haran, the city from which Jacob's grandparents, Abraham and Sarah, hailed, is located in Mesopotamia. Situated between the Tigris and Euphrates Rivers, Mesopotamia corresponds to modern-day Iraq and Kuwait as well as to northeastern Syria and also bits of Turkey and Iran. Haran was located in northern Mesopotamia in what is now Turkey. It would have been a journey of some five hundred miles. ■

Continuing his journey northward, Jacob finally arrives at a well. As God would have it, this is the very well at which his mother watered her flocks when she was a girl. Engaging the local shepherds in conversation, he discovers that he is near the home of his Uncle Laban.

"Look," they say, "there is Laban's daughter Rachel with her sheep." As Jacob turns to greet his cousin, he can't help staring. She is the most beautiful woman he has ever seen.

Determined to impress her, he rolls the huge stone from the mouth of the well so she can be the first to water her flock. After explaining that he is her aunt Rebekah's son, he kisses her and begins to weep.

As soon as Rachel's father hears the news, he hurries out to meet him, exclaiming, "You are my own flesh and blood!" As Laban and Jacob embrace, it is hard to ignore the similarity between them. The sharply arched brow, the calculating look, the clever smile. Indeed these two men—the older and the younger—spring from the same source. But for the difference in age, they could be twins.

As it happens, Laban has two daughters—the captivating Rachel and her weak-eyed, elder sister, Leah.

Though his heart is set on Rachel, Jacob has no money for the customary bride price. Instead he strikes a deal with his uncle, promising to work for him without pay for seven years, after which time Rachel will become his wife.

When his wedding finally arrives, Jacob is in high spirits. During the first day of the feast, he raises so many toasts to his beautiful bride that he needs a man on either side to steady him as he makes his way to bed.

In the morning, as Jacob opens the flap of his tent and the light streams in, he realizes his mistake. He has made love to Leah, rather than to Rachel!

When Jacob confronts the double-dealing Laban, his uncle is

ready with an explanation and another bargain. "It is not our custom here to give the younger daughter in marriage before the older one. Finish out the week with Leah and then you will have Rachel in return for seven more years of work." So Jacob agrees.

As time passes, it surprises no one—least of all Laban's eldest daughter—to learn that Jacob loves Rachel more than he loves her. But when God looks down and sees that Leah is unloved, he decides to bless her with children. She names her first son Reuben. Cradling the baby in her arms, she declares, "It is because the Lord has seen my misery. Surely my husband will love me now."

Then she conceives again, giving birth to Simeon and remarking, "Because the Lord heard that I am not loved, he gave me this one too."

Two more sons quickly follow.

Then Rachel cries out to Jacob: "Give me children, or I'll die!"

"Am I in the place of God, who has kept you from having children?" he fires back.

Instead of accepting her childless status, Rachel leads her maid to Jacob's bed. "Here is Bilhah, my servant. Sleep with her so that she can bear children for me and I too can build a family through her."

As Leah's maid Zilpah and Rachel's maid Bilhah give birth to more sons, it soon becomes a game of dueling maids. Finally Rachel becomes pregnant and gives birth to Joseph, and later to Benjamin.

Rachel's action would have been considered culturally acceptable. Since it was a woman's duty to produce heirs for her husband, the failure to do so brought shame. By giving Bilhah to Jacob as his wife, Rachel sought to perform her duty, which would also improve her social standing. Some wedding contracts gave the husband the right to divorce his wife if she failed to provide an heir within a preset time limit.[2] ■

With his quiver now full of arrows—eleven sons and one daughter—Jacob decides it is time to return home. Though Laban has made him taste the bitter fruits of deceit, yet God has blessed him and made him prosper despite his trials. And though a penniless fugitive when he left, he is returning home a wealthy patriarch.

As Jacob and his family head south, he considers the perils ahead. First among them is his brother Esau. Though his mother Rebekah had promised to send word as soon as it was safe to return, no word had ever come. Had Esau grown embittered over the years?

To gauge the state of his brother's heart, Jacob sends messengers to announce his homecoming. When he learns that his brother is coming to meet him leading a band of four hundred men, Jacob is seized with fear. Dividing his caravan into two groups, he hopes that at least one will survive an attack.

Then he falls on his face and pleads with God. "O God of my father Abraham, God of my father Isaac, Lord, you who said to me, 'Go back to your country and your relatives, and I will make you prosper,' I am unworthy of all the kindness and faithfulness you have shown your servant. I had only my staff when I crossed this Jordan, but now I have become two camps. Save me, I pray, from the hand of my brother Esau, for I am afraid he will come and attack me, and also the mothers with their children. But you have said, 'I will surely make you prosper and will make your descendants like the sand of the sea, which cannot be counted.'"

After that he selects a magnificent array of gifts for his brother—hundreds of animals, the best of his livestock. Instructing his servants, he tells them to go ahead of him, putting space between the herds. By showering his brother with successive waves of gifts, Jacob hopes to pacify him.

That night, after sending his wives and children ahead, Jacob remains behind. As shadows descend, a mysterious stranger appears and challenges him. The two wrestle for hours with neither gaining an advantage. When Jacob's adversary sees that he cannot overpower him, he touches Jacob's hip so that the bone is wrenched from the socket. Despite the pain in his thigh Jacob will not give up.

Jacob's gift is enormous, larger than what many towns would have been able to pay a conquering king.[3] ■

"Let me go, for it is daybreak," the stranger says.

But Jacob through gritted teeth declares, "I will not let you go unless you bless me."

"What is your name?" the man asks.

"Jacob," he says.

"Your name will no longer be Jacob, but Israel, because you have struggled with God and with humans and have overcome."

Jacob replies by asking his adversary to reveal his name. Instead of answering, his mysterious opponent blesses Jacob and then departs.

"This place will be called 'Peniel,'" Jacob declares, "because I saw God face to face, and yet my life was spared."

Israel means "he struggles with God." ■

———————————

Peniel means "face of God." ■

When Jacob looks up, he sees his brother approaching at the head of an army of men. Dismounting, Esau begins to run straight at him. Instead of attacking, he throws his arms around Jacob, greets him with a kiss, and then begins to weep.

Though Jacob is weeping too, he is uneasy. When Esau offers to escort him and his family south to the region in which he and his household have settled, Jacob defers, promising to follow as soon as his caravan has rested. Ever the deceiver, he heads north instead.

Before long, Rachel becomes pregnant with her second child. But the delivery is an agony, and she names her baby Ben-Oni, meaning "son of my trouble." But Jacob renames him "Benjamin," meaning "son of my right hand."

Though Rachel perishes in childbirth, Jacob will live on for many years. During that time he will suffer greatly, not from outsiders but at the hands of his deceitful sons. Though his last days on earth will be spent in a foreign land, he will be laid to rest with honor in the tomb of his fathers. In the centuries that follow, his body will repose next to his first wife Leah rather than his favorite wife Rachel, who was buried somewhere along the road[4] after dying in childbirth.

THE TIMES

Jacob and Esau's story took place from about 2006 to 1909 BC.
Their story is drawn from Genesis 27–33

Like his father and grandfather before him, Jacob and his family were frequently on the move. To imagine what their lives were like, think of modern-day Bedouins, who fold up their tents and move when conditions change. Rather than living entirely in Canaan, Jacob spent years living in foreign lands, first with relatives in northern Mesopotamia and then finishing out his life in Egypt, where he and his family took refuge in the midst of a severe famine.

More than any other account in the Bible, Jacob's story places special emphasis on the meaning of place names and personal names. Though names in the ancient world often worked, as they do today, distinguishing one person from another, they also functioned at a much deeper level, signifying a person's essence or destiny.

When Jacob met God in a dream, he named the place Bethel, meaning "house of God." When he wrestled with God he called the place Peniel, meaning, "face of God." At the conclusion of their wrestling match, God renamed him Israel, meaning "struggle with God."

The names of Jacob's twelve sons are also significant as each child's name expressed the anguish or hope of his mother.

LEAH AND HER MAID ZILPAH'S SONS

Reuben—"see a son," sounds like the Hebrew word for "he has seen my misery"

Simeon—"one who hears"
Levi—sounds like the Hebrew for "attached"
Judah—may be derived from a Hebrew word meaning "praise"
Issachar—sounds like a Hebrew word that means "reward"
Zebulon—"honor"

RACHEL AND HER MAID BILHAH'S SONS

Dan—"he has vindicated"
Naphtali—"my struggle"
Gad—"a troop" or "good fortune"
Asher—"happy"
Joseph—"may he add"
Benjamin—"son of my right hand"

Note that both Leah and Rachel could lay claim to six sons each and that Leah also gave birth to a daughter named Dinah, meaning "judgment."[5]

When Jacob returned to his homeland with his wives and children in tow, he discovered that his brother Esau had also prospered in his absence. By then, Esau was living in Edom, a mountainous region south of the Dead Sea.

Though Jacob and Esau achieved a semblance of peace during their lifetimes, the Edomites and Israelites would often be at odds in the future. During the Israelites' exodus from Egypt, the king of Edom refused them passage through his land. Both Saul and David fought against the Edomites, with David finally prevailing. Later on, the Edomites became known as Idumeans. Two of the New Testament's most notorious villains, Herod the Great and his son Herod Antipas, came from Idumean stock.

The Idumeans disappeared from history after the Romans destroyed Jerusalem in 70 AD.

THE TAKEAWAY

1. Place names and personal names are significant in this and in many biblical stories. If you know it, briefly share the meaning of your own name. In what ways, if any, does it reflect something significant about who you are or what you've experienced in life?

2. God spoke to Jacob in a dream, assuring him he would watch over and protect him wherever he went. Yet Jacob's life might not have seemed very "watched over." Describe times in our own life when circumstances caused you to doubt God's presence and care. How did you deal with your doubts?

3. Jacob is known as the man who wrestled with God. Is it ever ok for us to do the same? Are there matters over which it is never right to wrestle with God? Why or why not?

4. Have you ever refused to give up pursuing God for a blessing or an answer to prayer? If so, what was the outcome? If you were to wrestle with God in this season of your life, what blessing would you seek?

CHAPTER 6

THE STORY OF
SHECHEM

A Despicable Revenge on
a Despicable Prince

*Cursed be their anger, for it was fierce; and
their wrath, for it was cruel: I will divide
them in Jacob, and scatter them in Israel.*

GENESIS 49:7

*"It is mine to avenge; I will repay," says the
Lord.*

ROMANS 12:19

Though Joshua would later lead an Israelite invasion of Canaan, it was difficult to displace the people living there, many of whom continued to occupy the plains and valleys, the most fertile areas of the country. Without conquering the Canaanites, the Israelites were tempted to assimilate with the surrounding peoples, adopting their religious beliefs and practices as their own. ■

Though Abraham didn't purchase land to live on, he did purchase a cave in which to bury his wife Sarah. Known variously as the Cave of the Patriarchs (to Jews and Christians) or the Sanctuary of Abraham or the Ibrahimi Mosque (to Muslims), it is located in the Palestinian city of Hebron, which is nineteen miles south of Jerusalem. Also known as the Cave of Machpelah, it is the traditional burial site for Abraham and Sarah, Isaac and Rebekah, and Jacob and Leah. ■

Jacob leans on his staff, favoring his weak leg. As he gazes across the fertile plain that stretches out before him, he smiles. Here at last, on the outskirts of the Canaanite city of Shechem, his large family has come to rest. In sight of the walled city, he can lay down roots while his herds grow fat and strong.

After years of struggling with Esau and then Laban, Jacob, the heel grasper, is ready to let go. With little energy left for fighting, he wants only to live in peace. He is the first of his family—of Abraham and Isaac—to buy property in the land God has promised. But while Jacob is dreaming of peace, trouble is brewing at home.

Leah's twelve-year-old daughter Dinah,[1] a girl surrounded by ruffian brothers, has grown restless. Longing to explore life outside of camp, she does the unthinkable, slipping out on her own to mingle with the locals. Without the protection of father or brothers, she approaches a group of women who are sitting on the ground, not far from the city gates. As curious about her as she is about them, they break away from their tasks to greet her.

Eager to make friends, Dinah doesn't understand that she has become a spectacle. Many eyes, including a set of large, dark eyes, which belong to a prince of the city, are trained on her. Accustomed to ruling over others, this young man hasn't yet learned to rule himself.

Too late to warn her off, the women step away as they see him approaching, averting their eyes and busying themselves with their weaving. Shechem smiles warmly as he takes Dinah by the hand and then speaks softly to her. After a while he leads her out of sight and then rapes her.

After Shechem has satisfied his urges, he tries to soothe her, showering her with words of love. He tells her that he is the prince of the city and that she is destined to become his princess. Pledging his love, he assures Dinah that his father will speak to her father before the day is done so that the two can wed.

When the news of what has happened reaches Jacob's ears, he says nothing until his sons return from the fields. When they learn that their sister has been defiled, they are filled with rage. How could such a thing happen? What was Dinah thinking when she wandered off alone? Cursing the Hivites as filthy dogs, they vow to avenge her honor. But it is not easy to attack a walled city and prevail.

Some commentators believe this was a case of statutory rape. In other words, Dinah may have willingly slept with Shechem even though she would have been under the age of consent. Even if this were true, Shechem committed what would have been considered an outrageous offense against Dinah and her family. ▪

Before long, two men approach. One is the large-bellied ruler of the city, a man named Hamor, and the other is Shechem, his arrogant, self-absorbed son.

The Hivites were one of several Canaanite tribes. Though little is known of them, *Hivite* may mean "tent-dweller." When Solomon was king they were consigned to forced labor and eventually blended with the Israelites. ■

After greeting Jacob, Hamor begins: "My son Shechem has his heart set on your daughter. Please give her to him as his wife. Intermarry with us; give us your daughters and take our daughters for yourselves. You can settle among us; the land is open to you. Live in it, trade in it, and acquire property in it."

He offers no word of apology, no regret or hint of shame about what his son has done. Instead he speaks as though he is merely proposing a simple business venture, a political deal with obvious benefits for everyone. Surely Jacob will see the value of forging an alliance, especially since his daughter needs a husband to remove her shame.

Before Jacob can respond, Shechem speaks up. "Let me find favor in your eyes," he says, "and I will give whatever you ask. Make the price for the bride and the gift I am to bring as great as you like, and I'll pay whatever you ask me. Only give me the girl as my wife." He is confident that the right amount of cash will close the deal.

Though Dinah was victimized, she would have been shamed in the eyes of others. ■

As Shechem waits for an answer, he fails to notice how Dinah's brothers are staring at him, listening for something he hasn't offered—a word of remorse, an expression of regret, an acknowledgment of guilt. His conscience is so callous that it never occurs to him to be ashamed.

Calmly, as though their fury and grief has melted away, one of the brothers replies, "We can't do such a thing; we can't give our sister to a man who is not circumcised. That would be a disgrace to us. We will enter into an agreement with you on one condition only: that you become like us by circumcising all your males. Then we will give you our daughters and take your daughters for ourselves. We'll settle among you and become one people with you. But if you will not agree to be circumcised, we'll take our sister and go."

To Jacob and his sons, circumcision is an indelible sign of their relationship with Yahweh. It marks them, not only as Abraham's descendants, but also as men whose powers have been surrendered to God. At least that is the theory.

But now they are bent on taking power into their own hands. Why else would they invite a people who worship many gods to join them in a covenant they cannot understand?

Though surprised by his sons' offer, Jacob says nothing.

After agreeing to their proposal, Shechem and his father Hamor return to the city with only one thing in mind. They must convince the rest of the men that the temporary pain of circumcision is a small price to pay for the riches they will gain.

"Listen to me," Hamor tells them. "The men who've settled near us are friendly. If we let them live in our land and trade in it, we will all benefit. Think how rich we'll become. We can marry their daughters and they can marry ours. We only need to submit ourselves to circumcision. Let's do it my friends. What are a few days of pain compared to all we stand to gain?" So every man agrees.

Three days later, when all the men of Shechem are too sore to stand, two of Dinah's brothers, Simeon and Levi, enter the city and massacre every last male, even the smallest boys. Then they return home with Dinah in tow. When the rest of Jacob's sons discover the bodies, they loot the city, seizing flocks and herds and everything out in the fields. They take the women and girls as well.

When Jacob discovers that his sons have surpassed his own talent for deceit, he confronts Simeon and Levi, saying, "You have made me a stench in the nostrils of everyone who lives in this land. We are few in number, and if they join forces against us, we will all be destroyed."

Instead of apologizing, Leah's sons look him straight in the eye and say, "Should we have allowed him to treat our sister like a prostitute?"

Something in their tone bites and tears at his heart. They have called Dinah "our sister." But she is his daughter too. Would he have kept a closer eye on her had her mother been Rachel rather than Leah?[2]

For the first time, Jacob allows himself to wonder—have the sons of his less-loved wife felt the pain of being less loved too? This he does not know, though the years ahead will make the answer clear enough to any who will hear the story.

THE TIMES

The story of Shechem and his demise
took place around 1909 BC.
His story is drawn from Genesis 34.

Male circumcision was widely, though not uniformly, practiced in the ancient Near East. Performed at puberty, it was a rite of passage that emphasized a young man's sexual potency and marked his initiation into male society, a time when he was leaving behind his primary attachment to his mother and entering the world of his father.

Among the Israelites, circumcision took on a radically different meaning. Rather than being performed at adolescence, circumcision, then and now, was practiced on eight-day-old boys. Instead of touting a young man's masculine power, circumcision served as a visible sign of purification and commitment to the covenantal relationship with God. Rather than signifying male prowess, the ritual pointed to male responsibility.

Then as now, when Jewish fathers have their sons circumcised, they are, as commentator Leon Kass points out, "summoned to ratify the meaning of their own circumcision (and, therewith, of the community's view of manhood), each new father vindicating the promise made by his own father to keep him within the covenant. . . . They are reminded that bearing the child is the easy part, that *rearing him well* is the real vocation. They are summoned to continue the chain by rearing their children looking up to the sacred and the divine, by initiating them into God's chosen ways."[3]

Like other ancient peoples, the Israelites also realized that circumcision promoted cleanliness, which may be why it was closely associated with spiritual purity. The Bible refers to the Philistines and later to the Greeks with the derogatory term, the "uncircumcised," implying that they were not only physically unclean but also spiritually corrupt.

Why weren't Jewish females circumcised? There are probably several reasons. One is that males may have needed more inducement than females to take on the responsibilities of parenting. As Leon Kass points out, "Freed by nature from the consequences of their sexuality, probably both less fitted and less interested by nature than women for the work of nurture and rearing, men need to be acculturated to the work of transmission. Virility and potency are, from the Bible's point of view, much less important than decency, righteousness, and holiness."[4]

By the early first century, babies were circumcised by a priest, either at the Jerusalem Temple or in a synagogue. During the ceremony the child was also publicly named.

Though circumcision was a symbol of covenant community, at times it devolved into an outward sign of ethnic and religious pride with little internal meaning, which is why the prophet Jeremiah called on people to circumcise their hearts and not just their bodies (Jeremiah 4:4).

Listen to how *The Message* paraphrases Paul's words in his letter to the Romans: "Circumcision, the surgical ritual that marks you as a Jew, is great if you live in accord with God's law. But if you don't, it's worse than not being circumcised. The reverse is also true: The uncircumcised who keep God's ways are as good as the circumcised—in fact, better. Better to keep God's law uncircumcised than break it circumcised" (Romans 2:25–27).

THE TAKEAWAY

1. In light of the meaning attached to circumcision as practiced in the Jewish community, comment on how the males in the story—both the Shechemites and the Jews—behaved. How did they live up to or fail to live up to the commitment and responsibility of their circumcision?

2. In many ancient societies, women were stigmatized by or even considered responsible for sexual abuse or assault. In what ways, if any, do you think similar attitudes persist today?

3. How would you describe what it means to live with what the apostle Paul describes as a circumcised heart? Use the following sentences starters as part of your response:
   - I know I'm living with an *uncircumcised* heart when . . .
   - I know I'm living with an *circumcised* heart when . . .

4. After the incident with their pagan neighbors, God instructs Jacob to move away and settle in Bethel (Genesis 35:1–5), the place in which he experienced God in a dream when fleeing from Esau. What kind of things—ranging from an attitude, an influence, an atmosphere, or a relationship—has God instructed you to move away from in the past? What, if anything, might God be inviting you to move away from in this season of your life?

CHAPTER 7

THE STORY OF TAMAR

A Widow and a One-Night Stand

The Lord does not look at the things
people look at. People look at the outward
appearance, but the Lord looks at the heart.

1 SAMUEL 16:7

Jacob's talent for deceit is still winding its way through his off-spring. His son Judah is knee-deep in concocting a lie that will break old Jacob's heart. A reluctant liar, Judah has little idea that one day he will learn a lesson in deceit from his daughter-in-law Tamar. But for now he is the one mired in a lie.

Night has already fallen by the time Judah and his brothers arrive home, carrying with them the clothing of their seventeen-year-old brother, Joseph. When Jacob sees the richly ornamented robe he had given his favorite son ripped into shreds and smeared with blood, the old man wails, "It is my son's robe! Some ferocious animal has devoured him. Joseph has surely been torn to pieces."

Better, Judah thinks, for Jacob to believe his precious son had been eaten by wild beasts than to know the sorry truth—that Joseph is on his way to Egypt with a caravan of Ishmaelite and Midianite traders who've paid the going rate for a freshly minted slave.

Despite the fact that Judah has saved his brother's life by suggesting he be sold rather than murdered, as his brothers had intended, he is sickened by the whole sorry mess. No matter that Joseph has always been such a peacock of a boy and that his father has inflamed the situation by playing favorites. Judah knows it for what it is—a terrible betrayal.

The Midianites were Abraham's descendants through his wife Keturah while the Ishmaelites were his descendants through Hagar. That would have meant that the traders who purchased Joseph and sold him into slavery in Egypt were his second or third cousins. ■

Distancing himself from his grieving father and the wild donkeys who are his brothers, Judah moves to the town of

Adullam and stays with a man he knows there. Before long he meets and marries a Canaanite woman. Together they have three sons: Er, Onan, and Shelah.

As often happens, one bad decision has led to another. First Judah conspired against his brother Joseph. Then he lied to his father. Then he married outside his tribe, unlike his forefathers Abraham, Isaac, and Jacob. His marriage has opened the door to future difficulties. One of these will come into focus years later, after his eldest son marries a woman by the name of Tamar.

Instead of growing tall and straight, Judah's sons Er and Onan are like bent branches on the family tree, their ways twisted and deceitful.

Er is a sour, weedy-looking man who delights in punishing his wife, Tamar, for his many failings; he is the kind of man others easily overlook. But God does not overlook him. Instead, he notes every detail of Er's wicked ways and arranges for him to make an early departure from this life. At least that's what everyone says when he is found in bed one morning, purple-faced and choking on vomit.

By now Judah has become a man of means. But he is one son short. As is customary, he does the right thing by instructing his second son, Onan, to marry Tamar so that his dead brother may yet have an heir.

Onan is a "yes, Papa, anything you say Papa" kind of boy. But he has closed his fist around his dead brother's property as though it already belongs to him. Why would he want to sire a son who would eventually snatch it from him? So he merely plays at being husband. Whenever Onan sleeps with Tamar, he makes sure to withdraw before planting his seed inside her womb. There will be no child.

This story unfolds in a period in which God's command in Genesis 1:28 to "be fruitful and multiply" was an urgent necessity if the new nation was to survive. If a man died, it was the duty of his brother to marry his widow in order to perpetuate the dead brother's name. It was also a way to provide for his childless widow who otherwise might have no way to provide for herself. During the patriarchal period, the punishment for neglecting this duty was severe, which is why God killed Onan, Judah's second son, because he tried to prevent his wife, Tamar, from becoming pregnant. ■

Tamar says nothing. She is too afraid of what Onan may do to her if she speaks up, and so her tears go unnoticed by her father-in-law, Judah.

But the God who sees everything takes note of Onan's wickedness and puts Judah's second son to death.

Now Judah is two sons short. Who will carry on the family line?

Fortunately, he still has one son in his pocket, his youngest, Shelah. But what about Tamar? For a woman to marry a wicked man is tragedy enough. But to marry two wicked men in quick succession—that is more misery than one woman should have to bear. Still, Tamar is willing to hope for better things when Shelah comes of age.

So Judah instructs his daughter-in-law to return to her father's house to live as a widow until Shelah is old enough to marry. But this makes her uneasy. Why doesn't he let her stay as is the custom? Maybe he thinks her bed is cursed. Having lost two sons, perhaps he is reluctant to risk another.

Day after day Tamar sits inside her father's house, spending many hours at the loom. While her fingers ply the wool, she broods, watching other women do what she longs to. Like contented hens, they spend their days gathering their chicks beneath their wings. If only she could do the same, but the ache inside her tells her she has already become the thing she dreads, a widow without a future or a hope.

Time passes but still there is no wedding. Then Judah's Canaanite wife dies.

One day, Tamar hears that her father-in-law is planning to go up to Timnah for the sheep shearing. Because money is plentiful during the wool harvest, there will be women lying in wait. She knows this. But she is not like them, not in the least.

Even so, she trades her plain clothing for a colorful robe, covering her face with a veil. Then she sits down on the road that leads to Timnah and waits.

Judah catches sight of her. He thinks how hard it's been all these months without a wife to comfort him. "Come now, let me sleep with you," he says, his voice beguiling.

"How much will you pay me?" she asks.

"I'll send you a young goat from my flock."

The bartering continues.

"But how can I know you will keep your word? Let me have your seal and its cord, and the staff in your hands." These she knows are precious to a man.

So Judah agrees.

Afterward, Judah sends a friend to deliver the promised goat and to retrieve his property. But the woman has vanished. No one has seen a prostitute[1] on the road where she was. The answer is always the same: "There's never been a woman like that here."

Judah is puzzled. He never saw the woman's face because she kept it covered by her veil. So he merely shrugs and says, "At least I tried. Let her keep what she has. If I

Judah probably wore his seal on a cord around his neck. The seal was a stamp or engraving made of stone or metal that could be impressed onto clay or wax. Used to authenticate legal documents, it would have been decorated with a simple picture and may also have included his name. Staffs were often engraved, making the owner easy to identify. ∎

continue to look for her, the whole world will know about it, and I will become a laughingstock."

Three months pass until a shocking report reaches Judah's ears. "Your daughter-in-law Tamar is guilty of prostitution and now she is pregnant!"

Judah is incensed. How dare Tamar bring shame on his family!

He never considers that she is a childless widow with little means of provision. Nor does he think about what might have driven her to so desperate an act. Instead he thunders judgment, saying, "Bring her out and burn her to death!"

So the best men of the town hurry to do just that. But as they drag Tamar out of her house, she sends a message to her father-in-law along with particular items in her possession. "I am pregnant by the man who owns these. See if you recognize whose seal and cord and staff these are."

Judah is stunned. What excuse can he make? He has just condemned his daughter-in-law for sleeping with a man, but he is that man! So Judah makes his own shameful confession: "She is more righteous than I, since I wouldn't give her to my son Shelah."

Six months later, Tamar gives birth to two children. During their struggle to enter the world, one tiny arm emerges. Wrapping the baby's wrist with a scarlet thread, the midwife says, "This one came out first." To her surprise, the little hand retreats and his brother is born instead, prompting her to say, "So this is how you have broken out!"

Tamar's first son is named Perez, which means "breaking out." Her second son is named Zerah, which means "scarlet."

A widow who was all but forgotten by those who should have cared for her, Tamar has been remembered by God. Perez grew up and became the father of descendants who bore delightful names like Amminadab, Abijah, Jehoshaphat, and Zerubbabel. From him also came Boaz, King David, and the wise King Solomon.

As for Tamar, God made her a happy woman by rescuing her from two wicked husbands and then blessing her with two fine sons. As if that were not enough, she is among a handful of women listed in a genealogy in the first chapter of Matthew's gospel. Though their stories are laced with distasteful details, like incest, out-of-wedlock pregnancies, and murder, each woman in the list is remembered as part of a vital chain of human beings that stretches from Abraham to Joseph, the husband of Mary, of whom was born Jesus, who is called the Christ.

THE TIMES

Tamar lived around 1893–1833 BC.
Her story is told in Genesis 38. She is
also mentioned in Matthew 1.

The story of how Tamar tricked her father-in-law into sleeping with her so she could become pregnant by him sounds both sordid and bizarre. What's it doing in the Bible? Unlike contemporary readers, Jewish people who heard the story would have thought of Tamar as a hero rather than a villain.

In their world, one of the worst fates a woman could suffer was to be a childless widow because that meant you lacked everything you needed to survive: economic, legal, and social status. When Judah ordered Tamar to remain a widow though he had no intention of providing her with a husband, he was breaking the custom of levirate marriage, a common practice in many ancient cultures. To die without an heir was considered a curse. To prevent this, the dead man's wife was married to one of his brothers. Failing that, she could also be married to her father-in-law. Levirate marriage was a way to provide for the widow as well as to produce an heir to carry on her dead husband's name.

An ancient Hittite law read like this: "If a man has a wife, and the man dies, his brother shall take his widow as a wife. [If the brother dies,] his father shall take her. When afterwards his father dies, his [i.e., the father's] brother shall take the woman whom he had."[2]

Judah was also sinning against Tamar by preventing her from remarrying as other widows would have been allowed to do should the family not provide a husband. Despite her father-in-law's ill treatment, Tamar maintained her loyalty to his family by risking her life to produce an heir. Otherwise, the line of Judah, from whom the Messiah was to come, might have died out. Tamar's actions meant that Abraham's line would continue, not through Judah's wicked Canaanite sons but through the twins Tamar bore him.

THE TAKEAWAY

1. Why do you think the Bible includes sordid stories like this one?
2. Psalm 33:15 says that God watches everyone who lives on earth and considers everything they do. The words of the psalm would seem to be borne out by this story. How does this understanding shape the way you look at what's happening around you? How does it shape the way you look at your own life?
3. What does this story reveal about God's ability to redeem evil even in the midst of entrenched family dysfunction?
4. What kinds of things tend to make you feel worthless? What makes you feel worthwhile?

CHAPTER 8

THE STORY OF JUDAH AND HIS TERRIBLE BROTHERS

When God Surprises Everyone

You are a lion's cub, O Judah.

GENESIS 49:9

Judah remembers the story as though it happened yesterday. He feels it in his gut, like a knife turning. The pain of his treachery is so strong that it overwhelms every other sensation. Indeed, he had turned against his father and his brother, first by selling the conceited young Joseph into slavery and then by joining his brothers in the ruse they invented to explain his death.

"Here is Joseph's beautiful coat," they said, handing Jacob the bloodied garment of his beloved son.

"My son has surely been torn to pieces!" he cried. "Some ferocious animal has devoured him."

Jacob's agony was made sharper by what he suspected. Could his own sons have taken Joseph's life? Might they be the ferocious beasts who had torn him to pieces?

The ornamental robe had been a spectacular gift from father to son, marking Joseph not only as Jacob's favorite son but as the future ruler of his brothers. No wonder his older brothers had despised him. The garment he loved to wear was a constant reminder of their father's favoritism, which began with his preference for Rachel over their mother Leah.

Little brother Joseph had made things far worse by speaking openly about his insufferable dreams. Even his father had

Clothing in the Ancient Near East communicated something important about the status of its wearer. The quality of the fabric, the colors, the amount of ornamentation—all these sent a message about the person wearing a particular garment. In this case, Joseph's coat signified both favor and authority. Rather than a "coat of many colors," his garment might better be understood as a long-sleeve or full-length coat. ■

recoiled when he heard that his seventeen-year-old son had dreamt that the sun, moon, and stars—a code for his entire family—would one day bow down to him.

From the beginning, Jacob's family had been built on a fault line—the one that ran between Rachel and Leah and their children. What would happen when he died? Without their father holding everything together, it might splinter and disappear, blending in with the surrounding peoples.

Oddly, the brothers' betrayal of Joseph is what had united them, at least for a time. Reuben, Simeon, Levi, Judah, and all the others—every son but Benjamin—were complicit in the lie. Secretly, many of them—though not Judah—took pleasure in their father's pain.

When Judah distanced himself from his family by moving to a Canaanite town, he took no thought of the covenant God had made with his forefathers. Turning his back on everyone, including his grieving father, it never occurred to him to consider who might lead this broken band of brothers into the future. Nor did he gaze into the night sky recalling God's promise to his great grandfather Abraham: "Look up at the heavens and count the stars—if indeed you can count them. So shall your offspring be."

When we next hear of him, he is back with his father and his brothers. Threatened by a severe famine, Jacob sends Judah and his brothers (all except Benjamin) down to Egypt to purchase grain.

None of them suspect the surprise that awaits them in Egypt. For there they will discover the brother they betrayed years earlier. Neither do they recognize him when they encounter him.

Bowing before Joseph, who has become an influential Egyptian official, they explain that they have come to buy food to keep their family from starving.

Though his brothers fail to recognize the powerful man who stands before them, Joseph knows exactly who they are. Instead of disclosing his true identity, he initiates a game in which they will become pawns.

"You are spies," he accuses them.

"No, my lord," they protest. "Your servants were twelve brothers, the sons of one man, who lives in the land of Canaan. The youngest is now with our father, and one is no more."

"If you are honest men," Joseph replies, "let one of your brothers stay here in prison, while the rest of you go and take grain back for your starving households. But you must bring your youngest brother to me, so that your words may be verified and that you may not die."

"Surely," they whisper to each other, "we are being punished because of our brother. We saw how distressed he was when he pleaded with us for his life, but we would not listen; that is why this distress has come upon us."

When Joseph turns to hide his tears, they do not notice. Nor are they aware this Egyptian understands every word they say.

Leaving Simeon as a hostage, the brothers return home. Though their sacks are bulging with grain, their hearts are filled with anxiety. Judah wonders how they will find the courage to tell their father what has happened—that they have left Simeon behind to rot in an Egyptian jail.

As soon as Jacob hears the news, he exclaims, "You have deprived me of my children. Joseph is no more and Simeon is no more, and now you want to take Benjamin. Everything is against me! My son will not go down there with you; his brother is dead and he is the only one left. If harm comes to him, you will bring my gray head down to the grave in sorrow."

But as their rations dwindle, Jacob orders his sons to return to Egypt. Even so, he refuses to allow young Benjamin to go with them. Knowing they will perish without further stores of grain, Judah pleads with his father. "Send Benjamin along with me," he says, "so that we and you and our children may live and not die. I will guarantee his safety. If I fail to return him to you, I will bear the blame before you all my life."

So Jacob relents, and his sons set out for Egypt. As soon as they arrive, Joseph invites them to dine at his house, ordering his servants to fill their sacks with as much grain as they can carry. After politely inquiring about the health of their old father Jacob, he secretly instructs his steward to hide a silver cup in young Benjamin's sack. The next morning, after Judah and his brothers have left for home, Joseph orders his steward to pursue them and arrest the brother in whose sack he has hidden the cup.

When Benjamin and his brothers are dragged before Joseph, Judah once again speaks up, this time making the speech of his life. "If the boy is not with us when I go back to my father, we will have brought the gray head of our father down to the grave in sorrow. I myself guaranteed the boy's safety. Now then, please let me remain as your slave in place of the boy, and let him return to his brothers."

Judah's willingness to take Benjamin's place reveals the kind of man he has become. Not only has he returned to the heart of his family, but he has become willing to sacrifice himself so that his brother might live.[1]

His desire to pay the price to secure Benjamin's freedom makes Judah the rightful leader of the clan, the brother who will carry the covenant forward.

When Judah offers to enslave himself so that Benjamin can go free, Joseph can stand the tension no more. Bursting into tears, he exclaims, "I am your brother Joseph. The one you sold into Egypt!"

In a moment of stunned silence, the brothers step back. Surely this great man who stands before them cannot be the brother they despise! What will Joseph do? Shocked and confused, they expect the worst. Has God punished them by allowing them to fall into the hands of the brother they betrayed?

In a gesture surpassing even Judah's generosity, Joseph assures them, saying, "Do not be distressed, and do not be angry with yourselves for selling me here, because it was to save lives that God sent me ahead of you. For two years now there has been famine in the land, and for the next five years there will not be plowing and reaping. But God sent me ahead of you to preserve for you a remnant on earth and to save your lives by a great deliverance."

Then Joseph tells them to bring their families to live in Egypt so that their lives will be preserved.

So Jacob and his large family go down to Egypt. Before his death—and he will perish in Egypt—Jacob summons his sons and tells each of them what will happen to them in the days to come. When it is Judah's turn, his father says,

> Judah, your brothers will praise you;
> Your hand will be on the neck of your enemies;
> Your father's sons will bow down to you.
> You are a lion's cub, O Judah. . . .
> The scepter will not depart from Judah,
> Nor the ruler's staff from between his feet,
> Until he comes to whom it belongs
> And the obedience of the nations is his.

And so it is that despite their foolish, hateful ways, God preserves his fledgling people. He surprises everyone by bringing great good out of great evil and by raising up Judah as the leader of his people, from whose line will eventually be born the one who will be called the Lion of the Tribe of Judah, the Messiah of Israel.

THE TIMES

The story of Judah and his brothers took place about 1898–1859 BC.
Their story is drawn from Genesis 37–46, 49.

The ancient stories that thread their way through Genesis are fascinating and enlightening, repeating certain themes generation after generation. From the very beginning there is deception, struggle, violence, and incredible dysfunction, beginning in the garden of Eden, continuing with Cain and Abel, and then snaking its way through Jacob and his family.

Jacob must have felt that his own efforts to deceive his father and trick his brother out of a blessing had been paid back multiple times. Even Joseph, his favorite son and the innocent victim of this story, deceived his family in order to force his brothers to face the truth about what they had done to him.

Yet there is mercy and the evidence of God's remarkable power to preserve his people and carry his plan forward despite their brokenness.

To appreciate Judah's life and the transformation of his character, we need to think like someone in his world would have about his sacred obligations toward family. We also need to remember how fragile God's chosen people were at this stage in their history. Without the right kind of leader, it would have been easy for this fledgling clan to break apart, melding into the world around it.

After the brothers' betrayal of Joseph, Judah's move away from his family looks like another fracture. When the text says he "left his brothers and *went down*" to the town of Adullam, where he married a Canaanite woman (Genesis 38:1), it may be signaling that by abandoning his father and his crazy brothers, Judah has *gone down* the wrong path, one that could endanger the family's future.

Just as Judah turned his back on his brothers, his own sons, Er and Onan, turn their backs on their dead brother and his widow by deliberately preventing her from getting pregnant.

After the deaths of his first two sons, Judah once again neglects his family duty. Out of fear for the life of his youngest son, he fails in his responsibility toward both the living and the dead. By withholding his remaining son from Tamar, he relegates her to a difficult and lonely life. In Judah's world, childless widows had no social or economic standing. Without a male provider some women were even forced to sell themselves into slavery or prostitution in order to survive.

Judah also turns his back on his deceased sons by doing nothing to help insure that their names will live on through their descendants.

Fortunately his story doesn't end in failure. When faced with his sin, Judah reverses course by acknowledging his fault. From then on his story turns back toward his extended family. In the end we see Judah as a man who is capable of leading his clan because he refuses to leave his brother behind. He is willing to sacrifice his own life so that his youngest brother, Benjamin, can return to his father Jacob.

Though Jacob adopts Joseph's sons Ephraim and Manasseh as his own, and refers to his favorite son Joseph as "a prince among his brothers" (Exodus 49:26), the covenant promise will pass not through Joseph's line but through Judah's, from whom will come the Lion of the Tribe of Judah.[2]

THE TAKEAWAY

1. Judah's story once again highlights the dysfunctional character of the families whose stories populate the book of Genesis. They are rife with all manner of jealousy, betrayal, pride, self-seeking, greed, deceit, and more. What events or themes in Judah's story do you relate to most? In what ways, if any, does Judah's story help you understand something about your own family history or experience of family life?

2. Judah's story demonstrates God's ability to work for the good despite our struggles, hardships, and sins. What comes to mind when you consider this dynamic in your own life? How has God brought good out of your struggles, hardships, or sins—in the past or recently?

3. Through his failures and struggles, Judah becomes a different person. In what ways does his story challenge you? In what ways does it encourage you? What does Judah's life suggestions about the process of transformation—how God changes us?

CHAPTER 9

THE STORY OF MIRIAM

How a Good Woman Falters

For rebellion is like the sin of divination, and arrogance like the evil of idolatry.

1 SAMUEL 15:23

Papa, tell us the story about Joseph and his beautiful coat," she says. Her dark eyes shine in the firelight as she leans forward to hear the tale once more. Each time her father recounts it, the story of the young dreamer and his jealous older brothers comes alive in her mind as though it happened only yesterday.

Her father starts by reminding her that God had his hand on the youth from the very beginning, planting dreams of such magnificence inside him that the retelling of them drove his brothers crazy with envy. But even their betrayal could not stop God's plan to make Joseph a great man in Egypt—a man who would one day save the world—and his own family too.

Like Joseph's family, Miriam lives in the Nile Delta, in Goshen, not far from where the river flows into the Mediterranean. But unlike Joseph, this spirited girl has always been a slave. Her dreams of freedom are nurtured by stories about her people that have passed through the generations. They remind her not only that life has not always been this hard but that there is a God who loves them.

Though Joseph's memory lives on in the hearts of his people, a new ruler has arisen in Egypt who knows nothing of him. This man thinks only of how to control the Hebrew slaves, who are multiplying at an alarming rate. He fears they will soon grow too strong to subdue and that they may conspire with invaders on his northern border. So he decides to cull them, as though they are merely a herd of animals.

He begins by instructing the Hebrew midwives to slaughter every baby boy at birth. But the midwives fear God more than they fear Pharaoh, and so they contrive a lie that only a man would believe. They tell him that the Hebrew slaves are far heartier than Egyptian women. By the time the midwives reach the birthing stool, the baby has already been delivered and hidden away.

So Pharaoh commands his people to throw all the male infants into the Nile River as soon as they are discovered. Sometimes Miriam hears screaming in the middle of the night, and she can't keep the tears from rolling down her face, because she knows that another baby has just been fed to the river god.

Her mother, Jochebed, is one of those hearty Hebrew women who have recently given birth to a son. But instead of being a cause for celebration, his birth is a cause for worry.

By now Jochebed's baby is three months old, a lusty boy whose cries might easily give him away. Pressing her cheek to the softness of his, she holds him close and begins to pray. Day after day the words of her prayers rise up like incense to heaven. Hearing them, the great God above—the God of Abraham, Isaac, Jacob, Judah, and Joseph—the God of her fathers looks down with pity and answers.

Suddenly she knows exactly what to do. Pharaoh has ordered every baby boy to be consigned to the waters of the Nile. So be it. Carefully she covers a small papyrus basket with tar and pitch, making certain to coat the surface completely. When she is sure it is seaworthy, she lays her little boy inside. His brown eyes are so trusting that she is tempted to take him in her arms again and never let him go.

Miriam watches as her mother closes the lid of the waterproof basket and places it into the great river. Her heart is breaking too. How will the baby survive the pythons that lurk on its banks or the hippos and crocodiles that swim in the water? Standing at the edge of the river, she cranes her neck to see what will happen as the little ark floats away.

Suddenly she spots one of Pharaoh's daughters nearing the river bank. As soon as the princess notices the basket, she sends a slave girl to fetch it. The girl wades through the water, snatches it up, and then carries the basket to her mistress. She looks on as the princess opens the lid and exclaims, "This is one of the Hebrew babies." How tenderly Pharaoh's daughter lifts his little body from the basket and then holds him against her breast, swaying and cooing to quiet his cries.

Her heart beating wildly, Miriam steps forward to ask if there is anything she can do to help. Perhaps she can find a nurse maid for the infant. She knows of a Hebrew woman who has just lost a child. She holds her breath to see how Pharaoh's daughter will respond.

Fortunately, the princess is grateful for her help, and Miriam rushes home to fetch her mother. How convenient, the princess thinks, to have a woman close at hand who has just lost her own child. Could she be the baby's mother? But it's no concern of hers. What matters is that the baby survives.

Thanks to Miriam's boldness and God's unfolding plan, Jochebed is not only reunited with her son but she is being paid by a member of Pharaoh's household to care for him. After a few years, when the boy is weaned, he will leave his family and move to the palace. Until then, he is shaped by the love and guidance of his family. Miriam delights him with stories, like the one about Noah and the beasts that climb aboard the ark, or his favorite, the story of Joseph and his jealous brothers.

Time passes and the boy grows strong. One day, he walks down a path, holding hands with Miriam and his mother. He knows where they are going. He has always known because his mother is forever singing the princess's praises, telling how she rescued him from the Nile River. He wants to live in the palace but not yet, even though his mother and father say he must. Miriam squeezes his hand, as though to say everything will be all right.

Pharaoh's daughter welcomes them warmly. But when it's time for Jochebed and Miriam to go, the little boy's face contorts with fear and his arms reach out as though to drag them back. "Don't leave me!" he wails. Miriam turns away, hoping to hide her tears.

With her arm around Miriam's shoulders, Jochebed leads her out and whispers in her ear, "Hush child, your crying will only make things worse." Then a tear slides down her own cheek.

As for Pharaoh's daughter, she is delighted with her little boy. He will be a fine son, smart and strong. Now that he is safely past the age of weaning, she gives him a name. He will be called Moses, she says, "because I drew him out of the water." And so she had.

So Moses, a boy whom Pharaoh had tried to murder, grows up right under his nose, putting his feet up, living in his palace, eating his food, and getting the best education Egypt can offer. Whenever Miriam thinks of this, her pain eases. She laughs a little because it proves who is really in control.

Years pass. By now Moses is a grown man—forty years old. He is tall and broad—the picture of Egyptian dignity and power. Miriam wonders if he still remembers her. She hopes he recalls the stories she told him about a mighty God who has chosen their people and promised them a land to live in. Perhaps he will find favor with Pharaoh and become the one to lift them out of slavery, saving his family just as Joseph had saved his.

But this dream of hers, that God will deliver the lowly ones who cry out to him day and night, all but vanishes when she hears that Moses has been accused of murder and that Pharaoh intends to kill him as soon as he can lay his hands on him. What is his crime? He has slain an Egyptian slave driver who was beating a slave to death.

To her relief, Moses escapes, but to her sorrow, she hears nothing of him for another forty years.

After a while the king of Egypt dies, and another Pharaoh ascends the throne. This one, they say, is even worse than the last, with the heart of a viper. A golden cobra—the emblem of Wadjit, the protective goddess of the Delta region—adorns his crown, reminding his enemies of his strength and cunning. It proclaims his power, as though to say he will surely strike should anyone be fool enough to challenge him. With Wadjit's protection he feels secure.

But Pharaoh's smugness would soon vanish if he perceived the truth—that even now a Deity he does not know is stirring up trouble, calling forth a deliverer who will marshal the created world to fight against him.

By now Miriam's brother Moses is living in the desert of Midian, east of Egypt. It is the place where God shapes and molds him into the man he must become.

One day, as he is tending his flock near Mount Horeb,[1] God appears in the shape of a burning bush. Out of the fire he speaks a harrowing word:

"Moses, Moses! Take off your sandals, for the place where you are standing is holy ground. I am the God of your father, the God of Abraham, the God of Isaac and the God of Jacob . . .

"I have indeed seen the misery of my people in Egypt. I have heard them crying out because of their slave drivers, and I am concerned about their suffering. So I have come down to rescue them from the hand of the Egyptians and to bring them up out of that land into a good and spacious land, a land flowing with milk and honey. So now, go. I am sending you to Pharaoh to bring my people the Israelites out of Egypt."

Shielding his face with both arms, Moses is terrified lest he look into the flames and see the face of God and die.

Somehow he finds the courage to respond. "Since I speak with faltering lips, why would Pharaoh speak to me?" But the Lord assures him he is perfect for the job, not because he is strong or persuasive. He is neither of these. But because God himself will be with him.

When Moses returns to Egypt after an absence of forty years, he meets his family again. Though his parents are dead, his bond of love with his siblings, Miriam and Aaron, is renewed. The three take counsel together and then meet with the elders of Israel, and all concur: he and Aaron, who is to be his mouthpiece, are to go to Pharaoh and tell him what the Lord has said—that he must "let my people go."

So Moses meets with Pharaoh, but Egypt's arrogant ruler merely puffs up his chest and scoffs. "Who is this Lord you speak of?" He lingers on the word "Lord," drawing it out as a deliberate mockery. "I do not know him, and I will not let Israel go." Then he accuses the slaves of laziness and doubles their workload.

Myriam is distressed to hear many of her fellow Hebrews cursing Moses, accusing him of making things worse with all his foolish talk of freedom. But she takes heart when she hears what happened when her brothers paid a second visit to Pharaoh.

Issuing a challenge, Aaron had thrown down his staff, which quickly transformed into a snake. Trying to hide his surprise, Pharaoh called on his sorcerers to match the feat. When they threw down their staffs and the floor turned into a nest of writhing snakes, he crowed with delight. But Pharaoh's boasts were soon cut short as Aaron's staff devoured all the others.

The magicians quickly stepped back as each man weighed the unmistakable sign. The God of Moses and Aaron had challenged and defeated the goddess Wadjit, whose emblem was the cobra on Pharaoh's crown. Without the goddesses' mystical protection, how could his kingdom stand? But Pharaoh's stony heart would not admit the truth and he refused to let God's people go.

Snake charming was practiced in ancient Egypt by magicians who knew tricks that would put their snakes into a rigid, trance-like state.[2] ▪

So the battle continued with plague upon plague upon plague.

As the Nile turns to blood, the ground teems with frogs, the dust turns to gnats, great swarms of flies invade the land, the livestock is struck down, and festering boils break out on man and beast, Miriam wonders how long until Pharaoh will finally relent.

Joseph's God, the God of her people, is working to free them! She tells everyone to get ready. "We are going to leave Egypt," she says. "It could happen any day."

More plagues follow. Hail destroys the crops, locusts devour what's left, darkness covers the earth, and—worst of all—the beating heart of every firstborn son in Egypt is stilled, and there is mourning and wailing and grief such as the nation has never known. It has happened just as God and Moses said it would. Only the land of Goshen, where God's people live, is spared.

Finally, in the middle of the night, when the Egyptians are counting their dead, Pharaoh summons Moses. "Up! Leave my people," he cries, "you and the Israelites! Go, worship the LORD as you have requested. Take your flocks and herds, as you have said, and go."

In their haste to be rid of their former slaves, the Egyptians shower them with gold, silver, and fine clothing as though they have just been plundered by a conquering army.

So Moses, Miriam, and Aaron and all the ragtag band of Hebrew slaves and anyone else who wants to leave Egypt begin to march out. The women wear beautiful rings, necklaces, and golden bracelets reaching from wrist to elbow. The men are weighed down by pouches filled with silver. The children skip and play, oblivious to the dangers that lie ahead.

The great crowd of slaves go out from the land of their captivity singing and dancing, but not at first, because Pharaoh makes a last, brainless attempt to overtake them in their march to the sea.

On they come, the chariots. Great clouds of dust mark their passing and the people begin to panic. "We will be swallowed up," they cry, "trapped between the sea and Pharaoh's chariots!" Miriam and Aaron try to hold the line, to put a lid on the panic while Moses tells the people, "Do not be afraid. Stand firm and you will see the deliverance the LORD will bring you today. The Egyptians you see today you will never see again. The LORD will fight for you; you need only to be still."

Then Moses stretches out his arms and all that night the Lord holds back the Egyptian pursuers while he unleashes a strong east wind to uncover the floor of the sea so that the Israelites can march across.

A horde of people—young and old—along with all their herds, walk through the open trench with walls of water piled on either side. They march through the night.

With the deafening wind still beating back the waves, Pharaoh reaches the water's edge and urges his chariots forward, anticipating the slaughter he will wreak upon his fleeing slaves. But his chariots are soon mired in mud and he drives them so hard that their wheels fall off. By the time he realizes his mistake, it is too late to turn back.

With God's people now safely across, Moses lifts up his hands again, and great walls of water collapse on Israel's enemies. Every soldier, every horse, every chariot is smothered beneath the waves of the angry sea, forever buried in their watery grave.

Then Miriam takes a drum[3] and begins to lead a great, wild dance of victory as her people reenact the battle God has just won. Her skirts swirl and swing as she dances and sings a song that will not be forgotten.

> Sing to the LORD,
>> for he is highly exalted.
> Both horse and driver
>> he has hurled into the sea.

Then Moses along with Aaron and Miriam lead the people forward on their long and arduous journey through the wilderness. And as they march, God speaks. Sometimes he comes to Miriam in visions and dreams. She is a prophet, a woman he entrusts with words of wisdom.

One day she and Aaron begin to complain. The people are difficult to lead, the journey longer and harsher than they had expected. Why does Moses make all the decisions? Hasn't God spoken through them too? Their complaints mount up and spill over, and they begin to criticize him publicly. The pretense for speaking out is that Moses has taken a foreign wife.[4] But what they want is power, a bigger role to play. And the Lord hears them speaking against his servant Moses.

At once, God summons the three of them and has them stand before him. He calls Miriam and Aaron forward. "Listen to my words," he thunders from the pillar of cloud that hovers above the tabernacle.

> When there is a prophet among you,
>> I, the LORD, reveal myself to them in visions,
>> I speak to them in dreams.
> But this is not true of my servant Moses;
>> he is faithful in all my house.
> With him I speak face to face,
>> clearly and not in riddles,
>> he sees the form of the LORD.
> Why then were you not afraid
>> to speak against my servant Moses?

God's anger burns against them both, and when the cloud lifts, there stands Miriam—covered with white scales. She is leprous like snow.

Horrified by what has happened to his sister, Aaron begs Moses to intercede: "Please," he says, "ask God to lift the curse." Since Moses is more humble than anyone else on the face of the earth, he does what Aaron asks, crying out to the Lord, "O God, please heal her!"

And God replies with words that burn in Miriam's heart: "If her father had spit in her face, would she not have been in disgrace for seven days? Confine her outside the camp for seven days; after that she can be brought back."

So Miriam is healed and forgiven but not before she is exiled for seven days. During her confinement, she has time to reflect on the wickedness of what she and her brother Aaron have done. It is true that God has spoken to her. He has made her a leader and a prophet. But she is not Moses. She had not been drawn out of the waters and raised in Pharaoh's household. She had not done battle in Pharaoh's court. Nor had she met with God face to face as her brother had done.

She remembers the story of Joseph and his jealous brothers, and as much as she dislikes the thought, it occurs to her that she too has lost a fight with jealousy. She has been so blindly jealous that she did not realize she and Aaron were risking her people's future by challenging Moses and the words God spoke through him.

But why was she alone punished? Perhaps because God in his wisdom did not want the worship of the tabernacle to be disrupted by Aaron's absence as high priest.

After seven days, a mild punishment she thinks, Miriam is restored to the community and the people set out once again. After forty years of wandering and many difficult adventures along the way, God's people finally approach the land of promise. But Miriam will not reach it, nor will Aaron, nor will Moses. All three will die before they can enter the Promised Land.

So the people mourn them as they stand on the brink of taking hold of God's great promise to give them a land flowing with milk and honey—a paradise of their own. The task of leading them all the way in will fall not to Moses but to Joshua, a warrior who can safely guide them through every battle that lies ahead.

THE TIMES

Miriam's story may have taken place
from about 1533 to 1406 BC.
Her story is drawn from Exodus 2–3; 5;
7:1–13; 12:3–36; Numbers 12.

Unlike the Egyptians who worshiped as many as 1,500 gods throughout their history, the Israelites worshiped only one God, whose name is *Yahweh*.

It is only by listening to Yahweh and heeding his direction that Moses is able to lead the Israelites out of Egypt. And it is only by following Moses's leadership that Miriam, Aaron, and the people will survive the wilderness.

The battle between Moses and Pharaoh is an epic one that symbolizes the battle between good and evil. It is a battle not merely between humans but between God and all the false gods of the Egyptians who had enslaved his people.

Even today, the exodus story shapes the understanding of both Jews and Christians who believe that each of us are meant to identify with the story in a personal way. Just as the Israelites were in bondage to Pharaoh, who personifies evil, we too are beset by evils, from which only God can deliver us. If we follow him, he will lead us out of bondage and into a life of freedom.

Though Miriam is struck by leprosy for opposing her brother, there is little evidence of what we call Hansen's disease in the ancient Near East. The Hebrew term that is translated as "leprosy" probably refers to diseases like ringworm, psoriasis, or eczema.

As is often the pattern in Scripture, God uses unlikely heroes in unlikely ways to accomplish his purposes. Though Moses and

Aaron stand against Pharaoh, it is God himself who does the fighting. This epic battle, like all spiritual battles, cannot be won by human strength but only by God's power.

THE TAKEAWAY

1. Imagine that you are one of the characters who played a pivotal role in saving Moses—a Hebrew midwife, Jochebed, Miriam, Pharaoh's daughter. What goes through your mind and heart as you confront the circumstances? How has God worked in your own life to deliver you from evil?

2. People often think of Egypt as a vast desert, failing to understand the lushness of the land around the Nile River. The first forty years of Moses's life were spent in a fertile landscape. Why might God have allowed him to spend the next forty years in the desert before choosing him to lead his people for forty more years through the wilderness?

3. Moses first encountered God at Mount Horeb, also known as Mount Sinai. Instead of leading the Israelites on a straight path to the Promised Land, God led them first to the holy mountain, where they encountered him and received his commandments. Comment on the significance of this.

4. What adjectives would you use to describe Miriam? In what ways are you like her? In what ways are you unlike her?

CHAPTER 10

THE STORY OF PHARAOH, KING OF EGYPT

The Most Powerful Man on Earth
Learns Who's Really the Boss

Then a new king, to whom Joseph meant nothing, came to power in Egypt.

EXODUS 1:8

Pharaoh said, "Who is the Lord, that I should obey him and let Israel go? I do not know the Lord and I will not let Israel go."

EXODUS 5:2

Though Jacob is an old man by the time he and his sons move to Egypt, it will be several years until he is finally gathered to his ancestors. Before his death, he makes Joseph promise to bury him in the Cave of Machpelah, in the tomb where Abraham, Sarah, Isaac, Rebekah, and Leah have already been laid to rest.

When Jacob dies and Joseph asks permission to bury his father, Pharaoh provides a magnificent honor guard for the funeral procession. Jacob's body is embalmed and then escorted home by chariots, horses, and Egypt's leading men as well as by his sons and their families.

Jacob's final journey follows a circuitous route, crossing the desert and then entering Canaan from the east, by the Jordan River. Though no one knows it, this final passage of the patriarch hints of an event still hundreds of years in the future, when a horde of Hebrew slaves will escape from Egypt and take a similar route home, to the land God has promised.

After laying their father to rest, his children return to Egypt.

Many years later, when it is Joseph's turn to pass from this earth, he summons his remaining brothers and says, "I am about to die. But God will surely come to your aid and take you up out of this land to the land he

Rather than taking the most direct route by heading northeast and then continuing into Canaan via the coastal plain, the funeral procession seems to have taken a more circuitous route. Exodus 50:10–11 states twice, perhaps by way of emphasis, that Joseph and his entourage entered Canaan in a location near the Jordan River, which borders Canaan on the east.[1] ■

Jacob lived in Egypt for seventeen years until his death. Joseph lived another fifty years. ■

promised on oath to Abraham, Isaac and Jacob. God will surely come to your aid, and then you must carry my bones up from this place."

After Joseph, their great protector has passed, the descendants of Jacob remain in Egypt, and God blesses them.

Hundreds of years have passed and a new king rules in Egypt, one who does not honor Joseph's legacy, if he even remembers it. Fearing the Israelites' growing strength, he enslaves them. His successor does the same.

Oppressed by brutal taskmasters, the people cry out to God year after year, begging for deliverance. And the Lord hears their cries. As he looks down from heaven, his gaze rests upon the person who is at the heart of it all.

The Book of Exodus only refers to these two Kings of Egypt as "Pharaoh," leaving scholars uncertain about which ones played starring roles in the story. Possibilities include Thutmose I (1504–1491 BC) and Thutmose II (1491–1479 BC); Thutmose III (1483–1450 BC) and Amenhotep II (1450–1424 BC); or Seti I (1294–1279 BC) and his son, Rameses II (1279–1213 BC). ▪

Pharaoh is seated on his throne, ruling as a god among his people. His great power derives, at least in part, from the life-giving Nile River, which floods at regular intervals, depositing rich soil in which to grow abundant crops. While other nations struggle, Egypt prospers and grows strong.

But Egypt's kings have not always been so mighty. Ironically, it was Joseph, the beloved son of Jacob, the one they called the dreamer, who transferred power from the people to the pharaohs, lifting the kings of Egypt high above their subjects. He did it by filling Pharaoh's storehouses with grain during a time of plenty so that there would be enough to eat during seven years of famine.

Then he sold the food. When the people ran out of silver, he took their livestock as payment. When the livestock ran out, he took their land, transferring everything to Pharaoh's coffers.

The king who now reigns is the absolute ruler of his people. He is a demigod who keeps chaos at bay by serving as go-between, carefully balancing the relationship of the people and their gods, of which Egypt has a multitude.

Every day when Pharaoh leaves his house to perform his morning ablutions, he notices grass pushing through hairline cracks around the palace foundation. How is it, he wonders, that something as flimsy as grass can break through hard ground and cracked brick to sprout and grow?

It reminds him of another question that troubles him. Why do his Hebrew slaves continue to multiply and spread, despite his efforts to control them?

Though Egypt has been built on the backs of slaves, Pharaoh wants less, not more of them, at least of the male slaves. The ever-multiplying people, who live in the land of Goshen and who cling to their customs and beliefs, worry him. He suspects they are traitors who may one day form an alliance with his enemies, opening the northeastern flank of his kingdom to an invasion.

Even godlike Pharaoh must fear such possibilities. Since they are his possessions, he decides to control their numbers. Though he orders their midwives to kill every baby boy they deliver, the women fear God more than they fear him. As male children continue to multiply, Pharaoh calls the Hebrew midwives in and questions them.

"Our women," they explain, "are not like Egyptian women. They are so vigorous that they give birth before we arrive." It is the first of Pharaoh's many mistakes—to believe what they say.

Determined to suppress his slaves, he decrees that every newborn male should be thrown into the Nile. Odd that he decides to murder babies in the river that he and his people revere as the source of life.

Though many babies perish, one small boy survives. His mother hides him and then reluctantly complies with Pharaoh's decree by putting her infant into the river, but in a little basket boat that she has covered with pitch and tar. As he drifts down the river, one of Pharaoh's daughters plucks him out. Then she brings him up as her own boy, right under the nose of her wicked father.

So Moses is reared in Pharaoh's household and educated in the ways of the world's most advanced society. But God watches over him, making sure that there are places in his heart that Egypt cannot touch.

One day Moses spots an Egyptian mercilessly beating a Hebrew slave. Catching hold of the man's upraised arm, he snatches the whip from his hand before it can deliver a killing blow. Then he slays him and hides his body in the sand.

But word of what Moses has done spreads until it reaches Pharaoh's ears. Before he can kill his grandson, Moses flees north, disappearing into the vastness of the desert.

Forty years pass. By now the wilderness of Midian is as much a part of Moses as the cosmopolitan world of Egypt had been. One day, while tending his flock in a remote corner of the desert, God appears to him as a burning presence, assuring him that he has heard the cries of his people for deliverance. Moses will be his chosen servant to lead the Israelites out of Egypt and into the promised land.

By the time Moses returns to Egypt, a new pharaoh is on the throne. This one is young, confident, dynamic—ready, he thinks, for whatever the future holds.

Soon Moses and his brother Aaron approach this young king with a message from Yahweh. "This is what the LORD, the God of Israel, says, 'Let my people go, so that they may hold a festival to me in the wilderness.'"

But Pharaoh's heart is cold, and it has already formed a judgment. What is this talk about "my people"? The Hebrew slaves belong to him and him alone. They are his slaves, destined to build his cities, temples, and monuments.

Yahweh represents the personal, covenant name of God. Most scholars believe that the Hebrew word commonly translated as "LORD" in English translations of the Bible is "Yahweh."[2] ◼

He stares at Moses and Aaron, wondering how much trouble these two brothers can make. Are they capable of fomenting rebellion with all their talk of worshiping the Hebrew God?

And why just one God when Egypt has countless divine beings to choose from? There is Osiris, Seth, Isis, Horus, Anubis, Ra, and too many local gods to count. There are gods for healing, protection, fertility, and everything under the sun. As Pharaoh, it is his job to keep the peace by acting as intermediary between the gods and the people.

As if to confirm his exalted role, the golden cobra mounted on his headdress bobs slightly, as though ready to strike whoever might be foolish enough to oppose him. It is the emblem of the snake goddess Wadjit, the powerful protector and patron of the pharaohs.

Leaning forward, Pharaoh makes his reply: "Moses and Aaron, why are you taking the people away from their labor? Get back to your work!"

Then he commands his overseers to withhold the straw needed for brick making. Without it the mud will not adhere and the bricks will fall apart. "Let these lazy slaves find their own straw while making just as many bricks as before. Perhaps the extra work will teach them to stop listening to lies."

The strategy works. As Pharaoh has hoped, the slaves become angry with Moses the moment they hear what has happened. "You have made us obnoxious to Pharaoh and his officials and have put a sword in their hand to kill us," they accuse.

Though distressed, Moses returns to the king with Aaron as his spokesman. When Pharaoh demands a miracle, Aaron throws down his staff, and it turns into a snake.

Since Pharaoh believes in magic, he calls his own sorcerers, asking them to duplicate this feat. As soon as they throw down their staffs, the floor becomes a tangle of writhing snakes. Pharaoh claps his hands in delight. He will win this contest, he thinks.

Suddenly Aaron's staff begins to move across the floor and then devours all the other staffs. The sign is clear. The Hebrew God has challenged Pharaoh by devouring the staffs of his magicians and humiliating his great protector—the snake goddess Wadjit.

But the king is proud and he will cede power to no one. The next morning, when he arrives at the river with his officials to perform the usual rituals, he is annoyed to find that Moses and Aaron are already waiting for him. This time, when Aaron raises his staff, he strikes the Nile and it turns to blood.

Pharaohs were sometimes depicted on the walls of royal tombs holding a shepherd's staff, a symbol of their authority to rule. ▩

When Pharaoh's magicians repeat the feat, transforming water into blood, the king merely turns his back and walks into his palace.

After seven days have passed—enough time for a man to come to his senses—the Lord tells Moses to return to Pharaoh with the same request. This time, when Pharaoh refuses to allow the Hebrew slaves to journey into the wilderness to worship their God, Aaron stretches out his hand and frogs appear. They emerge from the river like an enormous rolling carpet, invading mud brick homes, spacious villas, and the palace itself. There are so many frogs that Pharaoh finds them swarming his bed, and people have to shoo them out of feeding troughs and ovens.

Once again, the court magicians repeat the feat. But the last thing Pharaoh needs is more frogs. What he does need is relief— somebody to rid him of these infernal pests!

Summoning Moses and Aaron, he bends a little. "Pray to the LORD to take the frogs away from me and my people, and I will let your people go to offer sacrifices to the LORD."

But the next day, after all the frogs have died and been piled into great, stinking heaps, he forgets his promise. He will not let even one Hebrew slave go out to worship his God.

More plagues descend.

An invasion of gnats
Dense swarms of flies
A plague on livestock
Festering boils on people and animals
Life-destroying hail
An army of locusts

The most powerful of Pharaoh's magic men cannot duplicate these feats nor can anyone explain why the land of Goshen, where the slaves reside, remains untouched.

Despite all these afflictions, the king refuses to let God's people go. By now, every act of resistance, every refusal to do what God has asked, has become compressed into a hard-fisted core in Pharaoh's heart.

Pride tells him that victory will surely come. All he needs to do is to stand fast against the demands of his lazy slaves. He does not yet suspect the enormity of the Power with which he is contending.

Then the Lord speaks to Moses and says, "Stretch out your hand toward the sky so that darkness spreads over Egypt—darkness that can be felt."

As soon as Moses reaches his hand skyward, Egypt is plunged into shadows. The nation that worships the great god of the sun, Amun Ra, is deprived of its light for three days running.

Three long days to wonder what appalling specters may lurk in the darkness is enough to unhinge Pharaoh's mind. Now he startles at every sound, pressing his hands against his ears in a vain effort to stop the laughter he thinks he hears. Is it coming from somewhere up above?

At the end of three days, Moses arrives and speaks for God again: "Let my people go!"

This time, Pharaoh is ready to give in—but not all the way ready. He tells Moses he will make every concession except one. The people may go out into the wilderness to sacrifice to Yahweh. Even the women and children may go. But the livestock must stay behind.

"Not a hoof is to be left behind," Moses insists.

"Get out of my sight," the king shouts. "Never appear before me again. The day you see my face you will die."

"As you like," Moses replies. "I will never appear before you again."

The words fall like an omen. Until now, the Lord has withheld the worst of his judgments. It will not be long before the hammer of judgment descends again, this time crushing the hearts of all Egyptians.

Before it does, Yahweh provides for his people by instructing them to hold a Passover meal. They must sacrifice an unblemished lamb, paint its blood on their doorposts, and then roast and eat it, along with unleavened bread.

At midnight when the moon is arcing through the sky, a shadow passes overhead and Pharaoh shivers in his sleep. Moments later, he wakes to full consciousness and unbearable pain.

His wife is already screaming.

Like a lion freshly wounded, he roars in anguish, the sound of his cries mixing with a great mournful wail that rises across the whole of Egypt. For no house is without its dead. Every firstborn son has perished. Even Pharaoh's son is dead.

Strangely, the cherished sons of those who live in the land of Goshen are still asleep on their mats. The lamb's blood painted on every doorpost has preserved them from the breathtaking power of the avenging angel.

In the middle of the night Pharaoh summons Moses and Aaron. "Up! Leave my people," he says. "You and the Israelites! Go, worship the LORD as you have requested. Take your flocks and herds, as you have said, and go."

After their sojourn in Egypt, the time has finally come for Jacob's children to return to the land God had long ago promised to their forefathers. Before departing, they ask their Egyptian neighbors for gifts of clothing, silver, and gold.

"Hurry, go! Before we all die!" The Egyptians are so eager to get rid of them they press treasures into their hands, loading them down with everything they can carry.

So it is that God's people leave Egypt, the land of their terrible oppression, not as beaten-down slaves who barely escape with their lives, but as a great, plundering army heading home with treasures of silver and gold.

But they are not yet home.

Exulting in their miraculous deliverance, they have no idea of the battle that lies ahead. If God were to tell them what is in his mind, they might never find the courage to leave behind the land of their bondage. For he is not yet finished with Pharaoh. Instead, he will lure him into the desert for the final battle.

Leading his people by means of a pillar of cloud by day and a pillar of fire at night, God brings them to the edge of the sea. The route they've taken bewilders the Egyptian scouts who follow. Clearly they are lost, trapped beside the sea with no way across.

When Pharaoh hears of this, hope returns to his heart as old prejudices rise up. That fool Moses has led the ignorant slaves into a trap. Mounting his chariot, he rides into the desert at the head of his army.

The Israelites are stunned when they catch sight of Pharaoh's chariots and horses thundering across the desert. Despairing, they wail, "Was it because there were no graves in Egypt that you brought us to the desert to die?"

Then God speaks to Moses. "Tell the Israelites to move on. Raise your staff and stretch out your hand over the sea to divide the water so that the Israelites can go through the sea on dry ground."

As Pharaoh and his army race on, the king begins to wonder why his soldiers make no headway. Though he and his men ride hard, they move no closer to their target. Is the desert playing tricks? He doesn't realize that the One who lives where time and distance cannot be measured is himself standing between the armies of Egypt and Israel's army.

Throughout the night the pillar of cloud and fire brings darkness to the Egyptians and light to the Israelites.

As Moses stretches out his hand to the sea, a strong east wind begins to blow. All night long it drives the sea back and turns it into dry land. Meanwhile, Pharaoh's horses maintain their furious pursuit.

In the darkness, the people begin to cross—the mothers with babies in arms, the children running free, the grandparents leaning on each other, the fathers driving the herds.

While people are still crossing, desperate to reach the other side, Pharaoh's chariot arrives at the edge of the sea. Framed against a backdrop of grey, billowing clouds, he looks like an angry god. But he is merely a man with a stubborn, cold-fisted heart. Lifting up a prayer to whatever god will listen, he urges his army into the sea.

Hell-bent they ride on, determined to overtake the slaves who are still struggling to cross. Suddenly, when they've drawn close enough to taste victory, the wheels of their chariots jam. The more they urge their horses forward, the more mired they become.

"The LORD is fighting for the Israelites against Egypt!" they shout. "Run!"

But it's too late for them to escape. At the command of God Moses stretches out his hand and the watery walls collapse. Over the chariots, over the horsemen the sea flows.

It is daybreak now. The battle is over. All is quiet . . . eerily quiet.

When the Israelites see the Egyptians lying dead on the shore, they sing a song so joyful it pierces the sky.

> The LORD is my strength and my defense;
> he has become my salvation.

He is my God, and I will praise him,
    my father's God, and I will exalt him.
The LORD is a warrior;
    the LORD is his name.
Pharaoh's chariots and his army
    he has hurled into the sea.
The best of Pharaoh's officers
    are drowned in the Red Sea.
The deep waters have covered them;
    they sank to the depths like a stone.
Your right hand, LORD,
    was majestic in power.
Your right hand, LORD,
    shattered the enemy.
In the greatness of your majesty
    you threw down those who opposed you.
You unleashed your burning anger;
    it consumed them like stubble.
By the blast of your nostrils
    the waters piled up.
The surging waters stood up like a wall;
    the deep waters congealed in the heart of the sea.
The enemy boasted,
    "I will pursue, I will overtake them.
I will divide the spoils;
    I will gorge myself on them.
I will draw my sword
    and my hand will destroy them."
But you blew with your breath,
    and the sea covered them.

> They sank like lead
>   in the mighty waters.
> Who among the gods
>   is like you, LORD?
> Who is like you—
>   majestic in holiness,
>   awesome in glory,
>   working wonders?
> You stretch out your right hand,
>   and the earth swallows your enemies.
> In your unfailing love you will lead
>   the people you have redeemed.

With a song in their hearts, God's people march on, continuing their journey across the wilderness and then finally, after years of struggle and trial, into the land they've been promised.

Over and over they will recount the tale of how God rescued them. And the hearts of the children will quake whenever they hear how their fathers and mothers—and all God's people—nearly perished at the edge of the sea. They will sigh with relief and knowingly nod when they hear once more the story of how God came down from heaven to deliver them with his mighty, all-powerful arm.

THE TIMES

The Exodus story is dated as early as
1445 BC and as late as 1260 BC.
Pharaoh's story is drawn from Exodus 1–13.

As the world's first nation state, Egypt was the most technically advanced civilization in the Mediterranean region when Jacob's family settled there.

Unlike other societies, the intense focus on the afterlife and on embalming corpses meant that the Egyptians were familiar with human anatomy—one reason they were renowned for their medical skills. Like all aspects of Egyptian society, medical practice was imbued with magic. Because illnesses were often attributed to demons, some remedies were intentionally noxious. What demon would want to stick around when a patient was being treated with fly droppings, animal dung, or boiled mice?

During the time of the pharaohs, the primary practitioners of magic were priests who could read the texts that preserved the secret knowledge that was thought to be imparted by the gods. Magic was a defense system that provided an illusion of security in the midst of visible and invisible forces that might otherwise wreak havoc.

Much of Egypt's wealth as well as its power derived from the Nile River, which the Egyptians simply referred to as "the river." Flowing from south to north, it traversed more than four thousand miles until emptying into the Mediterranean Sea.

Every summer, heavy rains from the Ethiopian highlands flow down into the Nile, inundating the land along the river and depositing rich, black silt, perfect for growing abundant crops. The Egyptians harnessed the river by practicing basin irrigation and by cutting canals to divert the water over a larger area. The rich soil around the river was known as the Black Land while the inhospitable desert region, a vast cemetery where tombs were built, was known as the Red Land.

Thanks to Hollywood, we often picture Hebrew slaves engaged in the backbreaking work of erecting elaborate stone tombs for Egypt's kings and queens, who were in search of a safe and comfortable passage to the afterlife. However, the ancient pyramids were constructed not by slaves but by several thousand permanent employees whose labors were supplemented by thousands of temporary workers. By the time Jacob's family settled in Egypt, pyramid building had generally gone out of style. Even so, the Israelites were subject to harsh forced labor for many years.

Like all ancient societies, the Egyptians were a deeply religious people, worshiping over two thousand gods during the course of their history. It must have seemed strange to Pharaoh and his subjects that the Israelites would rely on just one God—Yahweh—to protect and provide for their needs.

It is remarkable that Jacob's tribe not only multiplied in Egypt but that God's people maintained their unique identity in the midst of the seductive allure of the dominant culture.

Exodus showcases God's love and faithfulness as well as his absolute power over evil, for Pharaoh is a symbol not only of entrenched human evil but of satanic power as well. The story of Exodus highlights God's ability to use the intransigence of his enemies to bring glory to himself.

THE TAKEAWAY

1. The wise writer of Proverbs offers advice that would have benefited Pharaoh, had he been willing to listen: "Blessed is the one who always trembles before God, but whoever hardens their heart falls into trouble" (Proverbs 28:14). Describe times in your life when your heart wasn't as open as it should have been to God or others. How has God worked to soften your heart?

2. Imagine that you are a Hebrew slave, a powerless person living in the world's most powerful society. How do you respond to Moses's claims? Would you have trusted and believed him or perhaps grumbled about him? At what point during the journey out of Egypt would you have been most likely to doubt God's promised deliverance? Why?

3. Each of us is meant to identify with the Exodus story on a personal level. At some point in our lives, we have been enslaved to sin and oppressed by Satan. In what small or large ways has God "delivered you from Egypt"? How would you describe what it means to be brought into the promised land of his presence?

4. The story of Exodus depicts God as single-handedly delivering his people from Pharaoh's enslaving power. Describe what was required of Moses and the Israelites as God acted on their behalf. How might these responses apply to your own life?

CHAPTER 11

THE STORY OF RAHAB

She Told a Lie . . . and Saved the Day

> *Know therefore that the Lord your God is*
> *God; he is the faithful God, keeping his*
> *covenant of love to a thousand generations*
> *of those who love him and keep his*
> *commandments.*

DEUTERONOMY 7:9

Whenever she walks to the market, the women gather in little knots, shutting her out while the children snigger and point. But she just tosses her hair and swings her hips, provoking them all the more.

They are jealous, she thinks, because she makes a living that's five times better than theirs. Plus their husbands give her looks that tell her they are wondering what it would be like to caress her honey-gold skin and run their fingers through her thick, curly hair. The women retaliate by wagging their tongues. Their words are little slingshots aimed straight at her heart.

But Rahab doesn't care. She has the best of everything. A thriving business, good health, a quick wit. Plus she likes breaking molds. Surprising people. An enterprising woman, she owns a home, an inn really, that fits snugly inside the city's impenetrable walls. Because of its location near the city gate, she misses nothing, sees everyone as they pass through. Travelers from all over the region carry news of the world beyond. No wonder the king of Jericho sends his emissaries to her from time to time to gather the latest intelligence.

The term for "prostitute" may also have meant innkeeper. In that era innkeepers were often associated with prostitutes. ■

Some of her guests are only looking for a bed, while others want to share hers. She also works in linen, retting the long stalks of flax and then laying them out on the rooftop to dry before their soft fibers can be extracted and spun into thread. Today, though, it is not thread she's spinning but dreadful visions drawn from the rumors she is hearing. What will happen to her parents, her brothers and sisters and all their children if the tales are true?

Visiting merchants who are part of large caravans that criss-cross the region are buzzing about the presence of a great horde of people encamped at Shittim, ten miles to the east of Jericho, on the other side of the Jordan River. Rahab has heard the stories—how the Israelites left Egypt in triumph, and how their God reached down and parted the waves so they could walk across the sea to freedom. She knows these former slaves have been toughened by forty years in the wilderness and that they are fed with a mysterious food called manna. Perhaps that is what has made them so strong. Already they have annihilated the Amorite kings. Everyone says Jericho will be next.

But Jericho has survived the ravages of millennia. How can the world's oldest city possibly be conquered? Its walls are stout and tall, impossible to scale. Yet, still, its people tremble, and great waves of fear assail them as each new story builds upon the last, telling of the prowess of Israel's wonder-working God.

Like everyone else, Rahab is afraid. But her fears can't crowd out her curiosity. How is it that a band of slaves who lived in Egypt for more than four hundred years have slipped their bonds and become a mighty army? And why do they worship only one God, a God who speaks to them from a pillar of cloud by day and a column of fire at night?

Oh that she might know the protective power of such a God. That he might hold her in his all-sheltering arms and keep her safe. Despite her tough exterior, Rahab feels the need of belonging to someone stronger than herself.

But now night is drawing near—the busiest time of her day. Two strangers have just arrived. Something in the shape of their faces and the cut of their beards puts her on the alert. She is used to foreigners but not to men like these. Their skin is dark and weathered, their eyes bright and full of a singular purpose.

"You are Israelites!" she exclaims.

They try to hush her but don't deny it. In an instant she chooses sides.

"Come with me," she says.

Leading them to the rooftop where long stalks of flax are drying, she instructs them to hide beneath them.

Moments later, other visitors arrive. She opens the door a crack to see the king's men standing outside. "Bring out the men who are staying at your house," they demand. "They are spies."

Her fingers clutch her throat in feigned surprise, as though to say she is alarmed by what they've said. "Two men were here," Rahab answers, "but I didn't know who they were. They left the city at dusk, just before the gate closed. I have no idea where they've gone. If you leave now, you may still be able to catch them."

The code of Hammurabi (a set of laws in Mesopotamia that date back to about 1772 BC) state: "If there should be a woman innkeeper in whose house criminals congregate, and she does not seize those criminals and lead them off to the palace authorities, that woman innkeeper shall be put to death."[1] ■

As soon as they leave, she moves to the window, watching as they head in haste toward the fords of the Jordan River.

Steadying herself, she heads up to the rooftop to alert her guests, saying, "I know that the LORD has given this land to you and that a great fear of you has fallen on us, so that all who live in this country are melting in fear because of you. We have heard how the LORD dried up the water of the Red Sea for you when you came out of Egypt, and what you did to Sihon and Og whom you completely destroyed. When we heard of it, our hearts melted and everyone's courage failed because of you, for the LORD your God is God in heaven above and on the earth below.

"Now then, please swear to me by the Lord that you will show kindness to my family, because I have shown kindness to you. Give me a sure sign that you will spare the lives of my father and mother, my brothers and sisters, and all who belong to them, and that you will save us from death."

"Our lives for yours!" the men assure her. Then they instruct her to tie a scarlet cord in her window so that the Israelites will recognize her house when they invade the city. No matter what happens, she is to make sure that every member of her family—from the youngest to the oldest—stays inside the house. Stepping beyond the door will mean their deaths.

Agreeing, Rahab lowers the spies by rope from her window, telling them to hide in the hills for three days.

When the two scouts finally arrive at Shittim, they tell Joshua everything and watch as a smile quickly spreads across his face. "Surely," he says, "the LORD himself has flooded Jericho with fear." As Moses's successor, he will trust God for the victory. Though Joshua has no idea how he and his men will scale the walls of Jericho, he rallies his people, and they march until they arrive at the western banks of the Jordan River.

In the summer the river is only a trickling stream, but in the springtime it runs fast and high. A strong man might cross it, but everyone would be swept away. Even so, Joshua orders the priests to take up the ark of the covenant, which is a pledge of God's presence, and carry it into the river.

Aware of the danger, the priests pray that God himself will go into the river with them. Though mere boys when they left

Egypt, they remember how God had made a way through the Red Sea when they were trapped by Pharaoh's advancing army. Now they have become the advancing army, marching into the land God promised them.

As soon as their feet touch water, the river stops flowing and the ground begins to dry up. Slowly they advance, carrying the ark into the middle of the riverbed. Standing there, hour by hour, they wait patiently until every Israelite has crossed. Then they walk in procession to the other side. As soon as they and the ark are safe on the river bank, the water rushes back and the river closes in.

Now God's army is only five miles from Jericho.

Meanwhile, within the city walls of Jericho, no one goes in and no one goes out. There is too much fear. Panic has gripped the city because everyone has heard how the Israelites have just crossed the Jordan River.

By now Rahab's house is crowded with relatives. She watches from the window as the Israelite army marches toward the city. Instead of rushing the walls, they parade around them, carrying a golden box that glints in the sun. On top of the box sit two golden angels facing each other, their wings extended as though to shelter it. Carried on long poles, the sacred box is preceded by seven priests who are blowing seven ram's horns. Not a single word is spoken as the Israelites march around the city. Rahab hears only the tramping of feet and the blowing of horns. After the soldiers parade around Jericho once, they return to the Israelite camp.

No one knows what to make of this strange procession. It is not what the citizens of Jericho expected.

The same thing happens the next day and the day after that. For six days the Israelites march around the city carrying their beautiful golden box. If they mean to terrify Jericho's inhabitants, they have succeeded. Many people can no longer stand the sound of the blowing horns.

But Rahab is not one of these. Each time the golden ark passes by, she senses a presence that gives her peace.

On the seventh day, instead of processing around the city once, the Israelites keep on marching. They encircle the city seven times. On the seventh pass, when terror has reached a crescendo, a shout goes up from the Israelites. Like a great rolling wave of sound, it threatens to smash the world to bits. All at once, the encircling walls collapse. Rahab's small house tilts, cracks, and pitches slightly forward, but it does not fall. She prays that the spies will keep their word.

As she sits inside her house, she hears a great clash of weapons and screams that chill her heart. The city is quickly overwhelmed and then burned to the ground. Of all who lived inside its walls, only she and her family are spared.

Like Noah and his family, Rahab and her people escape the great destruction that comes as punishment for the sins of those who live in the land. Instead of a boat, this time it is a house that shelters them. Because Rahab has believed in Israel's God and has risked her life to help his people, she and her family are saved.

Had anyone from Jericho been able to tell the story, her role would have been described not with words like *courage* and *faith*, but with words like *treachery* and *deceit*. As it is, not one person was left alive who could contradict the story as it has been handed down through all the generations of God's people.

Leaving the ill-fated city behind, Rahab and her family settle with the Israelites. One of her descendants will be David, the greatest of Israel's kings. More remarkable than that, she will be known to later generations as the great, great, great-beyond-counting grandmother of Jesus, who is the Christ.

THE TIMES

*Rahab's story may have taken place about 1406 BC.
Her story is told in Joshua 2–3 and 6. She is mentioned in Matthew 1:5; Hebrews 11:31; James 2:25.*

Jericho was a fortified city, with perhaps as many as two thousand residents. Also called the City of Palms, it was located along important trade routes, just fifteen miles from Jerusalem. Archaeological evidence for its existence dates to the ninth millennium BC, which may make it the oldest city in the world.

Prior to advancing against Jericho, the Israelites celebrated Passover by eating some of the produce of the land. The next day, the manna that had nourished them throughout their wilderness journey stopped because they no longer had need of it (Joshua 5:11–12).

When the Israelite spies reached Jericho, they realized that God was already at work within the city to weaken it, spreading "a great fear" of them, as Rahab told them.

It was springtime when Joshua led the people across the Jordan River, a time when the river was at flood stage. The Bible says that "the water from upstream stopped flowing. It piled up in a heap a great distance away, at a town called Adam" (Joshua 3:16). Jericho is located in the Rift Valley, an unstable region with frequent seismic activity. It is possible that an earthquake caused the high banks of the Jordan to collapse upstream from where the Israelites were crossing, damning up the river. In 1997, an earthquake in the vicinity of Adam dislodged a 150-foot-high embankment, which stopped the flow of the river for twenty-one hours. The walls of Jericho may have collapsed because of a second earthquake, which could have enabled Joshua and his men to breach the city's defenses.

But how could Rahab's house have survived an earthquake? Excavations in the early twentieth century have revealed a portion of the lower city wall that did not collapse. Houses that were built against it were still intact.

THE TAKEAWAY

1. There are striking similarities and some differences in the way the Israelites began and ended their forty-year sojourn in the wilderness. Both involved a miraculous crossing of impassable water. Both occurred near the celebration of Passover. In the first case, Israel was being pursued. In the second, they were the pursuers. How do you account for the similarities and the differences?

2. The Israelite priests had to step into the Jordan River before it stopped flowing. Have you ever acted simply on the basis of your trust in God, taking a risk before experiencing the answer to a prayer or the fulfillment of a promise? If so, what were the results?

3. The command to march around Jericho seven times must have sounded bizarre to Joshua. How might the story have changed had he disobeyed God and relied on his own battle strategies? What are the implications for our own lives as people of faith?

4. Rahab was willing to risk her life to protect the spies. What kind of risks have you taken that express your trust in God?

5. In Exodus, Moses is the hero who grows up right under

the nose of his enemies. In this episode from the book of Joshua, God uses Rahab as the "insider" who will help his people overcome their enemies. What does this say about God's ability to work on behalf of those who belong to him?

CHAPTER 12

THE STORY OF DELILAH

A Wicked Woman Betrays Her Lover

At the window of my house I looked down through the lattice. I saw among the simple, I noticed among the young men, a youth who had no sense. He was going down the street near her corner, walking along in the direction of her house at twilight, as the day was fading, as the dark of night set in. . . . She took hold of him and kissed him and with a brazen face she said. . . . Come, let's drink deeply of love till morning; let's enjoy ourselves with love. . . . All at once he followed her like an ox going to the slaughter, like a deer stepping into a noose . . . Many are the victims she has brought down; her slain are a mighty throng.

PROVERBS 7:6–9, 13, 18, 22, 26

She sleeps in the crook of his arm, her head nestled against his chest. At times his snoring is so loud, she thinks it will lift the roof of her house. Then he grunts and moans, turning his head in a moment of fitfulness. Despite the occasional nightmare, he never wakes until the first ray of light begins to creep beneath her door. He slumbers so soundly that Delilah is sure he could sleep through the end of the world.

Before they go to bed, Samson tells her stories. Most of them are about his favorite subject—himself as a child, himself as a young man, himself as a leader in Israel. He says an angel foretold his birth and that he has always been consecrated to God. He regales her with tales of how he tore a lion apart with his bare hands and slew a thousand of his enemies with only the jawbone of a donkey. Oh, how he hates those asses, the Philistines.

Nothing will restrain his tongue when it comes to declaiming their worthlessness. He talks of setting their fields on fire to destroy their grain crops and of spreading terror wherever he goes. He considers it payback for how they've treated him and his people.

Quick to indulge his urge for power as well as for pleasure, he is confident that nothing can stop him because he is the Lord's anointed—the hero of the story God is telling. A one-man army, he has led his people now for twenty years.

Not long ago a group of men gathered inside the gates of Gaza. They were planning to murder him as soon as he departed. (He does not tell Delilah he was spending the night with a prostitute.) But as soon as he saw them, he took hold of the heavy wooden gates, together with the two posts, and tore them loose, the heavy bar and all. Then he lifted them up and threw them away, leaving the city of Gaza defenseless.

A great roar escapes his mouth as he recalls the details. His laughter is so loud Delilah jumps when she hears it, and that makes him laugh all the more.

But she already knows of his exploits. His power is what makes him so attractive—at least to Delilah. She likes the hardness of his muscles, the girth of his arms as they enfold her. He is invincible, she thinks, and tells him so.

Samson basks in her admiration, and it only takes a little flattery to keep him talking. She snuggles closer as he speaks about Abraham and Sarah and how God promised this land to his people. She knows of Moses and how Miriam led the victory dance at the edge of the Red Sea. His tale-telling is so vivid she can almost see Rahab peering over the ramparts of Jericho.

But if their God has done such marvels, she wonders why Israel is so weak. Samson has told her that two of the twelve tribes have been fighting each other and that the rest are harassed by outside enemies. But Samson only shrugs when she asks why they are weak. He doesn't bother to tell her about the people's unfaithfulness or about how keeping God's commands are tied to Israel's prosperity. Nor does he speak about the time when some of his own people betrayed him to the Philistines.

Samson is the biggest man Delilah has ever seen, but she knows he is not large enough to have performed so many wonders by himself. Some say that when the Spirit falls on him, he is strong enough to lift two mountains and hold them in his hands. She almost believes the tales they tell. For the moment, she is content to let the source of his strength remain a mystery. It is enough to bask in his power.

One day when Samson is away, Philistine rulers approach her. A fierce, seafaring people who have settled on the coast, they are used to being the ones who harass and oppress. If it were not for this one man, they could do as they please. But he is like a traveling avalanche, a man who wreaks havoc wherever he goes.

Though power has always been Delilah's favorite aphrodisiac, now they tempt her with something even more seductive—cold hard cash. Enough to keep her secure for the rest of her life.

"You are beautiful," they say, telling her what she already knows. "And Samson is under your thumb." She knows that too.

Then they offer her a bribe. "If you can lure him into telling you the secret of his power so that we are able to subdue him, we will each give you eleven hundred shekels of silver." It is an astonishing amount, an offer that reveals how desperate these Philistines are.

In the face of such a tempting offer, how should she choose? Her relationship with Samson has provided a sense of status, making her untouchable to those who would otherwise judge her. But money could do that and more, enabling her to live the kind of life that others dream of and that she dreams of too.

As her thoughts swing back and forth between two alternatives, she finally lands. The money will buy her everything she seeks. So she begins a game with Samson, asking him to reveal the secret of his great strength so he can be tied and subdued.

Samson loves this about her, that she is both beautiful and playful, and so he humors her, saying, "If anyone ties me with seven fresh bowstrings that have not been dried, I'll become as weak as any other man."

So the Philistines supply her with seven fresh bowstrings with which to bind him. Then, while his enemies are hidden in the room, she exclaims, "Samson, the Philistines are upon you!" But he simply snaps the thongs as though they are tiny strings and the secret of his great strength remains a mystery.

"You've made a fool of me," she scolds. "Come now, tell me the truth about how you can be tied." Then she caresses him as though to say she has already forgiven him.

Still toying with her, he replies, "If anyone ties me securely with new ropes that have never been used, I'll become as weak as any other man."

Delilah falls for the lie and ties him up again, crying, "Samson, the Philistines are upon you!" But as before, Samson merely snaps the ropes as though they are threads and his enemies quickly flee.

This time she sulks and swats at him. When he grabs her wrist to draw her close, she demands the truth.

Sighing, as though to signal she has finally won the game, he tells her: "If you weave the seven braids of my head into the fabric on the loom and tighten it with the pin, I'll become as weak as any other man."

One day, while he lies snoring, Delilah weaves his long hair into the fabric on the loom just as he has instructed.

In yet another comedic moment, Delilah cries out, telling Samson he is caught in the Philistine snare. But he simply sits up, yanking his hair from the loom.

Delilah's loom is possibly a horizontal loom fastened to the floor. ▪

Now she is angry. "How can you say, 'I love you,'" she accuses, "when you won't confide in me? This is the third time you have made a fool of me and haven't told me the secret of your great strength!"

Delilah's accusations are a never-ending siege that finally wears him down.

Finally, he tells her the truth. "No razor has ever been used on my head," he says, "because I have been a Nazirite dedicated to God from my mother's womb. If my head were shaved, my strength would leave me, and I would become as weak as any other man."

Sensing she has heard the truth at last, Delilah sends word to the Philistine rulers. This time they come loaded with a trove of silver.

Numbers 6:1–8 indicates that someone under a Nazirite vow was to abstain from three things: (1) any kind of intoxicating drink, including eating grapes or raisins; (2) cutting his hair; and (3) coming into contact with a dead body, either human or animal. ■

This trove would be approximately 140 pounds of silver. ■

As Samson sleeps with his head on her lap, a man shaves off his seven braids. When Delilah wakes him, exclaiming, "Samson, the Philistines are upon you!" he rouses himself, intending to break free just as he has always done. It takes a few moments for the truth to sink in. He is now as weak as other men because God has left him.

Cupping her hands over her ears to drown out his screams, Delilah turns away as the Philistines gouge out his eyes. Then they drag him off to Gaza. Later she hears the story of how they humiliate him in prison, forcing him to grind out grain as though he is a woman.

In a few months, she hears they are holding a great festival. The Philistines worship Dagon, the god of grain. At last, the man who tried to destroy their grain by setting their fields on fire is completely in their power. Thousands are gathered along with their rulers in Dagon's temple, eager for a glimpse of the strong man who is called out for their amusement. As soon as they see him, they praise Dagon, saying,

Blinding captives was a common practice in the ancient Near East when dealing with dangerous foes. ■

> Our god has delivered our enemy
>   into our hands,
> the one who laid waste our land
>   and multiplied our slain.

But the Philistines are in for a surprise. For Samson's God has entered the house, and Dagon is going down. Blind and shackled though he is, Samson's hair has grown long again and he can feel his strength returning. Confident that God is with him, he plots his revenge.

"Put me," he asks his guard, "where I can feel the pillars that support the temple, so that I may lean against them." To convince the guard, he slumps a little, as though he is only a blind man worn out from too much work. But once in position, he stretches out his arms, places each hand against a pillar and prays: "O Sovereign LORD, remember me. Please God, strengthen me just once more, and let me with one blow get revenge on the Philistines for my two eyes. . . . Let me die with the Philistines."

Then Samson pushes with all his might and Dagon's temple comes crashing down, crushing everyone beneath it and destroying three thousand men and women who were standing on the roof.

As the news of what has happened spreads throughout the region, Delilah can hear the wailing. The Philistines are grieving not only because so many of their own have died, but also because of the shame that has come to their god.

As for Delilah? She misses Samson for a time, but not too long. Instead of lament, her heart is filled with visions of the good life she has managed to secure for herself. No longer dependent on a man to meet her needs, she can do exactly as she pleases. Some would call her heartless, gullible, or stupid. But she merely calls herself lucky—free and rich beyond her dreams.

But what about Samson? How will he be remembered? Chosen by God for a singular role—to begin the liberation of his people—he managed to fulfill it, not by becoming wise and good, but by completing a final act of self-destructive violence. In death, Samson killed more of Israel's enemies than he had killed during his lifetime. Strong on the outside but weak on the inside, he ruled Israel for twenty years.

THE TIMES

Delilah's story probably took place about 1055 BC.
Her story is drawn from Judges 13–16.

Unlike the book of Joshua, which highlights a glorious period of conquest in Israel's history, the book of Judges tells of a time of terrible decline, in which "everyone did as they saw fit" (21:25). Samson was a primary example of this tendency, a man whose prodigious strength could not compensate for his moral weakness.

As they settled in Canaan, many of the Israelites began to practice idolatry, worshiping pagan deities like Baal (the god of storms and fertility) and Ashtoreth (the goddess of war and fertility). Repeating the pattern of Exodus, in which the journey from Egypt to Canaan should have been marked by days rather than years, the conquest and consolidation of Israel's power in the Promised Land took between three and four hundred years, showcasing the consequences of the Israelites' failure to trust God enough to obey him.

During the roughly two-hundred-year period described in the book of Judges, there is no clear evidence that any of the judges represented all the tribes of Israel. Sometimes judges arose concurrently in opposition to localized oppression.

Samson and Delilah lived in a period in which the Philistines ruled over southwestern Palestine. A seafaring people who had emigrated from the Aegean, they settled along the coast of Israel and then began to move eastward. The word "Palestine" is derived from their name.

Though the Israelites had not yet grasped Iron Age technology, the Philistines probably knew how to smelt and forge metal products, including those made out of iron. This knowledge gave them a strong military edge, helping them advance against the people who were already settled in Canaan. Though the Philistines had their own distinct culture, including language, dress, weapons, and pottery, they quickly adopted Canaanite religious practices, including the worship of the god Dagon.

Though the text does not identify Delilah's ethnicity, she may have been a Philistine.

THE TAKEAWAY

1. Delilah is one of the few female characters in the Bible who seems entirely negative. If you were to think of her as a more multifaceted character, what fears or insecurities do you imagine might have been behind her choices and behaviors?
2. In the story, Delilah appears to function primarily as a snare to a man who was chosen by God to lead his people. What kind of snares do you face in your efforts to live for God?
3. As a rule, women possessed little power in the ancient world in which Delilah's story unfolds. As often happens in such circumstances, Delilah used manipulation to get her way. How have you been tempted to use manipulation when you've felt powerless?

CHAPTER 13

THE STORY OF NAOMI AND RUTH

Two Desperate Women Look for a Home . . . and a Future

Give, and it will be given to you. A good measure, pressed down, shaken together and running over, will be poured into your lap. For with the measure you use, it will be measured to you.

LUKE 6:38

At least six hundred years have passed since Tamar disguised herself as a harlot and tricked her father-in-law into sleeping with her. Their one-night stand produced twin boys, the eldest of whom was Perez. It was through him that God preserved the tribe of Judah.

Now, in the time of the judges, when there is no king and chaos rules, a descendant of Perez whose name is Elimelek, dwells in a village called Bethlehem in the land of Judah. Though Bethlehem means "house of bread," there is hardly any bread to be found.

To preserve his family, Elimelek takes his wife, Naomi, and his two sons, Mahlon and Kilion, and heads east toward the rich highlands of Moab on the other side of the Dead Sea. In Moab there are rivers and rainfall and food enough for everyone. He leaves reluctantly, hoping this will be the briefest of sojourns, unaware that neither he nor his sons will see Bethlehem again.

Genesis 19:37 indicates that the Moabites were descended from Moab, who was the product of an incestuous relationship between Abraham's nephew Lot and Lot's eldest daughter. ▪

Though Naomi has little to eat, she is grateful that God has filled her house with the noisy banter of a husband and two sons. She is content as long as her family stays together.

But while they are in Moab, tragedy strikes. Elimelek falls ill and then dies. His passing is so swift and the pain of his loss so sharp that Naomi wonders how she will survive it.

As for her sons Mahlon and Kilion, they are now grown men with Moabite wives, named Orpah and Ruth, both of whom Naomi loves. In the midst of her grief, she makes a point of thanking God that even though she is a widow, she is not destitute. She has two loving sons and their wives to care for her.

She does not know that tragedy will strike again.

In quick succession both of Naomi's sons die. Now there is not merely one widow who needs looking after but three. To have no husband is a tragedy. But to be childless is a curse. With the loss of both husband and sons, Naomi is wild with grief and fear. A foreigner in Moab, she has no one to care for her. Surely God must be displeased with her to have taken her husband and both of her sons.

Before long, word reaches her that the land of Judah has been blessed with rain and abundant crops. The drought is finally over. Despite the fact that the road from Moab to Bethlehem is full of robbers, Naomi decides to risk the journey. Her daughters-in-law, Orpah and Ruth, insist on coming with her. God willing, the three women will arrive in time for the April harvest.

As much as she loves them, Naomi has misgivings. Before the three have journeyed far, she turns to her daughters-in-law, and says, "Go back, each of you, to your mother's home. May the LORD show kindness to you, as you have shown to your dead husbands and to me. May the LORD grant that each of you will find rest in the home of another husband."

As she kisses them in final farewell, the two young women weep and cling to her. They cannot bring themselves to let her face the dangers of the road alone.

But Naomi will not give up. "Return home, my daughters. Why would you come with me? Am I going to have any more sons, who could become your husbands? Return home, my daughters; I am too old to have another husband. Even if I thought there was still hope for me—even if I had a husband tonight and then gave birth to sons—would you wait until they grew up? Would you remain unmarried for them? No, my daughters. It is more bitter for me than for you, because the LORD's hand has turned against me!"

Naomi believes this. That God hates her.

But Orpah loves her. Even so, she agrees with Naomi. Why would anyone in the land of Judah want to marry an impoverished Moabite widow? Wishing the world was different than it is, she kisses her mother-in-law good-bye and then returns to Moab. But Ruth refuses to leave.

Once again Naomi presses her. "Ruth," she says. "Your sister-in-law is going back to her people and her gods. Go back with her."

But the young woman will not listen. "Don't urge me to leave you or to turn back from you. Where you go I will go, and where you stay I will stay. Your people will be my people and your God my God. Where you die I will die, and there I will be buried. May the LORD deal with me, be it ever so severely, if even death separates you and me."

Most people in the ancient Near East worshiped gods whom they believed operated only among their own people in a certain geographical region. Leaving Moab, Ruth must also leave behind the gods of Moab. ■

Beautiful, amazing Ruth! Naomi is relieved that her daughter-in-law has finally won the argument.

After several days, the two arrive safely in Bethlehem, an event that stirs considerable talk. "Can this be Naomi?" her neighbors exclaim, amazed that ten years have passed since she and her family moved to Moab.

"Don't call me Naomi," she replies. "Call me Mara, because the Almighty has made my life very bitter. I went away full, but the LORD has brought me back empty. Why call me Naomi? The LORD has afflicted me; the Almighty has brought misfortune upon me."

Then she speaks of her great anguish, of the emptiness she feels at losing her husband and sons.

Naomi has become what each of the women fears most, a widow with no means of support. A bitter fate indeed.

Naomi means "pleasant." *Mara* means "bitter." ◾

Though Ruth still feels the anguish of losing her husband, it eases her pain to think about taking care of Naomi. For all her complaints, her mother-in-law is not hard to love. With Naomi's blessing, she heads out to the fields to glean whatever the harvesters have missed. More than mere custom, the practice is enshrined in law—every landowner must refrain from reaping the edges of his field, thereby allowing the poor to gather whatever is left behind. If she's lucky, Ruth will harvest enough grain to keep herself and Naomi alive. But the work is rough and dangerous, especially for a young foreign woman without family members to avenge an insult.

Ruth begins working in a field that belongs to a man named Boaz. Mid-morning, she notices him talking with his foreman and then heading her way. A tall man with shoulder-length hair and a broad, welcoming smile, he greets her. "My daughter," he says, "listen to me. Don't go and glean in another field and don't go away from here. Stay here with my servant girls. Watch the field where the men are harvesting, and follow along after the girls. I have told the men not to lay a hand on you. And whenever you are thirsty, go and get a drink from the water jars the men have filled."

Surprised by his kindness, Ruth bows and then exclaims, "Why have I found such favor in your eyes that you notice me—a foreigner?"

"I've been told all about what you have done for your mother-in-law since the death of your husband," he says, "how you left your father and mother and your homeland and came to live with a people you did not know before. May the LORD repay you for what you have done. May you be richly rewarded by the LORD, the God of Israel, under whose wings you have come to take refuge."

His words feel like a benediction.

Later that day, Boaz offers Ruth a generous portion of bread and roasted grain to eat. Then he instructs his men: "Even if she gathers among the sheaves, don't embarrass her. Rather, pull out some stalks for her from the bundles and leave them for her to pick up, and don't rebuke her."

Ruth works hard until evening. After threshing the barley, she measures the day's haul—two thirds of a bushel, enough to feed Naomi and herself for several weeks! As she makes her way home, she notices a bird on its nest. Thinking of the chicks that shelter beneath its wings, she thanks God that she has found her own place underneath his all-sheltering wings.

Naomi is astonished by how much grain Ruth has harvested in a single day. "Whose field did you glean in? Blessed be the man who took notice of you!"

When Naomi learns that the field is Boaz's, she exclaims, "That man is our close relative; he is one of our guardian-redeemers."

As April passes into May, Ruth continues to work in Boaz's field. One day, her mother-in-law suggests a plan. "My daughter," Naomi says, "shouldn't I try to find a home for you, where you will be well provided for? Tonight Boaz will be winnowing barley on the threshing floor. This is what you must do. Perfume yourself and wear your best clothes and then go down to the threshing floor. But don't let him see you until he's finished eating and drinking. Note the place where he lies down. Afterward, go to him, uncover his feet, and lie down. He will tell you what to do."

So Ruth does exactly as Naomi tells her. She watches where Boaz lies down at the far end of the grain pile. He and his men will spend the night on the threshing floor in order to protect the harvest. Once all is quiet, Ruth lies down beside Boaz, uncovering his feet.

After the work was done, the threshers would feast together and then bed down for the night to protect the grain. Though the threshing floor at night was a male stronghold, it was sometimes visited by prostitutes. ■

She trembles as she does so, wondering how Boaz will react when he wakes up. Then she drifts off to sleep. And as she dreams, she sees an enormous eagle, hovering above her, singing these words: *If you make the Most High your dwelling, he will cover you with his feathers, and under his wings you will find refuge.*

At midnight Boaz awakens, startled to discover a woman lying at his feet. "Who's there?" he demands.

"I am your servant Ruth," she says. "Spread the corner of your garment over me, since you are a guardian-redeemer of our family."

Realizing that she is proposing marriage, Boaz replies: "The LORD bless you, my daughter. This kindness is greater than that which you showed earlier: You have not run after the younger men, whether rich or poor. And now, my daughter, don't be afraid. I will do for you all you ask.

kānāp is translated as "corner of your garment." It can also be translated as "wings." Covering someone with the corner of your garment symbolizes marriage and is a custom still practiced in parts of the Middle East. ■

Although it is true that I am a guardian-redeemer of our family, there is a another one who is more closely related than I. Stay here for the night, and in the morning if he wants to do his duty as your guardian-redeemer, good; let him redeem you. But if he is not willing, as surely as the LORD lives I will do it."

Ruth lies at his feet until morning but departs before sunrise so no one will notice her presence. Before she goes, Boaz pours six measures of barley into her shawl.

Then he heads straight into town and waits at the gate until the man who is Naomi's close relative passes by. When he finds him, he says, "Naomi, who has come back from Moab, is selling the piece of land that belonged to our relative Elimelek. I thought I should bring the matter to your attention and suggest that you buy it in the presence of these seated here and in the presence of the elders of my people. If you will redeem it, do so. But if you will not, tell me, so I will know. For no one has the right to do it except you, and I am next in line."

"I will redeem it," the man replies, glad for the chance to add more land to his holdings.

But there is a catch, which Boaz now reveals. "On the day you buy the land from Naomi and from Ruth the Moabitess, you also acquire the dead man's widow, in order to maintain the name of the dead with his property."

This is too much for the man, who quickly retracts his offer. He's in no position to acquire a new wife whose future offspring will take the name of Ruth's first husband and then inherit the land.

After Boaz has cleverly cleared the path for himself, he proclaims his love for Ruth in the presence of all the people. So Ruth becomes his wife, and she gives birth to a son. His name is Obed, and he will become the father of Jesse, who will become the father of David, who will become Israel's greatest king.

As everyone knows, it is from David's line that the Savior will be born.

Because of two desperate women and the God who cared for them, the world would one day come to know another Guardian-Redeemer. He would be the one to deliver his people, wiping out their debts and giving them a future filled with hope.

THE TIMES

Naomi and Ruth's story took place sometime between 1400 and 1050 BC.
Their story is told in the book of Ruth.

A widow without sons to support her might become so destitute that she would have to sell herself into slavery or prostitution to survive. Even though God commanded his people to care for widows, many of the Mosaic laws were ignored during the era of the judges. Though the law (Leviticus 19:9–10, 23:22; Deuteronomy 24:19–21) instructed landowners to leave some produce in their fields for the poor to glean, many landowners simply ignored this provision.

In addition to gleaning and levirate marriage, a widow could appeal to a guardian-redeemer, or *go'el*, to act on her behalf. In such cases, the closest male relative was expected to rescue or deliver her (or other impoverished family members) by paying off debts or buying back properties that had been sold, because without land people could barely survive.

The New Testament portrays Jesus as our great Guardian-Redeemer, the one who through his self-sacrifice pays off every debt our sins have incurred, delivering us from evil and setting us free.

THE TAKEAWAY

1. Though God sometimes renames people in the Bible, it is not God but Naomi who renames herself: "Don't call me Naomi . . . Call me Mara, because the Almighty has made my life very bitter." What does this reveal about her state of

mind? How would you rename yourself based on your own circumstances?

2. Naomi mistakenly thinks her suffering is a punishment from God. Have you ever felt that your hardships were evidence that God was displeased with you? Looking back, do you see it any differently now?

3. When Boaz first meets Ruth, he expresses the wish that God will repay her faith and kindness, never suspecting that he will become the answer to his own prayer. Have you ever become the answer to a prayer that you or others have prayed? What were the circumstances?

4. The story of Naomi and Ruth is marked by a series of blessings. First Ruth blesses Naomi by staying with her. Then Naomi blesses Ruth by helping her find a husband. Boaz subsequently blesses Ruth with a home, and God blesses them both with a child. Think back over the last two or three days. In what ways would you say that God has both blessed you and made you a blessing to others?

CHAPTER 14

THE STORY OF HANNAH AND PENINNAH

The Lord Judges between Two Rivals

My heart rejoices in the Lord; in the Lord my horn is lifted high. My mouth boasts over my enemies, for I delight in your deliverance. The Lord sends poverty and wealth; he humbles and he exalts.

1 SAMUEL 2:1, 7

A few years after Samson crushed the Philistines, a fat priest by the name of Eli is presiding as a judge in Shiloh. The last bad apple in the bowl, he is so heavy that the children speculate about how God could create another human being out of his excess.

Whenever he is not officiating as high priest, Eli rests in his favorite chair, the one specially crafted to hold his girth. He watches at the doorpost of the tabernacle as men and women pass in and out.

Shiloh is the religious capital of the new nation, the place where Joshua first divided the land and then apportioned it by lottery to the twelve tribes of Israel. The sacred center of the universe, it is the place where the golden ark has come to rest, sheltered inside the Tent of Meeting. Each year, thousands of pilgrims go up to Shiloh to celebrate the feasts.

One of these is a woman by the name of Peninnah. Though a lightweight on the scale of wickedness, she has a nasty habit of using her tongue to fling countless tiny arrows at her enemies. With a large mouth and a nose that is always looking down on someone, she is the least favorite of her husband's two wives. Unlike her rival, Hannah, she already has several children.

Every year a Levite by the name of Elkanah takes his two wives and his children up to Shiloh to worship the Lord and present their sacrifices. Along the way, Peninnah keeps pointing out the obvious. How sad that Hannah cannot have children. How fortunate for Elkanah that he has taken a second wife to perform the duty his first cannot. She thanks God for all the sons he has blessed her with so that she can make up for Hannah's lack. Truly God alone knows every heart—whom to bless and whom to curse. Blessed be the God of Israel.

As always, Peninnah's cruelty has found its mark in Hannah's heart, provoking her to tears. Each year the old wound opens up again as Peninnah's arrows thrust deeper.

Elkanah does his best to shush his disagreeable wife. Once he and Hannah are alone, he caresses her as she leans against his chest, trying to soothe her by asking, "Why are you weeping? Why don't you eat? Why are you downhearted? Don't I mean more to you than ten sons?"

How can Hannah tell her husband the truth—that though he is the best of men, he cannot heal the heartbreak that comes from not being able to bear a son?

The next day, Elkanah presents his offerings to God, and he and his family feast together as is the custom, partaking of their portion of the sacrifices. Afterward, Hannah makes her way to the sanctuary alone. There she enters the presence of the Holy One, who is the only one to whom she can pour out her heart's discontent. With tears spilling down her cheeks, and her lips moving inaudibly in prayer, she makes a vow: "LORD Almighty, if you will only look on your servant's misery and remember me, and not forget your servant but give her a son, then I will give him to the LORD for all the days of his life, and no razor will ever be used on his head."

As Hannah pours out her heart to God, the old priest Eli is watching from the shadows. When he sees her moving her lips without making a sound, he scolds her: "How long are you going to stay drunk? Put away your wine."

Prayers were usually prayed out loud. ▧

Jesus's disciples were also accused of drunkenness when they were filled with the Holy Spirit on Pentecost. See Acts 2:1–13. ▧

"Not so, my lord," she says. "I am a woman who is deeply troubled. I have not been drinking wine or beer; I was pouring out my soul to the LORD. Do not take your servant for a wicked woman; I have been praying out of my great anguish and grief."

"Go in peace," he tells her, "and may the God of Israel grant you what you have asked of him."

Afterward, Elkanah notices that Hannah's sadness has lifted. Once they arrive home, the two make love, and this time God blesses them with a son. Hannah names him Samuel, which sounds like the Hebrew word for "heard of God." Pledging him to the Lord, she plans to bring her boy to Shiloh once he is weaned, in about three years' time.

When the day arrives, she and Elkanah take their little son up to the house of the Lord. While Peninnah and her children look on, Hannah turns to Eli and declares, "Pardon me, my lord. As surely as you live, I am the woman who stood here beside you praying to the LORD. I prayed for this child, and the LORD has granted me what I asked of him. So now I give him to the LORD. For his whole life he will be given over to the LORD."

Animals often use their horns or antlers as weapons. Here Hannah invokes an image of strength and majesty, perhaps also suggesting prosperity and progeny. ■

Though it has been a long time since Eli has stood this close to a miracle, he merely nods his head in assent and takes the boy in hand. As Hannah kisses her only child good-bye, a solitary tear runs down her cheek. Before she leaves, she sings this prayer,

My heart rejoices in the LORD;
    in the LORD my horn is lifted high.
My mouth boasts over my enemies,

for I delight in your deliverance.
There is no one holy like the LORD;
    there is no one besides you;
    there is no Rock like our God.
Do not keep talking so proudly
    or let your mouth speak such arrogance,
for the LORD is a God who knows,
    and by him deeds are weighed.
The bows of the warriors are broken,
    but those who stumbled are armed with strength.
Those who were full hire themselves out for food,
    but those who were hungry hunger no more.
She who was barren has borne seven children,
    but she who has had many sons pines away.
The LORD brings death and makes alive;
    he brings down to the grave and raises up.
The LORD sends poverty and wealth;
    he humbles and he exalts.
He raises the poor from the dust
    and lifts the needy from the ash heap;
he seats them with princes
    and has them inherit a throne of honor.
For the foundations of the earth are the LORD's;
    on them he has set the world.
He will guard the feet of his saints,
    but the wicked will be silenced in the place
        of darkness.
It is not by strength that one prevails;
    those who oppose the LORD will be broken.
The Most High will thunder from heaven;

the LORD will judge the ends of the earth.
He will give strength to his king
    and exalt the horn of his anointed.

Even though Hannah will
give birth to six children, the
number seven in this prayer
symbolizes perfection. As such
it invokes her satisfaction at all
the ways God will bless her.

Though Peninnah feigns indifference, she cannot help but note the words of Hannah's song, especially the ones that pertain to her. Like arrows they pierce her heart.

As for Hannah, she becomes the happy mother of two daughters and three more sons. Every year, she and her family make the journey north to Shiloh to celebrate the feasts. Each time, she is amazed to see how much her boy has grown.

Unlike Eli, Samuel will grow up to become a great man of God. He will be the last of the judges, a prophet who will anoint Saul as Israel's first king and David as Israel's greatest king.

While Peninnah and her children will soon be forgotten, Hannah's story will echo through the centuries until another young mother lifts up her voice to proclaim the greatness of God.[1] Like Samuel, the child growing inside Mary will be born in answer to prayer, and he will be destined to cause the falling and rising of many in Israel.

THE TIMES

Hannah's story took place about 1105 BC.
Her story can be found in 1 Samuel 1:1–2:11. Echoes
of her prayer can be heard in Luke 1:46–55.

After Joshua led the Israelites on their initial conquest of Israel, he erected a tabernacle at Shiloh, about twenty miles north of Jerusalem. For more than three hundred years, Shiloh served as the religious center of the new nation, until it was destroyed by the Philistines in about 1050 BC. More than a century passed until Israel once again had a central religious site. This time it was located in Jerusalem, in Solomon's temple, which was built around 966–959 BC.

Like the peoples around them, the Israelites had a sacrificial system of worship. When we think of sacrificing something, we often think of giving something away. Ancient peoples would more likely have thought in terms of giving something *over*. To the ancient Israelites, sacrifice always involved transformation. Whenever something was sacrificed, it was transferred from the common realm to the realm of the sacred. When Hannah and Elkanah brought their sacrifices to God at Shiloh, they were giving him gifts he had already given to them—animals, grain, and wine. Through such sacrifices, they were seeking to deepen their relationship with God.[2]

In the early history of Israel, the practice of polygamy was generally reserved for wealthy families. Rather than stemming from uncontrolled sexual desire, it was more commonly practiced to achieve two ends—to continue the family line and to produce a large enough family to handle the labor-intensive demands of farming and raising livestock. Because ancient peoples believed that fertility was under divine control, infertility was often viewed as a curse.

THE TAKEAWAY

1. It is difficult to overestimate Hannah's pain at not being able to bear children, particularly given the culture in which she lived. How does her prayer (1 Samuel 1:10–16) point to a way out of despair?

2. Take a few moments to meditate on Hannah's song (1 Samuel 2:1–10). What words or phrases strike you? Why?

3. Hannah's song (page 166–68) emphasizes a series of reversals—the hungry are filled, the barren woman gives birth, the poor are lifted up. What does she mean by saying, "it is not by strength that one prevails?" In what ways might your life or perspective change if you took this statement seriously?

4. Hannah prayed for a child, but God gave her so much more. The son she prayed for was to become Israel's last judge as kingmaker, one who helped Israel make the transition from the chaotic period of the judges into the more ordered period of the monarchy. What might this imply about the potential ramifications of our own prayers?

CHAPTER 15

THE STORY OF SAUL

A King Falls into Despair

And without faith it is impossible to please God.

HEBREWS 11:6

Rubbing his cheek with his hand, the prophet Samuel feels the sting of their demands. He is troubled that the people keep clamoring for a king to rule over them. They want to be like every other nation in the world, but they are not every other nation. They are God's chosen people.

As the last of Israel's Judges, Samuel considers their request not only an insult to God but as a personal affront.

"It's not you they've rejected," God tells him. "No, they've rejected me as their king. Just as they've always done from the day I brought them up out of Egypt, forsaking me and serving other gods, so they are doing to you."

Then the Lord instructs Samuel to give them the king they desire.

❦

For the last three days, Saul has been roaming the countryside in search of runaway donkeys. Instead of donkeys, he encounters a white-bearded man of middling height, dressed in an elaborate robe. Could this be the man people speak of, the seer who will tell him where to find his father's donkeys?

Unbeknownst to Saul, the Lord has already spoken to the seer—the prophet Samuel—about him. "You will see him about this time tomorrow. He is the one chosen to deliver my people from the Philistines."

"Would you please tell me where the seer's house is?" Saul asks Samuel.

Reading nothing but potential behind the man's darkly lashed eyes, Samuel replies, "I am the seer. Go up ahead of me to the high place, for today you are to eat with me, and in the morning I will let you go and will tell you all that is in your heart. As for the donkeys you lost three days ago, do not worry about them; they have been found. And to whom is all the desire of Israel turned, if not to you and all your father's family."

Saul blushes, confused by the prophet's words. He has not been seeking his destiny, only looking for his father's donkeys.

"Am I not a Benjamite, from the smallest tribe of Israel," he objects, "and is not my clan the least of all the clans of the tribe of Benjamin? Why do you say such a thing to me?"

But Samuel insists that Saul join him for dinner. Seating him at the head of his guests, he serves him the choicest portion of meat.

The next morning, when Saul and Samuel are alone, the young man stands still while the prophet lifts a flask of oil and then pours it over his head. As the rich, aromatic oil soaks into his scalp and flows down his beard, his face tilts skyward, toward the rising sun.

Then he listens carefully as Samuels instructs him. "You are to travel to Gibeah of God, where there is a Philistine outpost. As you approach the town, you will meet a procession of prophets. The Spirit of the Lord will come upon you in power, and you will prophesy with them; and you will be changed into a different person. Once these signs are fulfilled, do whatever your hand finds to do, for God is with you.

"Then go down ahead of me to Gilgal. I will surely come down to you to sacrifice burnt offerings and fellowship offerings, but you must wait seven days until I come to you and tell you what you are to do."

Saul's subsequent encounters with God's Spirit transform him but only for a time. Like Samson, he is empowered by the Spirit to achieve particular tasks. ∎

As Saul journeys toward Gibeah, he reflects on the old man's words. Despite the expensive anointing oil and the prophet's surprising claims, he feels like the man he has always been, nothing more.

Later that day, God's Spirit rushes on him, and he begins to prophecy along with a group of prophets he meets along the way.

When neighbors and family members hear what has happened to Saul they press him for details. But he discloses nothing of what the prophet has said.

Sometime later, Saul learns that the tribes are gathering at Mizpah. He travels north with his clan, but not happily. He fears that Samuel might use the occasion to name him king.

When the tribes assemble, Samuel tells them, "This is what the Lord, the God of Israel, says, 'I brought Israel up out of Egypt, and I delivered you from the power of Egypt and all the kingdoms that oppressed you. But you have now rejected your God, who saves you out of all your calamities and distresses. And you have said, "No, set a king over us." So now present yourselves before the Lord by your tribes and clans.'"

Casting lots, the tribe of Benjamin advances and then Saul's clan and then Saul's family. When the lot finally falls to Saul the son of Kish, he is nowhere to be found.

The new king, the man whom God has chosen from among all the tribes of Israel, is hiding in the baggage, afraid of what will be asked of him. Despite his physical stature—he is a head taller than other men—he knows that he is a man of ordinary abilities. How can he fulfill the expectations of a people who are desperate for a king to deliver them from the Philistines?

But God, who sees everything, knows exactly who Saul is and where he is hiding. When Samuel leads him out, he places Saul in the center of the people and declares, "Do you see the man the Lord has chosen? There is no one like him among all the people."

Then a great shout goes up: "Long live the king!"

Instead of assembling an army on the spot, Saul returns to his father's house. One day, while he is plowing the fields, a messenger reaches him from Jabesh Gilead. The city is under siege and facing appalling terms of surrender. If its citizens capitulate, the Ammonites will spare their lives. However, they will also gouge out the right eye of every man to render him incapable of fighting. For how can a man do battle when his left eye is covered by a shield and his right eye is sightless?

When Saul hears of his countryman's plight, God's Spirit descends on him in a rush of power, and he calls on every tribe in Israel to come to the city's rescue. Then he and his men break into the enemy camp and slaughter them.

With the help of God, Saul has done precisely what a king should do, delivering his people from their enemies.

Soon after, Saul's son Jonathan attacks the Philistine outpost at Geba. But this victory is like a stick thrust into the eye of a lion. Enraged, the Philistines gather an enormous force to crush the Israelites.

During this period the Israelites faced numerous enemies, especially the Ammonites on the east and the Philistines on the west. The Ammonites descended from Abraham's nephew Lot and worshiped the god Molech. Their capital city was Rabbah (modern Amman, Jordan). ■

Saul has also gathered an army, but it is growing smaller by the day. The prophet Samuel had instructed him to go down to Gilgal and wait for him for seven days. Now Saul and his men are waiting at Gilgal, praying for Samuel to come quickly. Though this is the seventh day, there is still no sign of him. Meanwhile Saul's soldiers are scattering, running into caves and thickets and even across the Jordan River to flee from the Philistines.

The king fights to contain his doubts. What should he do? Trust the old prophet who claims to speak for God or take decisive action on his own? Why hasn't Samuel come as he promised?

Unwilling to wait a moment longer, he performs the pre-battle sacrifice himself and then prays to God for victory.

As soon as he completes the offering, Samuel arrives.

"What have you done?" the prophet asks.

"When I saw that the men were scattering," Saul says, "and that you did not come at the set time, and that the Philistines were assembling, I thought, 'Now the Philistines will come down against me at Gilgal, and I have not sought the Lord's favor.' So I felt compelled to offer the burnt offering."

"You acted foolishly," Samuel says. "You have not kept the command the Lord your God gave you: if you had, he would have established your kingdom over Israel for all time. But now your kingdom will not endure."

Again and again in the years that follow, Saul is put to the test. Each time he is challenged—either rely on God or on himself, either do what God tells him to or do what he thinks best. Saul finds it difficult to beat back his fear and the feeling that he should act on his instincts. But God insists on complete obedience. Get this right and Israel will flourish. Get it wrong and the king and everyone else will suffer.

But Saul keeps getting it wrong, keeps following his instincts, keeps trying to rationalize his disobedience and minimize his failings. Instead of becoming a king after God's own heart, he becomes the king of good excuses.

Failing test after test, he begins to retreat from God. The man who had thought so little of himself when Samuel first anointed him king will now do anything to cling to power.

Though he will occasionally admit his failings, Saul is not interested in real reform. So Samuel refuses to prop him up. One day they have it out. As Samuel tries to leave, Saul catches hold of the hem of Samuel's robe and tears it.

Turning around, Samuel tells him: "The Lord has torn the kingdom of Israel from you today, and has given it to one of your neighbors—to one better than you."

Then the Lord leads Samuel to a shepherd boy in Bethlehem, a young man named David who will become a king after God's own heart.

After that, Saul begins to suffer from nervous fits. One moment he is calm and the next crazed. All the time he grows more jealous of his power.

In the midst of his struggles he finds comfort whenever this same shepherd boy plays his lyre, soothing him with beautiful songs. He has no idea that Samuel has already anointed David as Israel's next king. He only knows that whenever the boy plays, he feels at peace.

But his kingdom is not at peace.

In the Elah Valley near the Philistine Plain the battle line is drawn, with the Philistine army on one side and the Israelites on the other. The Philistines have challenged Israel to one-on-one combat. Their champion Goliath will face off against Israel's fiercest warrior. But Goliath is a towering giant, standing over nine feet tall. His scaled, bronze armor, stretching across his massive chest, weighs over 125 pounds, and this is without his bronze helmet and the protective coverings he wears on his legs. The iron point on the tip of his enormous spear weighs 15 pounds.

Little wonder that no soldier from Israel's ranks has stepped forward to accept his challenge.

Visiting the Israelite camp one day, the shepherd boy hears Goliath bellowing his twice-daily challenge, one he has repeated for the last forty days: "Choose a man and have him come down to me. If he is able to fight and kill me, we will become your subjects; but if I overcome him and kill him, you will become our subjects and serve us."

To David's dismay, no one steps forward to accept the giant's challenge. Instead, men run when they hear his voice.

When Saul hears that David is willing to fight Goliath, he summons him to his tent.

"You're just a boy," he says.

But David assures him that he has already killed a bear and a lion in defense of his sheep. What's more, his eye is so sharp that he can sling a stone at a hair and not miss. Cannot the God who delivered him from the paw of the lion and the claw of the bear also deliver him from the hand of this Philistine?

Desperate to act, Saul dresses young David in his own armor. But the youth finds it cumbersome. Discarding it, he picks up five smooth stones from a nearby stream. With only a leather sling and a small bag of stones, he steps forward to meet the giant.

When Goliath sees that his adversary is a merely a boy, he mocks him: "Am I a dog, that you come at me with sticks? Come here and I'll give your flesh to the birds of the air and the beasts of the field!"

"You come against me with sword and spear and javelin," David shouts. "But I come against you in the name of the Lord Almighty, the God of the armies of Israel, whom you have defied. This day the Lord will hand you over to me, and I'll strike you down and cut off your head. Today I will give the carcasses of the Philistine army to the birds of the air and the beasts of the earth, and the whole world will know that there is a God in Israel."

Unaware of danger, Goliath moves to crush the boy. The last thing he sees is a leather sling swinging round and round above David's head. A moment later he falls face down on the ground with a stone embedded in his forehead. Before he can summon the strength to rise, David draws Goliath's sword from its scabbard and cuts off his head.

The Israelites are jubilant as the Philistines flee before them.

From then on Saul keeps David close. But it isn't long before problems emerge. For one thing, the boy wins too much. For another the people adore him. When Saul and David return from battle, the women rush into the streets crying, "Saul has slain his thousands, and David his tens of thousands."

It galls him to think that everyone in Israel is running after David. Even his daughter Michal is infatuated with him. But at least he can leverage that. Baiting David, he tells him he can marry his daughter if he can pay the bride price of a hundred Philistine foreskins. Saul has set the price so high that he is sure that David will die while trying to achieve the impossible. Instead the young warrior returns with double the number— two hundred Philistine foreskins.

One day, while David is playing the lyre, the king falls into a fit and tries to pin his son-in-law to the wall with a spear. But David escapes, leaving Michal behind.

In Hebrew poetry, ten thousand was used as a parallel for one thousand. So the women were probably not claiming that David had killed ten times more Philistines than Saul but that together the two men had slain thousands. Being compared equally to David was apparently enough to raise the king's ire.[1] ■

From then on, it will be a game of cat and mouse, with Saul pursuing and David eluding him in the desert wilderness. Years pass with two kings of Israel, one sitting on his throne and the other living by his wits in the wilderness.

One day, Saul hears that David and his men are hiding out in Engedi, an oasis west of the Dead Sea. Taking three thousand men, he heads south to hunt for David. When he enters a cave to relieve himself, Saul has no idea that David and his men are hiding deep within. While the king is taking care of business, David creeps up and cuts a corner off his robe.

As Saul goes on his way, David shouts after him: "My lord the king! Why do you listen when men tell you that I am bent on harming you? Today you have seen how the Lord delivered you into my hands in the cave. Some urged me to kill you, but I spared you; I said, 'I will not lift my hand against my master, because he is the Lord's anointed.'

The hem of a garment was considered a symbol of a man's authority. ■

"My father, look at this piece of your robe in my hand! I cut off the corner of your robe but did not kill you. Against whom has the king of Israel come out? Whom are you pursuing? A dead dog? A flea? May the Lord be our judge and decide between us."

As Saul listens to David's pleas, tears course down his face. "You are more righteous than I," he replies, "for you have treated me well and I have treated you badly. I know that you will surely be king and that the kingdom of Israel will be established in your hands."

After that, Saul stops pursuing David—at least for a while.

When Samuel dies, Saul mourns, not because of any fondness for the old man, but because the prophet was his only connection with God.

Though David can inquire of Abiather, his high priest, Saul has no one from whom to receive divine direction. How could he, since he has already murdered most of the priests, fearing they would take David's side?

Left to himself, he is unable to control his hatred for David as jealousy and paranoia descend on his heart again.

Sometime later, the Philistines gather in great force, hoping to defeat Israel once and for all.

By now the man who had seemed like the ideal king when Samuel first met him looks haggard and stooped. At night he finds it hard to sleep, and even when he does he wakes to nightmares. Tomorrow he will fight the Philistines. Will the Lord give him the victory? He has no word from God to guide him, no way to discern who will prevail.

THE TIMES

Saul reigned from about 1050 to 1010 BC.
His story is drawn from 1 Samuel 8–31.

When we hear of judges, we tend to think of people wearing black robes and presiding over courtrooms. By contrast, Israel's judges were usually heroic or charismatic individuals whom God raised up to lead his people prior to the establishment of the monarchy.

By contrast, many of the surrounding peoples had kings who went to war on their behalf. When the Israelites asked for a king, Samuel chided them for rejecting God's leadership, warning that a king would claim their sons as soldiers and their daughters to serve in his palace. Demanding the best of their fields, vineyards, and livestock, he would eventually enslave them all.

When Saul was anointed king, there was not much to be king over—no fortified city, no palace, no officials, no army, and no harem of beautiful women. Instead of the usual trappings of power, there was the unenviable challenge of fighting an enemy who was more powerful and technologically advanced than any other group in the region.

With the advent of the monarchy, the distinction between prophet and king became clearly demarcated. Unlike pagan prophets, who were expected to rubber stamp the policies of the reigning monarch, Israelite prophets were to operate independently, speaking the word of the Lord without reference to the king's pleasure or approval. When a king was unfaithful, they often played an oppositional role.

The biblical ideal of kingship differed radically from the ideal adopted by surrounding peoples. Rather than being a law unto himself, Israel's king was to rule humbly under the direction of God. He was to write down the law and read it "all the days of his life so that he may learn to revere the Lord his God and follow carefully all the words of this law and these decrees and not consider himself better than his brothers" (Deuteronomy 17:19–20). Neither was he to take many wives or accumulate large sums of money.

Unfortunately, many of Israel's kings, Saul included, were spectacular failures when it came to living up to the biblical ideal.

THE TAKEAWAY

1. Even though Samuel warns the people that exchanging God's leadership for that of a human king will cost them dearly, they persist in demanding a king. And even though God desires what's best for them, he gives in to their demands. In what ways, if any, does God's decision surprise you? Do you think it's possible that God sometimes responds to us in similar ways—saying yes to our demands even when he wants something better for us? Share the reasons for your response.

2. Before Samuel anointed David as king, God tells him, "The LORD does not look at the things people look at. People look at the outward appearance, but the LORD looks at the heart" (1 Samuel 16:7). Drawing on your own experiences, how would you describe what it's like to be assessed (positively and negatively) in these two ways: based on your outward appearance or based on your heart? When are you most likely to engage in similar assessments of others—judging by outward appearance or looking beyond it to the heart of the person?

3. Rather than repenting, Saul made a habit of excusing and rationalizing his willful failures. How does this tendency operate in your own relationship with God? What habits of thought or behavior are you most likely to try and justify?

4. Because of his failure to trust God, Saul missed out on the blessings God had for him. With each act of disobedience, his character was further marred and his heart hardened until he could no longer hear from God. In what ways, if any, do you recognize this pattern among God's people today?

CHAPTER 16

THE STORY OF THE
MEDIUM OF ENDOR

A Fortune Teller Conjures the Dead

*When you enter the land the Lord your God is
giving you, do not learn to imitate the detestable
ways of the nations there. Let no one be found
among you who sacrifices their son or daughter
in the fire, who practices divination or sorcery,
interprets omens, engages in witchcraft, or casts
spells, or who is a medium or spiritist or who
consults the dead. Anyone who does these things
is detestable to the Lord; because of these same
detestable practices the Lord your God will drive
out those nations before you.*

DEUTERONOMY 18:9–12

Doom. He feels it moving toward him though he cannot see it, snarly and bristling with malice. No matter how quickly he moves, pivoting to check his back, he can't seem to get out of the way. He can feel the hair standing up on his neck like hackles on a dog.

It's been like that for some time. Though Saul has men to guard him, he is afraid to close his eyes at night lest he be overtaken.

Some days are worse than others. Today is the worst.

How he longs for a word from God to shatter the darkness. To tell him all is forgiven and that his kingdom will endure. But there is only silence. He should ask the high priest to consult the Urim and Thummim for him, casting lots to discover whether he will prevail against the Philistines who have gathered in great numbers to attack him. But then he remembers that he has already murdered the high priest and many other priests as well. He fears they are in league with David, who has himself gone over to the Philistines.

Perhaps he should summon an interpreter to read his dreams, but these days he has no dreams because he sleeps so little.

If only he could ask Samuel for a word, but the old man has already been gathered to his ancestors and buried in Ramah.

Now there is only silence. No word from God.

Believing the priests were in league with David, Saul accused them of treachery and executed them. Only Abiather escaped, taking the special ephod, or garment, of the high priest with him. It contained the Urim and Thummim, which he brought to David so that he—and not Saul—could consult the Lord. ∎

Even when God had spoken to him in the past, the words were rarely to his liking. Before Saul had completed the first year of his reign, Samuel had accused him of being a flat-out failure. For just a small miscalculation God had rejected him as king. At least Saul thinks it was small. He had merely acted when God had told him to wait. But waiting was for women, not for soldiers under the threat of death.

For one offense and then another and another, Samuel, on behalf of God, had declared him unfit, saying,

> For rebellion is like the sin of divination,
> and arrogance like the evil of idolatry.
> Because you have rejected the word of the LORD,
> he has rejected you as king.

Though Saul has had his victories, the thing he wants most, he cannot have—to be at peace. To rest secure. After more than forty years of sitting on the throne of Israel, he is still uneasy. Philistines plague him. David eludes him. God abandons him.

He is alone.

⚬⚬⚬

The woman is alone too. She is a widow, doing her best to survive. She lives in Endor, not far from where Saul and his men are encamped. Today she feels restless and unsettled, though she cannot say why. Perhaps it is merely a phase of the moon or the souls of dead men who have gathered to

Though this scene is not in the Bible, some who practiced divination used this procedure to determine whether an army would prevail or a person would recover from an illness.[1] ▪

watch the looming battle. She only knows the air is electric. But as always, she wants to know more, so she fills a small bowl with water. Then she recites an incantation, asking for wisdom from the world beyond to know which way the fight will go. Carefully she pours a small drop of oil on the water's surface and watches as it splits in two, a sign that great men are about to fall.[2]

Late in the day, when night has fallen, she is startled to find strangers at her door. One of them is taller by a head than any man she has ever seen. Pushing through the door, he quickly states his business: "Consult a spirit for me, and bring up the one I name," he says.

But she is no fool. She knows King Saul has strictly forbidden the practice of necromancy, citing the Scripture that says: "If a person turns to mediums and necromancers, whoring after them, I will set my face against that person and will cut him off from among his people." Perhaps these are Saul's men, seeking to entrap her.

"Surely you know," she replies, "what Saul has done. He has cut off the mediums and spiritists from the land. Why have you set a trap for my life to bring about my death?"

But the big man, the one who had to fold himself in half, stooping low to get through her door, invokes an oath, promising her, "As surely as the LORD lives, you will not be punished for this."

He is such a mixture of earnestness and power that she believes him. "Whom shall I bring up?" she asks.

"Bring up Samuel," he says.

She is good at the art of deception. Since she is the only one who can see the visions and hear the voices she summons from beyond, she need only play her part convincingly. So she speaks in guttural tones, rolls her eyes, and makes her body tremble.

What is so bad about reassuring a mother that her dead child

is well, uniting lovers across impassible boundaries, conveying posi-
tive omens to those who seek them? She merely wants to do good,
to bring hope, and, yes, to find a way to support herself.

So now she makes a show of asking the reigning powers to raise
Samuel up from the grave. But before she can engage in the usual
pretense, something terrifying happens. She stares wide-eyed and
then looks accusingly at Saul.

"Why have you deceived me? You are Saul!" she exclaims.

"Don't be afraid. What do you see?" the king asks.

"I see a spirit coming up out of the ground."

"What does he look like?"

"An old man wearing a robe is coming up."

Trembling, Saul kneels with his face to the ground.

"Why have you disturbed me by bringing me up?" the old man
accuses.

"I am in great distress," Saul tells him. "The Philistines are
fighting against me, and God has turned away from me. He no
longer answers me, either by prophets or by dreams. So I have called
on you to tell me what to do."

"Why do you consult me, now that the LORD has departed
from you and become your enemy?" Samuel asks. "The LORD
has done what he predicted through me. The LORD has torn the
kingdom out of your hands and given it to one of your neighbors—to David. Because you did not obey the LORD or carry out
his fierce wrath against the Amalekites, the LORD has done this
to you today. The LORD will hand over both Israel and you to
the Philistines, and tomorrow you and your sons will be with me.
The LORD will also hand over the army of Israel into the hands
of the Philistines."

The prophet's words rush at Saul with nightmare force and he collapses. He is too weak to rise, overcome by fear and hunger, for he has eaten nothing for a day and a night.

Seeing how shaken he is—and she is shaken too—the woman pleads with him, saying, "Look, your servant has obeyed you. I took my life in my hands and did what you told me to do. Now please listen to your servant and let me give you some food so you may eat and have the strength to go on your way."

At first he refuses. But his men urge him to eat and he relents.

Slaughtering a fattened calf, the woman quickly prepares it along with some bread.

After they have eaten, she watches the king and his men depart. Staring out, she notes a shadow that is darker than the moonlit night. Hungry and bristling with malice, it trails a little distance behind the king. She knows that it will not be long until it overtakes him. With a shudder and a prayer, she closes her door.

THE TIMES

The medium of Endor's story probably
took place about 1010 BC.
Her story is told in 1 Samuel 28.

Fortunetellers used various means of divination, including observing patterns of oil dropped into water, interpreting dreams, reading the stars, and drawing meaning from the entrails of animals.

Though condemned in the Bible (Leviticus 19:31; 20:6), the practice of necromancy—of attempting to communicate with the dead—was practiced throughout the ancient Near East, where people employed magic in an attempt to control their lives by controlling the gods. Such practices were usually motivated by fear and the desire for power.

By contrast, Israel's all-powerful God could never be controlled, though he could be trusted to watch over those who remained faithful to him. Unlike pagan gods, he communicated, not through secret patterns revealed in the entrails of animals but through prophets and occasionally through dreams.

At times of national emergency, the Israelites also consulted the Urim and Thummim for revelation. These sacred objects may have been small sticks inscribed with symbols, or they may have been metal objects or stones carried in the breastplate worn by the high priest. They could be cast as lots so that God's will could be ascertained through a series of yes or no questions.

Deuteronomy 18:9–12 indicates that God considered magic an abomination, something his people should shun lest they be defiled by the superstitions of those around them, which could open them up to the influence of false gods and demonic powers.

THE TAKEAWAY

1. What three to five words would you use to describe the character of the woman of Endor?

2. Have you or has anyone you know ever engaged in the practice of magic? For example, by way of astrology, tarot cards, a Ouija board, or visiting a fortuneteller? What motivated you? Were you aware at the time that such practices are off limits for those who believe in God?

3. The story showcases how far Saul had fallen. Though a courageous and naturally gifted man, he met a tragic and pathetic end. What does this story reveal about the consequences of trusting yourself more than God?

4. Ancient people believed the supernatural world was real. How is that worldview both affirmed and denied in our culture today? How does your understanding of the existence of the supernatural world shape your daily life?

CHAPTER 17

THE STORY OF MICHAL

A Trophy Princess Falls Out of Love

Those who want to kill me set their traps,
those who would harm me talk of my ruin;
all day long they scheme and lie.

PSALM 38:12

Michal's father is a head taller than most—strong, handsome, decisive. He hails from the warrior tribe of Benjamin. She cannot remember a time when her father was not king and she not a princess. She has heard how God instructed the prophet Samuel to anoint Saul as Israel's first king.

She knows too that the old prophet is not altogether happy about his choice. She has heard rumors that the two men have fallen out and that Samuel has told her father point-blank that God is done with him. Apparently, her father is too much like the kings of other nations to meet with divine approval.

Despite Samuel's disapproval, Saul remains king. Though he is sturdier than most men, Michal senses something brittle within. He blows hot and cold, as though fast-moving clouds cast sinister shadows across the future. One moment he seems confident that his kingdom will last while the next he is dejected and sour.

Though Michal is sensitive to prevailing winds, she is not interested in politics. Instead, a young warrior has turned her head. Handsome and lithe, they say he routed the Philistines by felling their champion, a god-awful man by the name of Goliath. While Saul's army cowered before this giant, only David was willing to engage with him in single combat. Michal has heard the tale—how, refusing the protection of her father's armor, David prevailed with merely a sling and a stone.

Everything David does succeeds. Just days ago, she watched as women poured out of the city gates to greet David as he and Saul returned from battle. Hailing them, they sang,

Saul has slain his thousands,
and David his tens of thousands.

Their singing makes her father furious. "They have credited David with tens of thousands. . . . What more can he get but the kingdom?" Saul complains.

She notes the way her father eyes David, as though he is no longer a favorite but an enemy.

Her brother Jonathan is oblivious to Saul's jealousy. Instead of distancing himself from David, he draws him into his inner circle. The two men are like brothers. Jonathan has even handed him his tunic, sword, and belt. It is as much as saying that on the day David becomes king, he, the son of a king, will serve him.

Whenever Michal spots David in her father's court, she tries to catch his eye. Caring nothing for Saul's disapproval, she is unaware of how murderous his jealousy has become. Twice he has tried and failed to pin David to the wall with a spear. Now he can think of nothing but how to get rid of him.

One day, the king learns of his daughter's infatuation with David. The knowledge delights him, because she is just the bait he needs. So Saul instructs his servants to approach David with an offer: "Look, the king is pleased with you," they say; "he wants you for his son-in-law. All he asks for a bride price is that you take revenge on his enemies by bringing him a hundred Philistine foreskins." Saul knows that such a task will likely lead to David's death, for the Philistines are fierce fighters.

When Michal hears of it, she is thrilled to hear that David will attempt the challenge.

Mutilating enemies in this way was not uncommon. Unlike many of the surrounding peoples, the Philistines did not practice circumcision. By requesting a hundred foreskins, Saul can be sure that David has killed Philistines. ■

Before long, David returns from his quest with not one hundred but two hundred Philistine foreskins!

So Michal and David marry, and even though they are living under the shadow of Saul's jealousy, they are happy for a time. At night, when they are alone, David sings to her:

> How beautiful you are, my darling!
>> Oh, how beautiful!
>> Your eyes behind your veil are doves.
> Your lips are like a scarlet ribbon;
>> your mouth is lovely.
> Your breasts are like two fawns,
>> like twin fawns of a gazelle
>> that browse among the lilies.
> Until the day breaks
>> and the shadows flee,
> I will go to the mountain of myrrh
>> and to the hill of incense.
> You are altogether beautiful, my darling;
>> there is no flaw in you.[1]

Michal loves the poetry that flows from David's soul. No wonder Saul once welcomed his songs with their strange power to drive away demons and soothe his mind.

Her new husband is everything a princess could desire—passionate, strong, courageous, attentive, intelligent, and handsome. Other women envy her, and that pleases Michal even more.

One day word reaches her that her father is about to arrest David. Rushing to his side, she counsels him, "If you don't run for your life tonight, tomorrow you'll be killed." Then she lets her husband down through their open window and watches as he disappears into the night.

After David leaves, she takes a large statue[2] and lays it on the bed, covering it with a garment and putting goat hair at the head. A crude ruse, it fools the slow-witted soldiers who come looking for David. "He is ill," Michal explains, "and cannot rise from his bed."

But Saul is furious when they return without him. "Bring him bed and all if you must!"

When he discovers the statue, his rage explodes, and he accuses Michal of betraying him. "Why did you deceive me like this and send my enemy away so he escaped?"

A lie slips quickly off her tongue: "David said to me, 'Let me get away. Why should I kill you?'"

In the months ahead, Michal yearns for her husband. She wonders how long it will be until he climbs through the window and carries her away. From time to time she hears rumors of his exploits in desert regions to the south. Night after night she lies alone and lonely in their bed, feeling like the woman who sang:

> All night long on my bed
>   I looked for the one my heart loves;
>   I looked for him but did not find him.
> I will get up now and go about the city,
>   through its streets and squares;
> I will search for the one my heart loves.
>   So I looked for him but did not find him.

Michal does not encounter David for many years. By now she has stopped looking for him because she has been married off to a man named Paltiel. She knows that Saul was merely spiting David by giving her away to another man. It is just as Samuel said it would be when he warned the people what would happen when a king ruled over them. "You yourselves will become his slaves," he had said.

Now Michal feels the truth of this. Princess though she is, she knows she is merely a bird in a cage, a pawn for her father's power alliances. At least Paltiel loves her, and she has learned to love him too.

Though Michal doesn't know it, the days of her father's reign are coming to a close. Before long he and three of her brothers, including Jonathan, will be killed and mutilated by Philistines during fierce fighting on Mount Gilboa.

After Saul's death, the twelve tribes of Israel split in two. Some declare their allegiance to Saul's remaining son Ish-Bosheth while others follow David. Now that the king is dead, David demands Michal's return, and Ish-Bosheth agrees. Once more and without being consulted, Michal is torn from the husband she loves.

When Michal encounters David again, she is amazed. Instead of the youth she married, she sees a man hardened by war and determined to rule. The people flock to him, just as her father had feared they would. But despite his ascendancy, Michal cannot bring herself to love him again. Too much time has passed. Too many questions remain unanswered. Why had David not returned for her? She could have fled with him into the desert away from her father's wrath. But he never came.

David wants her back, she thinks, but only to secure his power.

As for the young woman David married, she is gone forever. In her place stands a woman who has been thrown by fate into a life she does not want. Queen though she is, Michal feels bitter and forsaken.

Not long after she is returned to David, Michal's brother Ish-Bosheth is killed by two of his own henchmen. Now all the tribes of Israel pledge loyalty to David. At last he holds the kingdom in his hands.

One day Michal walks to the window of David's palace and peers out. She listens as a large crowd winds its way up to Jerusalem with shouts and the clamor of trumpets. At the head of a great procession is the king himself. Instead of his royal robes, David wears the simple garments of a priest. He is dancing with all his might to the sound of songs and the music of harps, lyres, tambourines, and cymbals. Slowly the great golden ark of the covenant, the sacred place where God has decided to dwell, advances into the city. Yahweh has come to live among his own people once again!

David leads the crowd in praise, singing,

> Look to the LORD and his strength;
>> seek his face always.
> Remember the wonders he has done,
>> his miracles, and the judgments he pronounced. . . .
> Sing to the LORD, all the earth;
>> proclaim his salvation day after day.
> Declare his glory among the nations,
>> his marvelous deeds among all peoples.

But Michal is not in the mood for singing, nor does she feel like rejoicing. She thinks only of her dead father and brothers. This moment should belong to them and not to David. This is their kingdom, not his, she thinks. She looks on as David leaps about, contorting his body in a wild dance of praise to God. When the

200 LESS THAN PERFECT

dancing is over, he gives gifts to everyone present, and then he returns home to bless his household.

Michal daughter of Saul comes out to greet him, not with rejoicing as one might expect the queen to do, but with words designed to shame and scald: "How the king of Israel has distinguished himself today, going about half-naked in full view in the sight of the slave girls of his servants as any vulgar fellow would!"

But David merely answers: "It was before the LORD, who chose me rather than your father or anyone from his house when he appointed me ruler over the LORD's people Israel—I will celebrate before the LORD. I will become even more undignified than this, and I will be humiliated in my own eyes. But by these slave girls you spoke of, I will be held in honor."

The Bible doesn't indicate whether Michal was childless because of barrenness or because David refused to sleep with her. By refusing to have relations with her, he would have been ensuring there would be no rival claimants to his throne from the house of Saul. Those who heard her story would have likely seen Michal's childlessness as a curse. ■

And so it is that even to this day, David's memory is revered by all God's people.

As for Michal, her story ends sadly. Living in David's palace she remained who she always was, a little bird confined in a big cage, a pretty thing to please a man. Childless until the day of her death, she had no one who could rise up and call her blessed.

THE TIMES

Michal lived sometime between 1040–970 BC.
Her story can be found in 1 Samuel 18:20–29;
19:11–17; 25:44; 2 Samuel 3:13–16; 6:16–23.

Michal lived during a time of great transition, when Israel was leaving the chaotic period of the judges behind and entering the period of the monarchy. During the rule of the judges, Israel had great difficulty completing the conquest of Canaan and becoming a unified nation. But once the monarchy was established, Saul and David helped the Israelites defeat many of their surrounding enemies.

During this period many of the great powers in the region were in decline. The Hittites, Assyrians, Babylonians, and Egyptians had too many problems of their own to try to extend their influence into Canaan. Their weakness allowed David to extend the borders of his kingdom with great success. Only the Philistines who lived along the coast proved too hard to dislodge.

Though Samuel had anointed Saul as Israel's first king, it wasn't long before Saul proved himself unworthy by repeatedly disobeying the word of God as it was delivered by the prophet Samuel. Though Saul had rejected God, he reigned for forty-two years, until he committed suicide to avoid capture by the Philistines. David ruled for an additional forty years, and his son Solomon ruled for forty more. After that, the nation was divided into the southern kingdom of Judah and the northern kingdom of Israel.

Unlike the rulers of other nations, Israel's king was called to be humble rather than proud. He was to read God's word and live by it. Rather than dominating the people, he was to consider himself one of them (Deuteronomy 17:19–20). The king was to be devoted to God, which Saul was not. Unfortunately, Michal suffered the consequences of her father's repeated disobedience and unfaithfulness.

THE TAKEAWAY

1. Michal's story is a sad one. Born to royal privilege, she became a pawn of powers she could not control. What parts of Michal's story impact you most? In what ways, if any, do you relate to her?

2. Michal repeatedly finds herself at the mercy of forces she cannot control. What circumstances in your life have made you feel as though you have too little control? How have you responded? In what ways have you experienced or failed to experience God in such circumstances?

3. Michal experienced the loss of two husbands, a father, and four brothers. Her grief and bitterness over her losses made it difficult for her to move into a renewed relationship with David. How have your own hardships and losses affected your most important relationships?

CHAPTER 18

THE STORY OF DAVID

The Godly Man with a Shadow Side

*The LORD does not look at the things
people look at. People look at the outward
appearance, but the LORD looks at the heart.*

1 SAMUEL 16:7

There is no one who does good, not even one.

PSALM 14:3, ATTRIBUTED TO DAVID

Early in Saul's reign, God had already been at work raising up a successor to the disappointing King Saul.

The youngest of Jesse's eight sons, David is surprised when he is summoned home. Though still a youth, he has been busy tending his father's sheep, a job that requires both courage and constant watchfulness.

Whenever the rains fail, as they frequently do, David must lead his sheep to remote pastures far from the safety of home. Like all shepherds, he knows how quickly his flock can get into trouble.

Easily distracted, sheep are prone to wandering. Easily panicked, one frightened sheep can lead an entire flock to ruin. Despite their foolishness, David is determined to watch over his sheep so that not even a single one goes missing. At night he counts each one, herding them into a ready-made pen and then lying down in the entranceway to insure their safety with his own body. With his rod and staff at his side, he is confident that he can protect them from the worst of their enemies, even lions and bears.

At night sheep were often kept in caves or simple enclosures made from bushes. The shepherd would have used his staff to probe for snakes or scorpions before guiding his sheep into a cave. ■

The young shepherd prizes his time alone, often playing the lyre to pass the days, and singing songs that he composes.

The LORD is my shepherd, I lack nothing.
He makes me lie down in green pastures,
he leads me beside quiet waters,
he refreshes my soul.

Today David is tending his flock close to home, watching over them as they chew on the long grasses that sprout in Bethlehem's rocky hills. When one of his brothers arrives, he is surprised to hear that the prophet Samuel has been asking for him.

The old man has come to Bethlehem on a mission—to anoint one of Jesse's sons king. When Samuel meets the eldest son, he thinks he has discovered the one God has chosen. But he is merely repeating a familiar mistake. Like a young Saul, Eliab is tall and well muscled with strong hands that seem capable of any task.

Before Samuel can anoint him king, he hears an unmistakable voice: "Do not consider his appearance or his height, for I have rejected him. The LORD does not look at the things people look at. People look at the outward appearance, but the LORD looks at the heart."

So if Eliab is not God's choice, who is? Jesse's son, Abinadab, passes before Samuel. But he is not the one. Then comes Shamah. But God rejects him too. Four more of Jesse's sons pass before Samuel, but each time the answer is no. This is not the Lord's chosen one.

Vexed, Samuel asks Jesse if he has any more sons. When he learns that the youngest is off tending the sheep, he asks Jesse to summon him.

As Samuel waits for David to arrive, he feels two tensions rising in his heart—his resolve to do God's will and terror at the thought of anointing a new king while Saul still reigns.

When Jesse's youngest finally arrives, the prophet feels a divine yes welling up inside and dissolving all fear. "Rise and anoint him," the Lord says. "This is the one."

As Samuel pours the aromatic oil over the boy's head, the Spirit of the Lord descends on David and remains with him. It will not

be long before the boy is led into battle with Goliath and then
into the courts of a king who will try to murder him, not once but
several times.

The Spirit's presence is so evident in David that at first not even
Saul can resist him. When the young shepherd plays his lyre, Saul
finds peace. As David wins battle after battle, capturing the imagination of everyone in Israel, Saul's jealousy flashes and David flees.

Living by his wits in the wilderness, David gathers a group
of disaffected men to himself. Everyone in his father's household,
including his brothers, flocks to him as do many others who are
troubled by debt or distress. With a band of four hundred men at
his back, he hires himself out as a mercenary.

Afraid that his rival will try to take the throne, Saul hunts him.
But David is a fast-moving shadow that cannot be captured.

Years later, when David learns of Saul's death, he laments him,
not as a failed king but as a mighty warrior, a fallen hero. And as
for Jonathan, David expresses the keenness of his loss.

> How the mighty have fallen!
>   Saul and Jonathan—
> in life they were loved and admired,
>   and in death they were not parted.
> They were swifter than eagles,
>   they were stronger than lions.
> Daughters of Israel,
>   weep for Saul,
> who clothed you in scarlet and finery,
>   who adorned your garments with ornaments of gold.
> How the mighty have fallen in battle!
>   Jonathan lies slain on your heights.

I grieve for you, Jonathan my brother;
>   you were very dear to me.
Your love for me was wonderful,
>   more wonderful than that of women.
How the mighty have fallen!
>   The weapons of war have perished!

Though the men of Judah quickly rally to David, proclaiming him their king, the rest of Israel pledges loyalty to Saul's remaining son Ish-Bosheth. But this son of Saul neither looks the part nor plays it well. When two of his own men stab him and then cut off his head and carry it trophy-like to David, he surprises everyone by sentencing them to death for daring to kill a king. Soon after, all the tribes of Israel acclaim David as their king.

In the years that follow, he expands the borders of his kingdom, winning every fight he undertakes. Philistines, Moabites, Edomites, and Ammonites—all of them fall beneath David's mighty sword. Indeed, the Lord gives him the victory wherever he goes.

But one day he simply does not go.

Though spring is the time for kings to march off to war, David stays behind. After years at the head of his army, he sends his commander, Joab, to besiege the Ammonite city of Rabbah, forty miles northeast of Jerusalem.

Modern readers may be tempted to think that David and Saul's son Jonathan were lovers. But that would be to read our own cultural assumptions into the text. As V. Philips Long has remarked, "Some modern readers, unaware or neglectful of the biblical and ancient Near Eastern background to such expressions of love, have tried to read a homosexual nuance into David's words. But not only is such a reading unwarranted and inadmissible in terms of the broader biblical context and ancient Near Eastern attitudes toward homosexual practice generally, so far as the minimal evidence allows us to determine, it also flies in the face of the fact that 'love language' was often used to express loyalty in legal contexts."[1]

Springtime was a good time to conduct battle since the winter rains had stopped and able-bodied men were not yet needed to bring in the harvest.[2] ▪

Instead of camping out on the hard ground alongside his men, David sleeps in his own soft bed. But not well. Tonight he is restless. Strolling around the rooftop garden of his palace, he surveys the land below. Closing his eyes, David inhales the honeyed fragrance of almond trees, whose pink blossoms bless the landscape with their soft beauty.

When he opens his eyes, he sees something even more beautiful—and unusual. A young woman is bathing in the courtyard of her home. He watches as she rubs a cloth slowly and rhythmically across delicate, wheat-colored skin. Dark tresses fall in languid curls across her back. Hers is a face more beautiful and exotic than any he has seen.

Though David is already past the middle years of life, he feels ready for this new adventure that presents itself unbidden. So he sends for her, this woman named Bathsheba. When he discovers who she is, that she is the wife of one of his best soldiers and the granddaughter of a trusted advisor,[3] he feels a twinge of guilt. But why should he, as Israel's conquering king, refuse himself the pleasure of her company?

When she enters his private chambers he gathers her into his arms and makes love to her.

A few weeks after Bathsheba returns home, she discovers she is pregnant. Since she had just completed a ritual bath marking the end of her monthly period when David summoned her, the truth is painfully obvious. Both know that the punishment for adultery is death.[4]

As king, David is used to solving problems. Since Bathsheba's husband is off fighting the Ammonites at Ramah, David calls him home.

When the soldier arrives, the king greets him warmly, and then sends him home to spend the night with his wife. But instead of sleeping with Bathsheba, Uriah the Hittite[5] spends the night in the entryway of the palace, along with some of David's servants.

The next day, David asks Uriah why he has refused the comfort of his own bed. "How could I go to my house to eat and drink and make love to my wife," the soldier explains, "when my commander Joab and my lord's men are camped in the open country? As surely as you live, I will not do such a thing!"

Alarmed, David convinces Uriah to linger. This time he invites him to dinner and gets him drunk. Surely Uriah will return to Bathsheba tonight. But once again, Uriah spends the night at the palace.

As a way of maintaining ritual purity, David and his soldiers refrained from having sexual relations with their wives whenever they went to battle. ▪

Feeling cornered, David sends Uriah back to the battle, entrusting him with a message addressed to Joab. When the soldier hands the letter to his commander, he has no idea he is delivering his own death warrant.

"Put Uriah out in front, where the fighting is fiercest," David wrote. "Then withdraw from him so he will be struck down and die."

The next day Joab does what no good commander would do— ordering one of his best men to take up a position within striking distance of the city walls where the archers are thickest.

When Bathsheba's husband and the soldiers with him are cut down, Joab sends word to the king, saying, "Uriah the Hittite is dead."

Though David has killed many men in the course of battle, he has never before committed murder. Though he tries to excuse his crime, his conscience troubles him. At night, when shadows multiply, he sees the sad, accusing face of Uriah in the darkness. Before long, the vision fades as do the pangs of guilt assailing his heart.

As soon as the customary period of mourning ends, he marries Bathsheba, and she bears him a son. Celebrating the boy's birth, David begins to think he has weathered the crisis. But his troubles are just beginning.

For the Lord, whose eyes are always roaming the earth, searching for someone to bless, is dismayed when he looks down at his servant David. Knowing that darkness begets darkness, he decides to bring David's secret into the light.

Before long, God stirs up the prophet Nathan. Gathering his courage, Nathan goes to the king and tells him a story, one that reminds David of his early years tending his father's sheep.

The prophet speaks of two men, one rich and the other poor. Though the wealthy man owns large numbers of sheep and cattle, the poor man has only one little ewe to call his own. Instead of raising her in an outside pen, he brings her into his house and treats her like one of his children. He is so attached to the lamb that she becomes like a daughter to him, sharing his cup and even sleeping in his arms.

One day the rich man entertains a guest. Instead of culling an animal from his own flock, he steals the poor man's ewe, slaughters it, and feeds it to his visitor.

David is so incensed by the story that he can hardly wait for Nathan to stop talking. "As surely as the LORD lives," he exclaims, "the man who did this deserves to die! He must pay for that lamb four times over. Because he did such a thing and had no pity."

"You are the man!" Nathan replies.

"This is what the LORD, the God of Israel, says: 'I anointed you king over Israel, and I delivered you from the hand of Saul. I gave your master's house to you, and your master's wives into your arms. I gave you the house of Israel and Judah. And if all this had been too little, I would have given you even more. Why did you despise the word of the LORD by doing what is evil in his eyes? You killed Uriah the Hittite with the sword of the Ammonites. Now, therefore, the sword will never depart from your house, because you despised me and took the wife of Uriah the Hittite to be your own.'

"This is what the LORD says: 'Out of your own household I am going to bring calamity on you. Before your very eyes I will take your wives and give them to one who is close to you, and he will sleep with your wives in broad daylight. You did it in secret, but I will do this thing in broad daylight before all Israel.'"

In the silence that follows, tears roll down Nathan's cheeks and David knows them for what they are—the tears of God.

In a choking voice, David admits the truth: "I have sinned against the LORD."

He makes no excuse. Does not try to shift the blame. Instead he opens his heart and exposes the darkness inside. Sorrow, guilt, disgust at what he has done and who he has become overwhelm him.

"The LORD has taken away your sin," Nathan tells him. "You are not going to die."

David weeps loudly, making no effort to quiet his sobs.

But Nathan is not finished. "Because by doing this you have shown utter contempt for the LORD, the son born to you will die."

With a loud cry David tears his robes and falls to the ground.

What God has given, God has taken away.

A few days later, when the child falls ill, David begs for mercy. Fasting and lying on the ground for seven days, he pleads for the Almighty to spare his baby's life. He is so distraught, that his servants are afraid to tell him when the boy dies, fearing he will do something desperate.

But David surprises them. Instead of spiraling into depression, as they expect him to, he gets up from the ground, bathes himself, and dresses. Then he goes to the house of the Lord to worship. Bowing his head in the presence of the Almighty, he prays:

> Have mercy on me, O God,
>> according to your unfailing love;
> according to your great compassion
>> blot out my transgressions.
> Wash away all my iniquity
>> and cleanse me from my sin.
> For I know my transgressions,
>> and my sin is always before me.
> Against you, you only, have I sinned
>> and done what is evil in your sight;
> so you are right in your verdict
>> and justified when you judge.
> Surely I was sinful at birth,
>> sinful from the time my mother conceived me.
> Yet you desired faithfulness even in the womb;
>> you taught me wisdom in that secret place.
> Cleanse me with hyssop, and I will be clean;
>> wash me, and I will be whiter than snow.
> Let me hear joy and gladness;
>> let the bones you have crushed rejoice.
> Hide your face from my sins
>> and blot out all my iniquity.
> Create in me a pure heart, O God,

and renew a steadfast spirit within me.
Do not cast me from your presence
    or take your Holy Spirit from me.
Restore to me the joy of your salvation
    and grant me a willing spirit, to sustain me.
Then I will teach transgressors your ways,
    so that sinners will turn back to you.
Deliver me from the guilt of bloodshed, O God,
        you who are God my Savior,
        and my tongue will sing of your righteousness.
Open my lips, Lord,
    and my mouth will declare your praise.
You do not delight in sacrifice, or I would bring it;
    you do not take pleasure in burnt offerings.
My sacrifice, O God, is a broken spirit;
    a broken and contrite heart
    you, God, will not despise.
May it please you to prosper Zion,
    to build up the walls of Jerusalem.
Then you will delight in the sacrifices of the righteous,
    in burnt offerings offered whole;
    then bulls will be offered on your altar.[6]

Returning to the palace, David asks his servants to prepare a meal for him.

Perplexed, they exclaim, "While the child was alive, you fasted and wept, but now that the child is dead, you get up and eat!"

"While the child was still alive," David explains, "I fasted and wept. I thought, 'Who knows? The LORD may be gracious to me and let the child live.' But now that he is dead, why should I go on fasting? Can I bring him back again? I will go to him, but he will not return to me."

After that David comforts his wife Bathsheba and makes love to her and she gives birth to a son named Solomon.

As soon as David had heard the story of the poor man's lamb, he delivered his judgment against the rich man, decreeing that he would be required to pay for the lamb four times over. But he is the one who will have to pay four times over.

Solomon sounds like the Hebrew word for "peace" and the word for "replacement."[7] ■

Having lost one son, he will lose three more in the years ahead. Four times he will be reminded that even a king—perhaps especially a king—cannot place himself above God's law. He will learn the painful truth— that breaking God's commandments will not only break a man but will fracture the lives of those he loves.

THE TIMES

*David reigned from 1010–970 BC, first over the
tribe of Judah and then over a united Israel.
His story is drawn from 1 Samuel 16 and 2 Samuel 1–12.*

Both Saul and David came to power during a time in which the
superpowers of the region were receding. The Anatolian kingdom
of the Hittites had already been destroyed, the Egyptians had with-
drawn from Canaan, Babylon was facing pressure from Assyria, and
Assyria was dealing with its own persistent troubles.

The eclipse of these great powers made it possible for David to
set up a mini-empire as, one by one, he defeated Israel's enemies,
including the hated Philistines who had for so long oppressed and
harassed them.

Some of these regional powers—the Moabites, Aramites,
Edomites, and Ammonites—were eventually forced to pay tribute
to David. By reducing his enemies to tributary status, David not
only increased Israel's wealth but siphoned off resources that might
otherwise have strengthened the surrounding peoples, enabling
them to rise up against him.

Both the Old and New Testaments use the imagery of the shepherd to characterize God's care for his people. It was also common
imagery for kings, even among surrounding cultures, including
that of Egypt.

Psalm 23, which is attributed to David, speaks of a rod and a
staff as items that comfort the psalmist. While the rod was used like
a club to beat back predators, the staff had various uses. It could
guide sheep away from the edge of a cliff or pry them free when
their wooly coats became entangled in thickets and brambles.

At lambing time, when several sheep were giving birth at once, lambs and ewes would sometimes become separated. When that happened, a watchful shepherd would use the crook of his staff to lift the lamb and place it near its mother so the two could bond. Using the staff rather than his hands would keep the shepherd from transferring his scent to the lamb, causing the ewe to reject her offspring.[8]

David was the ideal shepherd king, a man after God's own heart.

Given David's personal history, Nathan's parable was designed for maximum shock value. Instead of protecting his sheep, the shepherd king had turned into a predator, sleeping with Bathsheba and then murdering her husband.

To his credit, David neither railed against God nor blamed him for his subsequent troubles. Instead he repented of his sins and accepted the consequences.

THE TAKEAWAY

1. Though David displayed a great heart for God during most of his life, at some point his heart changed and hardened, which ultimately led him to commit serious sins. How can his story act as a cautionary tale today?

2. Whether or not someone confronts you directly, how do you respond when you are found to be in the wrong? For example, do you tend to rationalize, avoid, deny, or defend, or are you more likely to take responsibility for your behavior immediately?

3. Take a moment to consider a time when someone sincerely repented of wrongdoing by apologizing to you or to

someone you know. How did the apology impact you and your relationship with that person?

4. Though God showed mercy to David by sparing his life and forgiving his sins, he didn't wave a magic wand and erase the consequences of those sins. What does David's story tell us about the nature of God's forgiveness and the damage sin can do?

CHAPTER 19

THE STORY OF BATHSHEBA

How Bathing in Public Caused No End of Difficulty

Can a man scoop fire into his lap without his clothes being burned? Can a man walk on hot coals without his feet being scorched? So is he who sleeps with another man's wife; no one who touches her will go unpunished.

PROVERBS 6:27–29

Bathsheba feels an ache inside, an emptiness so deep she cannot fill it no matter how hard she tries. Her husband, Uriah, is a good man, but he is preoccupied by battles and duty and talks only of warfare. But soldiering bores her. How she wishes he was not merely strong but sensitive, able to enjoy the things she loves, like music and poetry. If only he were home more often. If only he were home right now.

But all the men are gone. They are off fighting the Ammonites, besieging their capital at Rabbah, forty miles northeast of Jerusalem. Curiously, even though it is the spring of the year, a time when kings march off to battle, David is the only able-bodied man left in the city. Though the king is nearing fifty, he is still good-looking, still remarkably strong. Everyone says so, and Bathsheba agrees.

Springtime in the Middle East marks the end of the rainy season, making for passable roads and plenty of fodder for animals. ■

Because Jerusalem is crowded and compact, built on a mere fifteen acres of land, everyone knows when the king is at home. What's more, her single-story homestead is close to the palace.

Though it is evening, Bathsheba longs for a fresh breeze to dry the sweat from her brow. Perhaps a bath will cool her down and soothe her restlessness. Like all women, she bathes inside, in the privacy of her home. When Uriah is there, he helps by wetting the sponge and running it back and forth across her back. But since her period has just ended, she will manage the ritual bath by herself as she always does.

She thinks of how refreshing it would be to simply bathe outside in the courtyard. She has never heard of a woman doing such a thing, but why not? Since only the rich can afford multistory homes, there is little danger of nosy neighbors spying her out. There is only the palace to worry about.

Inside his palace, the king is trying to rest. He sleeps fitfully, perhaps because he cannot stop thinking of the battle raging to the north. Though he is confident of victory, he thinks of the toll it will take on his men. God knows how many times he's had to bed down hungry and exhausted, waiting for a city to fall. At least his soldiers are well-provisioned, and they are well-led, too, with Joab in command.

No, it is not anxiety that disturbs his rest but the nagging sense that he should not be sleeping in his soft bed but encamped outside of Rabbah alongside his men. Yet here he is, enjoying a life of comfortable luxury, while they risk their lives for him. With a sigh, he gets up and begins to stroll around the rooftop garden of his palace.

Despite the fact that Jerusalem is built on a mountaintop, the air is oppressive. David feels it like a damp blanket wrapping him from head to toe. If only lightning would cleave the sky and a sudden storm would break the humidity. Perhaps his restlessness would ease. From his vantage point, he enjoys a commanding view of the Kidron Valley. At twilight, he sees cooking fires glowing in the courtyards below.

Suddenly he catches his breath. His gaze is fixed on a woman, shapely and young. He admires the long, dark hair that cascades in wild tangles down her back. She is bathing inside her courtyard. He knows he should look away. But he has not felt this alive for some time. So he continues to stare.

When she is finished, she suddenly looks up. Is it only his imagination or is she looking at him the way he has been looking at her? Quickly, before desire fades, he sends for a servant to discover who she is.

It doesn't take long to receive the report: "She is Bathsheba, the daughter of Eliam and the wife of Uriah the Hittite."

Uriah was a foreign mercenary who was also a worshiper of the Lord. He is numbered as one of David's thirty mighty men (2 Samuel 23:39; 1 Chronicles 11:41). ▪

––––––––––

If Eliam is the same man mentioned in 2 Samuel 23:34, he was numbered among David's mighty men and his father would have been Ahithophel. ▪

The news is disappointing, for the woman he covets is related to men he knows, men who are among his elite troops. The woman's husband is one of his best soldiers. What's more, her grandfather Ahithophel is David's personal counselor. How can he disregard close bonds like these? For a moment he hesitates. But then he recalls her beauty, and he reminds himself that he is king.

Before long, Bathsheba is surprised by a knock at the door. It is the king's men. She knows by the look in their eyes that she cannot refuse to go with them.

When Bathsheba enters the king's private quarters, David tells her she is beautiful beyond all women. Before dawn, she leaves the palace and returns home, and few are the wiser. But it isn't long before she notices the signs. A little cramping, sore breasts, fatigue. She waits until she is certain and then she sends a message to David: "I am pregnant."

These three words will change not only their own lives but the history of Israel, though neither Bathsheba nor David knows it at the time. But both know the law, that adultery is punishable by death. What will the king do?

A few days pass before Bathsheba learns that her husband,

Uriah, has been recalled from the front. Relief floods her because she realizes that David has not let the matter drop. She plans to welcome Uriah home like a loving wife so no one will suspect the child isn't his. Though she waits all night, he never comes. And then the next night, but her husband doesn't return.

She has no idea that David shares her desperation.

When Bathsheba finally hears that her husband has perished, she weeps. And as she mourns, she tries to hide the truth from herself, that half her tears well up from guilt, not grief.

So David, Israel's great hero king, falls prey to lust and then to murder. Though Bathsheba suspects the truth, it will be a while until she hears the details from David's lips. Meanwhile, she and David marry, and people say this proves the goodness of their king. How generous he is to honor the memory of one of his fallen soldiers by providing his widow with a home. When Bathsheba bears David's son, they say this proves it—that God is smiling on the king and on Uriah's memory.

But if you could stand in heaven and gaze upon God's holy face, you would not detect the slightest hint of a smile. Indeed, while David and Bathsheba's sordid story is unfolding, he is sitting on his great throne, looking down as David strolls the ramparts of his palace. He notes the first spark of desire and then watches it grow into a raging fire that devours the lives of several men. Displeased with David, God speaks to the prophet Nathan about the matter and Nathan tells David:

"This is what the LORD says: 'Out of your own household I am going to bring calamity on you. Before your very eyes I will take your wives and give them to one who is close to you, and he will sleep with your wives in broad daylight. You did it in secret, but I will do this thing in broad daylight before all Israel.'"

This prophecy was fulfilled when David's son Absalom slept with his father's concubines in a tent erected on the roof of the palace in sight of all. Interestingly, it was Ahithophel, the man who was David's counselor and possibly also Bathsheba's grandfather, who counseled Absalom to undertake this action in order to claim the throne. (See 2 Samuel 16:21–22.) ■

David is devastated. He has become the kind of man he has always despised.

As for Bathsheba, no one can say for certain what was in her heart the night she slept with David. Was she powerless against a king's abuse—first raped, then widowed, then rendered childless because of his egregious sin? Or was she a seductress, bent on obtaining a place in David's palace regardless of the cost? Throughout the long years that have transpired since her passing, storytellers have spun the tale both ways.[1]

THE TIMES

Bathsheba probably lived sometime between 1050 and 950 BC. Her story appears in 2 Samuel 11–12 and 1 Kings 1–2. She is also mentioned in Matthew 1:6.

To a greater degree than any of the surrounding peoples, the Israelites possessed detailed laws regarding ritual purity and the methods for restoring it once a person had become ritually unclean. These laws stressed the holiness of God and set out clear stipulations for living in his presence. Since defilement could occur by coming into contact with certain diseases, having sexual intercourse, menstruating, giving birth to a child, eating unclean foods, touching a corpse, having or coming into contact with a bodily discharge, or touching something dead, it was impossible to maintain ritual purity at all times.

In Bathsheba's case, the text makes it clear that she was taking a ritual bath because her period had just ended. By including this detail, the author is making it clear to his readers that David and not Uriah is the father of her child.

Though some commentators cast Bathsheba as co-villain of the story, painting her as a social-climbing seductress, others argue that Nathan's story of the innocent ewe lamb depicts her as the victim of David's crime. They point out that it would have been nearly impossible for her to refuse the king given the extent of his royal power. If this is the case, her story becomes even more tragic because in addition to being raped and having her husband murdered, she suffered the loss of a child because of David's sin.

Instead of being named in Matthew's genealogy of Jesus, she is listed only as "Uriah's wife." Was this Matthew's way of holding his nose when he mentioned the woman he held responsible for David's fall? Or was it one more instance in which Scripture was underlining human sin—in this case, David's sin—and God's gracious provision of a Savior?

Kenneth Bailey, an expert on Middle Eastern New Testament studies who spent more than forty years living and teaching in the Middle East, contended that no self-respecting woman then or now would ever have taken a bath in plain sight of the palace, pointing out that Bathsheba knew exactly what she was doing.

So which is she, villain or victim? We may never know. What we do know is that even the Bible's greatest heroes are fragile characters whose hearts, like ours, are in need of redemption.

Though our culture may see sexual dalliances as naturally occurring behaviors, God sees them in another light, knowing the consequences they wreak on families and on the larger community in which they occur.

THE TAKEAWAY

1. The punishment for adultery was death. Take a few minutes to imagine that you are Bathsheba and that you have just sent a message to King David, telling him you are pregnant. Describe how you are feeling and what you are thinking.
2. Unlike ancient biblical culture, our society often glamorizes adultery and sexual immorality. What are the benefits of resisting the cultural tendencies?
3. Bathsheba had to deal with multiple tragedies. Yet God eventually blessed her with a son who would become the king of Israel and the world's wisest man. If you had to sum up her life in one sentence, what would you say?

4. Describe the progression of David's sin. What do his actions reveal about the consequences of entertaining temptation? How have you seen this process at work in yourself and others?

5. Where in the story do you see evidence of God's goodness and mercy? How have you experienced his mercy with regard to your own failings?

CHAPTER 20

THE STORY OF DAVID'S SONS—AMNON, ABSALOM, AND ADONIJAH

Three Men Who Would Be King

And he passed in front of Moses, proclaiming, "The LORD, the LORD, the compassionate and gracious God, slow to anger, abounding in love and faithfulness, maintaining love to thousands, and forgiving wickedness, rebellion and sin. Yet he does not leave the guilty unpunished; he punishes the children and their children for the sin of the parents to the third and fourth generation."

EXODUS 34:6–7

AMNON'S DECEIT

Amnon is bored. With no aptitude for learning and little interest in music, song, or soldiering, he seeks pleasure and pleasure only. And today he is not pleased.

Instead of rising early, he lies in bed thinking only of what he cannot have. As David's eldest, the thing he desires most is not his father's throne. That will come someday, he thinks. No, the thing he cannot have and desperately wants is not a thing at all but his beautiful half-sister Tamar. He can think of no one else.

He tells himself he will not be happy nor at peace until she is allowed to come to him. But that will never happen. For she is his sister, a princess whose purity is carefully guarded.

Inflamed by powerful desires that cannot easily or safely be named—though he will speak of them—he feels unwell.

His close friend and cousin is a shrewd man whose sharp eye misses nothing. "Why do you, the king's son, look so haggard morning after morning?" Jonadab probes. "Won't you tell me?"

Amnon is sick of hiding what he feels. Why must he, the some-day king, deny the deepest desires of his heart?

"I'm in love with Tamar, my brother Absalom's sister," he confides.

Ah, so this is what's been troubling him! Lusting after his own flesh!

Clever Jonadab, the man who is in on every secret and who never tires of reminding Amnon that he is the king's son, advises him, "Go to bed," he says, "and pretend to be ill. When your father comes to see you, say to him, 'I would like my sister Tamar to come and give me something to eat. Let her prepare the food in my sight so I may watch her and then eat it from her hand.'"

So Amnon does exactly as Jonadab advises. And David falls for it. An unwitting pawn in his son's deceitful game, he sends word to his daughter, telling her that her brother is ill and requires her presence.

When Tamar arrives, Amnon is still languishing in bed. Refusing the bread she baked especially for him, he orders everyone else to leave. As soon as they are alone, he catches her roughly by the arm. "Come to bed with me, my sister."

"Don't, my brother! Don't force me," she cries. "Such a thing should not be done in Israel! Don't do this wicked thing. What about me? Where could I get rid of my disgrace? And what about you? You would be like one of the wicked fools in Israel. Please speak to the king; he will not keep me from being married to you."

But Tamar is a solitary sparrow, unable to fend off the swooping hawk. By now Amnon is beyond caring whether the king would ever bless their marriage.

Pulling her to himself, he rapes her. After satisfying his lust, there is nothing left but shame. Unwilling to own the disgust he feels, he blames her. "Get up and get out!" he shouts.

Shaking uncontrollably, the tears streaming down her cheeks, his sister stands her ground. "No!" she screams. "Sending me away would be a greater wrong than what you have already done to me."

Turning his back on her, Amnon calls his servant, commanding him to throw his sister out and bolt the door.

Tearing the ornamental robe that marks her as a virgin princess, Tamar stoops down and picks up ashes from the evening fire.

Modern readers may be shocked by the implication that Tamar is asking her rapist to marry her, but the Old Testament prescribes this law for a man who has raped a virgin: "If a man happens to meet a virgin who is not pledged to be married and rapes her and they are discovered, he shall pay her father fifty shekels of silver. He must marry the young woman, for he has violated her. He can never divorce her as long as he lives" (Deuteronomy 22:28–29). ▪

Throwing them on her head, she weeps loudly as she goes.

When her brother Absalom discovers what has happened, he tries to console her. "Be quiet now, my sister," he says. "He is your brother. Don't take this thing to heart."

But Absalom takes it to heart. Though he says nothing, he is enraged by what has happened.

As for Tamar, she is beyond consolation, her shattered heart filled with pain. Because of Amnon's sin, she will never be able to marry. No children will rise up to call her blessed. Though only a young woman, she will live the rest of her life as a widow in Absalom's house. Losing her virginity has meant that she has lost her future too.

No one asks whether such consequences are fair or whether Tamar should have to bear the shame she feels. They do not challenge the status quo. They only know that this is how things have always been.

When David hears the news, he is furious but silent. There is no denouncement, no punishment, no consequence. Amnon is still heir apparent to his throne. Why this passivity, this failure to discipline his son and comfort his daughter with justice? Could it be that the heart of the king is governed by memories from his own troubled past?[1]

David's failure to punish his eldest son creates a vacuum that Absalom rushes in to fill. But instead of justice, he seeks revenge.

Two years after Amnon assaulted his sister, Absalom invites

the entire family to a feast to celebrate the wool harvest. But David begs off, telling Absalom he doesn't want to burden him with the expense of entertaining a king.

"Then please let my brother Amnon come," Absalom responds. So David, who is now a pawn in Absalom's game, sends Amnon and his other sons to the sheep-shearing party.

Once the celebration is in full swing, when Amnon is too drunk to defend himself, Absalom orders his servants to slay him. As soon as his other brothers catch wind of what has happened they scatter.

Since the economy was largely based on wool, the spring shearing time would have been treated as a time of abundance and celebration.[2]

When he hears the news, David collapses, weeping bitterly. Day after day he grieves for his son. But no one knows which son the king mourns. The one who raped his sister or the one who murdered his brother?

And what about poor Tamar? Isn't she worthy of at least a few tears? Though she is David's daughter and therefore a royal princess, she has been like a lamb led to slaughter—her life ruined, not by her failures but by her father's failure to protect her from her brother's unbridled lust.

ABSALOM'S REBELLION

After killing his brother, Absalom flees north to take refuge with his grandfather, the King of Geshur. Now that the eldest is out of the way, he has a clear path to the throne,[3] except for one small detail. Returning to Jerusalem would mean risking the full force of his father's anger.

He doesn't realize that his father's heart is empty of wrath but full of longing. David wants only to see his son again. After a while,

David had several wives, including Talmai, the mother of both Absalom and Tamar and the daughter of the ruler of the small Aramean kingdom of Geshur. ∎

Joab, the commander of David's army, decides to try to bring the two together.

Hiring a shrewd woman, known for her persuasive gifts,[4] Joab instructs her to seek an audience with the king. She is to play the part of a widow mourning the death of her son. Though what he proposes is mere trickery, he flatters himself that it is Nathan and David all over again.

When the woman comes before the king, she pleads for help, saying, "I am a widow, the mother of two sons. One of them killed the other during an argument when they were alone in the fields, and now my clan demands the life of my remaining son. When he dies, his inheritance will pass to another male relative, extinguishing the only burning coal I have left and leaving my husband neither name nor descendant on the face of the earth."

Taking pity on her, the king says, "Go home, and I will issue an order on your behalf. If anyone says anything to you, bring them to me, and they will not bother you again. As surely as the LORD lives, not one hair of your son's head will fall to the ground."

Though her voice quavers a little, because it is never safe to confront a king, she makes her case more directly. "Since the king has agreed to protect my son, does he not convict himself? For why has he not brought back his banished son? Like water spilled on the ground, without hope of recovery, so we must die. But God devises ways so that a banished person does not remain banished from him."

Sensing another mind behind her words, he asks: "Isn't the hand of Joab with you in all this?"

"As surely as you live," she says, "no one can turn to the right or to the left from anything my lord the king says. Yes, it was your servant Joab who instructed me to do this and who put all these words into the mouth of your servant. Your servant Joab did this to change the present situation. My lord has wisdom like that of an angel of God—he knows everything that happens in the land."

Though David has seen through her charade, the woman's words have moved him. After she leaves, he instructs Joab to bring Absalom back to Jerusalem. But there is one condition. Absalom must live in his own house and never enter David's presence.

So Absalom returns to Jerusalem, but he soon grows restless. Tired of treading water, he wants a complete pardon. But Joab is reluctant to intervene again and ignores Absalom's repeated requests for help.

Since Joab owns a field adjacent to Absalom's property, the young prince sets the field on fire. When Joab comes running, Absalom explains himself. "I sent you many messages. Why did you ignore them all? I want to see the king's face, and if I am guilty of anything, let him put me to death."

When Absalom is finally ushered into David's presence, he prostrates himself before the throne. At once, he feels his father's hands lifting him up and then embracing him.

As David kisses his prodigal son, tears roll down his face, but Absalom's eyes are dry.

After that, the young prince's popularity soars. The most handsome man in the kingdom, he is the picture of royal strength. Clever, vainglorious Absalom—his eyes are always on the throne. Wearing his hair long, he cuts it only once a year and his shorn locks weigh in at five pounds according to the royal standard.

Providing himself with a chariot and horses, he hires fifty men to run before him. Arriving at the city gates[5] early each day, he begins his campaign by asking everyone he meets what town they're from. Then he says, "Look, your claims are valid and proper, but there is no representative of the king to hear you. If only I were appointed judge in the land! Then everyone who has a complaint or case could come to me and I would see that they receive justice."

Whenever anyone bows to him, Absalom lifts him up and kisses him. In this way, he steals the hearts of everyone in Israel.

One day, he asks the king for permission to travel to the city of Hebron so that he can fulfill a vow. This storied city, located in the hill country of Judah, just twenty miles from Jerusalem, contains the tombs of Abraham and Sarah, Isaac and Rebekah, and Jacob and Leah. As David's first capitol, it is an excellent city from which to launch a coup.

Two hundred prominent men, unaware of Absalom's planned revolt, accompany him on his journey. Clever Absalom has made them look like co-conspirators, thereby forcing them to support him.

David reigned in Hebron for seven and a half years before moving his capitol to Jerusalem. ■

Once Absalom arrives in the ancient city, he sends secret messages to his supporters throughout Israel urging everyone to join him. "As soon as you hear the sound of the trumpets, then say, 'Absalom is king in Hebron.'"

After that he summons his father's wisest counselor. This is the chance Ahithophel has been waiting for. Embittered by David's treatment of his granddaughter, Bathsheba, and her husband, Uriah, the old man seeks revenge.[6] As soon as Ahithophel throws his weight behind Absalom, the conspiracy gains strength.

When David hears of this and learns that Absalom has stolen the hearts of many in Israel, he flees Jerusalem, taking his household with him. Ten concubines stay behind to care for the royal palace.

As David departs, the whole countryside gathers to watch. The king is weeping and walking barefoot, with his head covered as a sign of sorrow. Those who watch are weeping too.

While making his retreat, David meets his good friend Hushai. Asking him to act as a spy, he instructs Hushai to go to Jerusalem and swear loyalty to his rebellious son.

After gaining Absalom's confidence, Hushai listens in as Ahithophel advises the would-be king. His first suggestion is a stunner: "Sleep with your father's concubines whom he left to take care of the palace. Then all Israel will hear that you have made yourself obnoxious to your father, and the hands of everyone with you will be more resolute."

Pleased by his advice, Absalom pitches a tent on the roof of the palace, close to where David had first seen Bathsheba. One by one, he lays down with his father's concubines in the sight of all Israel.

Then Ahithophel advises him to choose twelve thousand men and set out in pursuit of the king immediately. "If you act quickly," he says, "you will crush the king and all his men."

To sleep with a king's wives or concubines was tantamount to proclaiming yourself the king. ▪

Knowing the wisdom of this plan, Hushai counsels the opposite.

"Even now," he says, "your father is hidden in a cave or some other place. If he should attack your troops first, whoever hears about it will say, 'There has been a slaughter among the troops who follow Absalom.' Then even the bravest soldier, whose heart is like the heart of a lion, will melt with fear, for all Israel knows that your father is a fighter and that those with him are brave.

"Take time to gather the tribes of Israel, and then with overwhelming force defeat the king," he tells Absalom.

Though Ahithophel's advice is a sure course to victory, God sees to it that Absalom listens to Hushai.

When Ahithophel realizes that his advice has been ignored, he despairs. Unwilling to receive a traitor's reward when David regains his throne, he puts his house in order and then hangs himself.

By the time Absalom finally ventures out in pursuit of his father, David has already regained his footing. Though he is ready to lead his men into battle, they plead with him, saying, "You must not go! If we are forced to flee, they won't care about us. Even if half of us die, they won't care; but you are worth ten thousand of us. It would be better now for you to support us from the city."

Before they leave, David issues a strict command. "Be gentle with the young man Absalom for my sake," he says.

The battle is soon engaged in a nearby forest, and there are heavy losses. In the ensuing confusion, Absalom is separated from the rest of his army. Riding alone through a tangle of trees, his luxuriant hair is suddenly caught in the branches of a large oak tree. Comically, though his mule plods on, he stays behind, his body swinging in midair.

Responding to a soldier who has just informed him that Absalom is hanging in an oak tree, Joab exclaims, "What! You saw him? Why didn't you strike him to the ground right there? Then I would have given you ten shekels of silver and a warrior's belt."

"Even if a thousand shekels were weighed into my hands," the soldier replies, "I would not lift my hand against the king's son. In our hearing he commanded you, saying, 'Protect the young man Absalom for my sake.'"

But Joab has no scruples about ignoring David's wish. To spare Absalom will risk a second rebellion if he is allowed to regather his strength. Better to be done with him once and for all. Plunging three javelins into Absalom's chest, he orders ten of his men to finish him off.

When the king hears what has happened to his son, he cries, "O my son Absalom! My son, my son Absalom! If only I had died instead of you—O Absalom, my son, my son!"

But David's lament cannot raise his son from the grave. Hung on a tree, he has been cursed by God. Later, as the story is passed from generation to generation, wise men ponder it, pointing out that just as Absalom lost his seat on his royal mount, so he lost his seat on Israel's throne. Suspended in midair, he was left hanging between heaven and earth, without any solid ground to stand on.[7]

When Absalom lived, he had raised a pillar of stone to mark his memory. When he died, another monument rose up—a heap of stones to mark the hole into which his broken body lay.

ADONIJAH'S FOLLY

David shivers beneath the covers of his royal bed despite the summer heat. To warm his ice-cold body, a beautiful young virgin is brought to lie down beside him. Abishag is neither wife nor concubine but only a soft blanket to ease the old man's suffering.

Absalom's was a type of burial often used for enemies or criminals.[8] ◾

At seventy, the aging monarch has outlived most men by twenty years.[9] While David languishes, his son Adonijah grows restless. Now that Amnon and Absalom are no more, he is next in line to be king, though some insist that the throne has already been promised to Bathsheba's son, Solomon.

Because his father has always been preoccupied with affairs of state, Adonijah is used to doing as he pleases. And now it pleases him to ascend his father's throne.

Adonijah was the son of David and Haggith, and he would have been next in line for the throne. In 1 Chronicles 3:1–9, we learn that David had nineteen sons by various wives and many other sons by concubines. Even without his governing responsibilities, it would have been impossible for him to provide proper oversight for so many sons. ■

He begins by enlisting the help of powerful officials, men like Joab who are ready to abandon their old loyalties. Together they hatch a plan that will allow Adonijah to claim the throne.

Learning that Adonijah has invited every brother but Solomon to offer sacrifice at En Rogel, a spring just outside of Jerusalem, Nathan the prophet raises the alarm. But not to David. He goes straight to Bathsheba instead.

"Have you not heard that Adonijah has become king? Our lord David knows nothing about it. Now then, let me advise you how you can save your own life and the life of your son Solomon. Go in to King David and say to him, 'My lord the king, did you not swear to me your servant: "Surely Solomon your son shall be king after me, and he will sit on my throne?" Why then has Adonijah become king?'"

Though years have passed since Bathsheba and David were lovers, she is still cherished. Kneeling beside his bed, Bathsheba makes her case. "My lord, you yourself swore to me your servant by the LORD your God: 'Solomon your son shall be king after me, and he will sit on my throne.' But now Adonijah has become king, and you, my lord the king, do not know about it. He has sacrificed great numbers of cattle, fattened calves, and sheep, and has invited all the king's sons, Abiathar the priest and Joab the commander of the army, but he has not invited Solomon your servant. My lord the king, the eyes of all Israel are on you, to learn from you who will sit on the throne of my lord the king after him. Otherwise, as soon as my lord the king is laid to rest with his ancestors, I and my son Solomon will be treated as criminals." Indeed, she knows they will be killed.

While Bathsheba is still speaking, Nathan arrives. Bowing before the king, he confirms everything she has said. Afterward, David swears to Bathsheba: "As surely as the LORD lives, who has delivered me out of every trouble, I will carry out this very day what I swore to you by the LORD, the God of Israel: Solomon your son shall be king after me, and he will sit on my throne in my place."

Though his body is frail, the king's mind remains clear. Commanding his key men, he instructs them to act quickly. "Have Solomon my son mount my own mule and take him down to Gihon. Zadok the priest and Nathan the prophet shall anoint him king over Israel. Blow the trumpet and shout, 'Long live King Solomon!' Then he is to come and sit on my throne and reign in my place. I have appointed him ruler over Israel and Judah."

The signs of David's choice are unmistakable. Solomon is given the rare privilege of riding on the king's mule. He is accompanied by the royal bodyguards. He is anointed by both prophet and priest. Lastly, the coronation ceremony takes place at one of Jerusalem's primary landmarks. David has made his intentions clear to everyone.

As soon as the trumpet is blown, a cheer thunders across the valley. "Long live King Solomon!" As the new king makes his way back up to the city, the people play flutes, rejoicing loudly as they go. There is so much noise that the earth shakes with the sound of their joy.

Less than a mile away, Adonijah is still celebrating with his guests, sharing a feast that serves as a pledge of friendship, loyalty, and protection. But how can an

Gihon was the main water source for the city of Jerusalem. It would have eclipsed En Rogel, the spring that Adonijah had chosen for his coronation. ∎

unlawful king protect his guests when the ground begins to shift beneath him?

"Solomon has taken his seat on the royal throne," a messenger informs the gathering. "The king himself has bowed down in worship on his bed, saying, 'Praise be to the Lord, the God of Israel, who has allowed my eyes to see a successor on my throne today.'"

It is mayhem in Adonijah's camp—every man for himself as the traitor-in-chief clings to the altar and begs for mercy.

Despite the attempted coup, Solomon begins his reign by sparing his brother Adonijah on the condition that further treachery will not be tolerated.

But Adonijah still covets the throne. After David dies he approaches the queen mother. Perhaps it is Bathsheba's age or her gender that makes him think her a fool.

"Please ask King Solomon—he will not refuse you—to give me Abishag the Shunammite as my wife," he says.

For a moment, she catches her breath. What is he asking? To wed a woman who once shared the king's bed—even one who is still a virgin—would be to advance a claim to the throne.[10]

Before she can refuse, Bathsheba thinks better of it. Why not pass this request to her son and let him settle the matter once and for all?

At the next opportunity, while Bathsheba sits at her son's right hand, she turns to him and says, "I have one small request to make of you. Do not refuse me."

"Make it my mother, I will not refuse you."

"Let Abishag be given in marriage to your brother Adonijah."

When the expected explosion occurs, she is relieved. Turning to her, Solomon says, "Why do you request Abishag the Shunammite for Adonijah? You might as well request the kingdom for him."

That very day, the new king orders his rival and brother Adonijah to be put to death. In years to come, when people mention the names of the king's despicable sons, they will nod their heads in knowing fashion, recalling Nathan's parable about the rich man who stole the poor man's lamb. Hasn't it happened just as David decreed? The guilty man has paid four times over for his sins, first with the life of his infant son and then with the lives of three other sons—Amnon, Absalom, and Adonijah.

THE TIMES

The story of David's sons took place in the tenth century BC. The story of Amnon is told in 2 Samuel 13, of Absalom in 2 Samuel 13–18, of Adonijah in 1 Kings 1–2:35.

It's impossible for today's readers to read the stories of David and his sons without considering the plight of the women who were used and abused by them. Bathsheba, Tamar, the king's ten concubines, Abishag—all were at the mercy of the men in the stories.

Even though women in Israel had fewer rights than men, their position was generally better than that of women in surrounding cultures. For instance, according to the Middle Assyrian laws (from around 1114–1076 BC), a married man who raped an unmarried woman would have to marry her. While that mode of "punishment" would be unthinkable in modern societies, it was also practiced in ancient Israel (see Deuteronomy 22:28–29).

But the Middle Assyrian laws went even further. The rapist would have to turn over his own wife so that she too could be raped. Additionally, the Middle Assyrian laws allowed husbands to punish their wives by plucking out hair, whipping or beating, or even by mutilating their ears.

Whenever the Old Testament commands diverged from the laws of the surrounding cultures, they tended to move in the direction of more respect for human life and greater equality between the sexes.[11]

As the king, David had an enormous family—nineteen sons by multiple wives and an unknown number of sons by concubines. He must have had many daughters as well.

Though multiple wives could make for dysfunctional house-holds, they were a status symbol for wealthy and powerful men. In ordinary society, most men could not afford to marry more than once. When they could, it was often for practical reasons since multiple wives meant multiple children to work on the family homestead.

In the case of royal marriages, wives were often acquired as a way of forging alliances. Though concubines were an accepted part of the household, they held lesser status than wives and were often acquired as captives of war or as slaves.

Little wonder that with wars to fight, a kingdom to run, and an enormous family to care for, David did not always do well by his children.

THE TAKEAWAY

1. The writer of Proverbs says, "When pride comes, then comes disgrace, but with humility comes wisdom" (Proverbs 11:2). Where do you find evidence of pride and humility in these stories?

2. Each of David's three sons engages in deceit. What simi-larities and differences do you recognize in the motives for their deceit? How does the desire for power play out in each son's story?

3. It's been said that "wounded people wound people." In other words, what starts out as a relational wound can become a launching pad for sin. How do you recognize this dynamic in David's family? How do David's moral failures lead to dys-functions and subsequent failures within his family? In what ways, if any, might your relational wounds wound others?

4. Take time to think about the women in these stories—
   Tamar, the shrewd woman hired by Joab, David's
   concubines, Abishag, Bathsheba. In what ways were these
   women powerless? In what ways did they wield power?.

5. In "Letter from Birmingham Jail," Martin Luther King
   wrote, "Injustice anywhere is a threat to justice everywhere."
   How is the truth of this observation played out in these
   stories?

CHAPTER 21

THE STORY OF JONAH

How a Prophet Who Refused to Swallow His Pride Got Swallowed by a Fish Instead

*Where can I go from your Spirit? Where
can I flee from your presence? If I go up to
the heavens, you are there; if I make my bed
in the depths, you are there. If I rise on the
wings of the dawn, if I settle on the far side of
the sea, even there your hand will guide me,
your right hand will hold me fast.*

PSALM 139:7–10

Go to Nineveh. Go to Nineveh. The voice is quiet but so insistent that Jonah ben Amittai cannot sleep. Huddled in a corner of his house, he pulls a blanket over his head, hoping to muffle the sound. But there is no stopping the voice he would rather not hear.

Go to the great city of Nineveh and preach against it, because its wickedness has come up before me.

The words come in a whisper but fall like a hammer. As he tries to shut them out, Jonah feels a steady ache building between his temples.

He cannot fathom the message. Why would God ask one of his prophets to travel five hundred miles north and east to a city full of warmongers and cheats, vicious people who hate God's people and care nothing for his laws? Like most Israelites, Jonah fears and loathes the Assyrians, who have always been their oppressors. How in God's name can he preach to degenerates like them?

For Jonah is among Israel's most patriotic prophets. Hadn't he foretold Jeroboam II's prosperous rule? Despite the king's obvious flaws, Jonah is glad that God is working through this powerful man to expand Israel's borders at a time when Assyrian power is finally ebbing. At last, Israel has become what it has always longed to be—the head and not the tail—one of the most powerful nations in the region.

But now God is asking him as a loyal prophet of Israel to travel to a large Assyrian city in order to proclaim the word of the Lord. Because Jonah would sooner preach to pigs, he runs as fast as he can in the opposite direction.

Leaving home in a hurry, Jonah travels south and west until he reaches Joppa, a seaport on the Mediterranean. As he approaches the harbor, he spots several Phoenician ships. Selecting a single-masted vessel with a large rectangular sail, he climbs aboard and then heads below deck to rest. This tub-shaped boat will carry him and a few others across the Mediterranean to Tarshish and far away from Nineveh.

By the time the ship sets sail, the sun is shining in a clear blue sky. But soon heaving thunderclouds roll in with great bolts of lightning streaking across the sky and threatening to tear the firmament to shreds. The ship pitches so violently that the sailors fear it will break apart. To lighten their load, they toss the cargo overboard. But the storm still rages.

Jonah was from Gath Hepher, a town three miles north of Nazareth. He is the only Old Testament prophet who hails from the region of Galilee. ■

Terrified, they cry out to their gods: "Baal Hadad, save us!" "Baal Shaman, come to our rescue!" "Baal Malage, hear our prayers, we are dying!" Perhaps one of these deities will intercede on their behalf, rescuing them by appeasing the god of the chaotic sea.

Meanwhile, Jonah remains below deck, curled comfortably on a makeshift bed where he has fallen asleep, no doubt weary from the effort of running away from God.

Desperate to find out who has offended the deity, the captain wakes him, shouting to make his voice heard above the howling wind. "How can you sleep in this storm? Get up and call on your god! Maybe he will take notice of us and we will not perish."

As soon as Jonah arrives on deck, the sailors hit on a plan to discover the source of the trouble. "Come, let's cast lots to find out who is responsible for this calamity." So each man places a small token into a large cup. They believe the offended god will reach down as the cup is shaken up and down and pluck out the guilty man's token. When one of the pieces comes flying out, they realize the lot has fallen to Jonah.

Turning to him, the crew peppers him with questions. "Where do you come from? What do you do? What is your country? Who are your people?"

"I am a Hebrew," Jonah replies. "I worship Yahweh, the God of heaven, who made the sea and the land."

They are amazed because no deity in their pantheon has that much power—a god who not only created the sea but also rules over it.

When Jonah confesses that he is running away from this all-powerful God, they are incredulous. "What have you done! Tell us now what we should do to you to make the sea calm down?"

"Pick me up and throw me into the sea," Jonah replies, "and it will become calm. I know that it is my fault that this great storm has come upon you."

But the sailors are principled men who fear the gods. They have no desire to shed innocent blood, nor do they want to risk angering a powerful deity by killing his servant. So instead of casting the reluctant prophet into the sea, they decide to attempt landfall. But as they dig their oars into the furious sea, the storm only intensifies.

Desperate, the sailors cry out to Jonah's God, "O Yahweh please do not let us die for taking this man's life. Do not hold us accountable for killing an innocent man, for you, O Yahweh, have done as you pleased." Then they lift Jonah up and heave him into the raging sea.

As Jonah descends to his watery grave and the sea becomes suddenly quiet, the sailors bow before Yahweh and offer sacrifice.

They are grateful for the pity Jonah's God has shown them. But what about pitiful Jonah? He has fallen into the water with his eyes wide open. Kicking his legs and flailing his arms, he tries to resist its downward pull. No matter how hard he kicks, he can't break the surface. As Jonah struggles toward the light, he prays for rescue. Instead, he keeps sinking. The darkness is so complete and the current so strong that he no longer knows which way is up. He has only seconds to live. Finally, when he can stand it no longer, he opens his mouth to exhale and the sea rushes in.

After that Jonah feels only peace. Forgetting what made him panic, he is content to float along in the vast, dark sea, his body undulating with the current. But in the moment before his heart stops beating and his soul escapes to the netherworld, something strange and wonderful happens. An enormous sea creature swims into view, opens its cavernous mouth, and scoops him up.

Lying inside the creature's mouth, Jonah coughs and sputters and then falls in and out of consciousness. Periodically the monster surfaces for air before swimming back into the deep. Gradually Jonah regains his senses. He remains in the fish for three long days and three interminable nights.

Finally, from inside the fish he opens his mouth and begins to pray, saying:

The Bible speaks of a great fish but does not specify a whale. If it was a whale, it may be that Jonah was in its mouth. Technically, whales are not fish but mammals that need to surface periodically for air which they inhale and exhale through a blowhole. ■

> In my distress I called to Yahweh,
>   and he answered me.
> From deep in the realm of the dead I called for help,
>   and you listened to my cry.
> You hurled me into the depths,

into the very heart of the seas,
and the currents swirled about me;
all your waves and breakers swept over me.
I said, 'I have been banished
from your sight;
yet I will look again
toward your holy temple.'
The engulfing waters threatened me,
the deep surrounded me;
seaweed was wrapped around my head.
To the roots of the mountains I sank down;
the earth beneath barred me in forever.
But you, Yahweh my God,
brought my life up from the pit.
When my life was ebbing away,
I remembered you, Yahweh,
and my prayer rose to you,
to your holy temple.
Those who cling to worthless idols
turn away from God's love for them.
But I, with shouts of grateful praise,
will sacrifice to you.
What I have vowed I will make good.
I will say, "Salvation comes from Yahweh."

Even though Jonah is dwelling in deep darkness in the utter-most parts of the sea, God hears his desperate prayer and rescues him by commanding the creature to vomit Jonah onto dry land.

Sputtering and coughing as he wipes slime and seaweed from his salty face, Jonah attempts to stand, but the most he can manage is a crawl. Though he looks half dead, he feels like celebrating because God has reached down and rescued him.

Yahweh speaks to him saying the same thing as before, *Go to the great city of Nineveh and proclaim to it the message I give you.*

This time there is no dissembling. Jonah hastens to Nineveh where he spends three days crisscrossing the city, preaching on every street corner: "Forty more days and Nineveh will be overturned. Forty more days and Nineveh will be overturned." But his heart is not in it.

To his great surprise, enthusiastic crowds begin to gather. The Ninevites are eager to see this foreign prophet and to hear the message he conveys. The more he rails against their sinfulness, the more the people welcome him, beating their breasts and confessing their guilt. Instead of stoning him, they hang on his every word.

Since Assyria has been wracked by revolt and successive plagues, its peoples are desperate for relief. Because they worship many gods, there is always room for one more. So they embrace Jonah's God, taking his message to heart. As soon as the prophet's message reaches the ears of the king of Nineveh, he strips off his royal robes, covers himself with sackcloth, and sits down in the dust. Then he issues a proclamation:

> By the decree of the king and his nobles: Do not let people or animals, herds or flocks, taste anything; do not let them eat or drink. But let people and animals be covered with sackcloth. Let everyone call urgently on God. Let them give up their evil ways and their violence. Who knows? God may yet relent and with compassion turn from his fierce anger so that we will not perish.

When the great God above looks down on the king of Nineveh

and upon all his nobles and all his people humbling themselves and wearing sackcloth, he responds with compassion. Because they are willing to turn from their evil ways, he will turn away from the destruction he has threatened.

Instead of rejoicing at this remarkable turnaround and thanking God for his great mercy, Jonah stamps his feet and shakes his fist.

Sackcloth was the usual dress of the poor and of prisoners and slaves. Frequently made from goat hair, it was also worn by people who were in mourning. As a sign that they were mourning the sins of the people, prophets also wore sackcloth.[1] ■

"O, LORD," he prays, "isn't this exactly what I said, when I was still at home? That's why I tried to flee to Tarshish. I know that you are a gracious and compassionate God, slow to anger and abounding in love, a God who relents from sending calamity. Now, LORD, take away my life, for it is better for me to die than to live."

"Is it right for you to be angry?" Yahweh replies.

Bitter and disappointed, Jonah leaves Nineveh and plants himself on a small rise in view of the city. He builds a little shelter, sits in it, and waits to see what will happen. To his great delight, God provides a vine, making it grow up over his head so that he can sit in comfort beneath its leafy shade.

But at dawn the next day, the Lord provides a worm, which chews up the plant and causes it to wither. With the rising sun comes a scorching east wind. Jonah is so hot he thinks he will faint. Depressed and angry, he says, "It would be better for me to die than to live."

But God says to Jonah, "Is it right for you to be angry about the plant?"

"It is," he says. "And I'm so angry I wish I were dead."

"Look how concerned you are about this plant," the Lord

replies, "though you did not tend it or make it grow. It sprang up overnight and died overnight. Should I not be concerned for the great city of Nineveh, in which there are more than a hundred and twenty thousand people who cannot tell their right hand from their left—and also many animals?"

So Jonah's story ends with a question we must all answer for ourselves. If God has compassion for those who are far from him, what should our attitude be toward such people? Furthermore, if the people of a wicked city like Nineveh can repent and turn to the God who loves them, why can't we, as people who are beloved by God, humble ourselves by turning away from our sins and trusting in his mercy?

By contrast, it is likely that there were only about thirty thousand people living in Israel's capitol city of Samaria at that time. Even fewer people were living in Jerusalem.[2] ∎

THE TIMES

Jonah's story may have taken place between 770–750 BC.
His story is told in Jonah 1–4.

From the period 782 BC to 745 BC, Assyria was weakened by a series of military reverses, domestic uprisings, and famines. What's more, in 763 BC there was an eclipse of the sun, which the Assyrians would have regarded as an ill omen. These factors may have contributed to the quick repentance displayed by the Ninevites when they heard Jonah's warning.

During this period, while the Assyrians were growing weaker, Israel was growing stronger and more prosperous. King Jeroboam II had successfully restored the boundaries of Solomon's day, just as Jonah had predicted he would. Even though Israel prospered, there was a growing gap between rich and poor and widespread spiritual complacency. Jonah's story was meant to confront the Israelites with their own sins.

The book of Jonah is one of the most controversial books of the Bible because some scholars view it as history and others as a fictional story that was meant to be read as such. Those who view it as fiction would date the book to a later period, sometime after the sixth century BC. ■

In the eighth century BC, Nineveh and Tarshish stood at opposite ends of Jonah's world. Clearly, he meant to run as far away as possible in order to avoid preaching a message that might enable the hated Assyrians to repent and avoid God's judgment.

To escape from God, Jonah boarded a ship that was probably manned by Phoenician sailors. Like others in the ancient Near East, the Phoenicians believed that their gods had tamed but not abolished the forces of chaos. It was thought that these threatening forces were especially present in the chaotic sea. The ship's captain urged Jonah to pray because with so many gods, one never knew which one might be displeased or which might come to the rescue.

God showed his power by taming the sea and by rescuing Jonah. The Book of Jonah not only showcases God's power but his compassion and mercy. By sending his reluctant prophet to preach to the Ninevites, God was sending a message to everyone in Israel. If even their worst enemies were capable of repenting, surely they were too.

THE TAKEAWAY

1. Many people tend to think of God as angry or eager to condemn those who do wrong. This story challenges that perspective by portraying not God but Jonah as the one who is eager to mete out condemnation and punishment. Are there times when you recognize a similar Jonah tendency in yourself? What situations tend to make you quick to judge and condemn? Why?

2. When are you most likely to try running from God—to put distance between yourself and his clear command?

3. Though the story of Jonah speaks of impending judgment against sin, it also reveals God's compassion. Where do you see evidence of this in the story?

4. What does God do—and not do—in an effort to bring Jonah around? Has God ever used a similar approach to bring you around? If so, describe the circumstances and the results. What does Jonah's story reveal about how we should think of our enemies and about individuals, communities, or nations who seem far from God?

CHAPTER 22

THE STORY OF JEZEBEL

A Bad Queen Learns It's Not Smart to Fight with God

The kings of the earth rise up and the rulers band together against the Lord and against his anointed, saying, "Let us break their chains and throw off their shackles." The One enthroned in heaven laughs; the Lord scoffs at them. He rebukes them in his anger and terrifies them in his wrath.

PSALM 2:2–5

Her lips blush red against skin the color of the seashore. As she walks, you can hear the tinkling of tiny ornaments fastened to feet and ankles. Locks of black curly hair are woven tightly into a braid that snakes halfway down her back with two shorter braids falling at each side. On her wrist is a golden bracelet with a serpent's tail at one end and a lion's head at the other. Back straight, head held high, a gold band encircling her forehead, she is the picture of a wealthy and powerful Phoenician woman. If not for the sly look that dances around her eyes, she would be quite lovely.

What plot is she hatching now? Not long ago one of her neighbors, a man named Naboth, had been executed on trumped-up charges because Jezebel wanted to confiscate his vineyard to present it as a charming little gift to Ahab, her husband. While residing at his winter palace in Jezreel, King Ahab had offered to buy Naboth's beautiful vineyard, but the stupid man had refused to sell. Thwarted by this nobody, Ahab had taken to his bed, sulking and refusing to eat.

Here is what the Bible says about Jezebel's husband: "There was never a man like Ahab, who sold himself to do evil in the eyes of the LORD, urged on by Jezebel his wife. He behaved in the vilest manner by going after idols, like the Amorites the LORD drove out before Israel" (1 Kings 21:25–26). ∎

Astonished that a king would not simply take whatever his heart desired, Jezebel soon hatched a scheme. She arranged for Naboth to be convicted of crimes so grave he would forfeit his life and land. Weeks later, the unlucky man's screams still echo in the minds of those who watched as he was buried beneath a volley of stones.

Power is a terrible thing in the hands

of a wicked person, but it is worse when that person happens to be intensely religious, as Jezebel is. And no wonder. Her daddy is Ethbaal, priest king of Sidon. He serves the Cloud Rider, Storm God, bringer of rain and prosperity. This is the god they call Baal, the one she and her father adore.

Just as all royal marriages should be, the marriage of Ahab and Jezebel is a strategic one, giving the Phoenicians access to inland markets while providing Israel with access to the rich markets of the Mediterranean. Despite her rising power, Jezebel has enemies, one in particular. The man's name is Elijah, and, oh, how that wily prophet vexes her.

After marrying Israel's king, Jezebel works hard to sway the hearts of the people away from their God, Yahweh. Determined to establish Baal as Israel's highest reigning deity, she massacres every true prophet she can find. But some elude her, and the worst of these is Elijah, the meddling fool who claims to have shut up the heavens, causing drought and famine because neither she nor Ahab will kowtow to Israel's God.

Even now, she feels enraged as she recalls the worst of his escapades on what has become the most humiliating day of her life. Yesterday, King Ahab returned from Mount Carmel with appalling news.

"Elijah has made us a laughingstock!" he told her.

Jezebel's old enemy had been at it again, chiding the king for surrendering to his wife's influence and building a temple to Baal: "You have abandoned God, choosing to follow the Baals and making trouble for Israel," Elijah had charged.

What insolence! How dare he scold a king?

Ahab continued his sorry tale. "'Invite 850 prophets of Baal and Asherah,' Elijah told me, 'the ones your wife feeds at her table, to meet with me on Mount Carmel. Then we will settle the question once and for all about who God really is—Baal or Yahweh.

"'Bring two bulls, and let the prophets of Baal cut one into pieces and put it on the wood without lighting a fire. Then I will prepare the other bull, laying it on the wood but not lighting a fire. Then let Baal's prophets call on the name of their god, and I will call on the name of mine. The god who answers by fire—he is God.'

"It would have seemed weak," Ahab confided, "to refuse his challenge. Plus, I thought it was an easy wager, one that would finally rid us of that wild ass of a man.

"So I called the prophets together. They presented their sacrifice on the altar, shouting and dancing, praying and imploring:

> Baal, God of Thunder,
>> Storm God who rides upon the clouds,
> throw down your lightning bolts,
>> burn up the offering we have prepared.
> Lord of the fertile earth,
>> greatest of all warrior gods,
> vindicate your great name
>> and show forth your might!

"'Surely Baal will respond to such passionate entreaties,' I thought. But we waited for hours and there was nothing. No bolt of lightning, not a single spark from heaven.

"Meanwhile, that old fool, Elijah was shaking with laughter. 'Shout louder!' he yelled. 'Perhaps Baal is sleeping and cannot rouse himself. Or maybe he's away on a trip or perhaps he has stuffed his ears with cotton.'

"I wanted to slap the look off his face.

"Then it was his turn. Incredibly, he started by making the challenge worse—pouring four jars of water on his sacrifice. Elijah drenched everything, not once but three times.

"'How stupid you will look when nothing happens,' I thought. Then Elijah cried out, invoking the God of Abraham, Isaac and Israel.

"Suddenly the sky tore open and fire came streaking down, running across the altar and licking up every drop of water in the trench! It consumed the sacrifice, the wood, stones, and even the dirt beneath it."

Recounting the scene, the king struggled to finish. "The people fell on their faces and kept crying out, 'The LORD—he is God! The LORD—he is God!'

"After that Elijah whipped the people into a frenzy and they slaughtered the prophets! No one escaped."

A day after hearing the story, Jezebel is still trembling, not with fear but with an all-consuming rage that makes her feel invincible. She neither knows nor cares about how Elijah has worked his magic. Her heart has no room for curiosity, but only for revenge. One thing she does know. The old man has to be punished. He cannot be allowed to humiliate her. She will please the lord Baal, uphold his honor by crushing the man who has troubled them both.

At once, Jezebel dispatches a messenger to Elijah with this threat: "May the gods deal with me, be it ever so severely, if by this time tomorrow I do not make your life like that of one of the prophets you slew."

As it happens, the gods do deal with Jezebel, but to tell you just how this transpires would be to rush the story.

264 LESS THAN PERFECT

With the help of an angel, Elijah flees, hiding away in the far reaches of the land, and the wicked queen soon realizes that it is impossible to kill a man she cannot find.

Time passes.

But Jezebel remains the same, only more wicked than she had formerly been, gloating now over her most recent triumph—the matter of Naboth and the stolen vineyard.

But the God who sees all things—the God of Abraham, Isaac, and Israel, the one called Yahweh—has his eye on Jezebel and her wicked husband. And this God rouses his servant Elijah, saying, "Go down to meet Ahab king of Israel, who rules in Samaria. He is now in Naboth's vineyard, where he has gone to take possession of it. Say to him, 'This is what the LORD says: "Have you not murdered a man and seized his property?" This is what the LORD says: "In the place where dogs licked up Naboth's blood, dogs will lick up your blood—yes, yours!" . . .

"'And also concerning Jezebel the LORD says: "Dogs will devour Jezebel by the wall of Jezreel."'"

King though he is, Ahab hardly dares carry the news of this latest threat back to the queen. To his surprise, Jezebel merely throws back her head and laughs when she hears it. She laughs so long and so hard he thinks she might never stop.

Years pass.

One day, with Jehoshaphat, the king of Judah, Ahab rides out to battle. "I will enter the battle in disguise," he tells Jehoshaphat, "but you can wear your royal robes."

Meanwhile, their enemy, the king of Aram instructs his commanders: "Don't fight with anyone, small or great, except Ahab, the king of Israel. As soon as he is finished, the battle will be finished." When the soldiers spot Jehoshaphat, decked out in royal robes, they assume they have found their target. But when Jehoshaphat cries out in his own defense, they realize their mistake. Leaving him alone, they keep up the hunt for Ahab.

Suddenly, a random arrow sails swift and straight through long ranks of men until at last it reaches its target—the disguised king Ahab—piercing him between sections of his armor. Mortally wounded, the king dies slowly, the life blood draining out of his wound and onto the chariot floor. Then the dogs lick up Ahab's blood just as Elijah's God had foretold.

More years pass.

By now Elijah has gone up to heaven and his understudy, Elisha, has taken his place. Though Jezebel's son Joram is reigning in Ahab's place, Elisha gives secret orders for a bold man named Jehu, a commander in Joram's army, to be anointed the new king of Israel.

The man he sends to convey this dangerous prophecy locates Jehu, whisks him off to an inner room, pours oil onto his head, and then quickly declares: "This is what the LORD, the God of Israel, says: 'I anoint you king over the LORD's people Israel. You are to destroy the house of Ahab your master, and I will avenge the blood of my servants the prophets and the blood of all the LORD's servants shed by Jezebel. The whole house of Ahab will perish. As for Jezebel, dogs will devour her on the plot of ground at Jezreel, and no one will bury her.'" Then he runs for his life.

Wasting no time, Jehu marches toward Jezreel where Jezebel's son, Joram, resides. When the palace lookout spots him, he calls out, "I see troops coming."

"Get a horseman," Joram orders. "Send him out to meet them and ask, 'Do you come in peace?'"

The horseman rides off to meet Jehu and says, "This is what the king says: 'Do you come in peace?'"

"What do you have to do with peace?" Jehu replies. "Fall in behind me."

The lookout reports, "The messenger has reached them, but he isn't coming back."

So the king sends out a second horseman. When he reaches Jehu and his men, he asks, "Do you come in peace?"

Jehu replies, "What do you have to do with peace? Fall in behind me."

Once again, the lookout reports, "He has reached them, but he isn't coming back either. The driving is like that of Jehu son of Nimshi—he drives like a madman."

"Hitch up my chariot," Joram commands. King and commander advance toward each other, meeting on the exact plot of ground that Jezebel had stolen from Naboth.

"Have you come in peace, Jehu?" Joram demands.

"How can there be peace," Jehu replies, "as long as all the idolatry and witchcraft of your mother Jezebel abound?"

Too late, Joram tries to escape. But Jehu's arrow finds its mark right between the shoulders. Tossing the body onto the ground, Jehu keeps riding with only a backward glance at the dead king, whose body sprawls awkwardly on the plot of land that had once belonged to Naboth.

Jehu keeps on riding.

When Jezebel hears he is coming for her, she makes no attempt at escape. Too late for that. Instead she goes straight to her makeup table. Picking up a silver mirror, she surveys her face. By now, the slyness around her eyes has hardened into deep lines, and her lips form a thin slash across her face. With a trembling hand she paints her eyes. Though outwardly calm, she can't still the wild beating of her heart. After arranging her hair, she stands by the window, watching as Jehu approaches.

Is the queen planning to seduce him or resist him, her attendants wonder. But her next words make everything clear. As soon as Jehu is within earshot, Jezebel shouts: "Have you come in peace, you murderer of your master?" Instead of replying, Jehu treats the queen as though she is a nobody. Looking up at the servants who stand next to her, he shouts: "Who is on my side? Who among you? Throw her down!"

In an instant, the woman who had made herself God's enemy by murdering his prophets and stealing the hearts of many who belong to him, tumbles out of the window, landing with a sickening thud. There, she is trampled by horses.

Afterward, while Jehu is recovering from the hard work of committing regicide by consuming a large meal, it occurs to him that Jezebel ought to be buried. "Take care of that cursed woman and bury her, for she was a king's daughter," he instructs.

But it is too late for that.

By the time his men reach her, next to nothing of Jezebel is left. Not the purple linen robe she had been wearing, not a single strand of her beautifully coifed hair. Only a rather small skull, with feet and hands that are strewn like garbage on the ground.

When Jehu hears the news, he simply shrugs and says: "This is the word of the LORD that he spoke through his servant Elijah. 'On the plot of ground at Jezreel dogs will devour Jezebel's flesh. Jezebel's body will be like refuse on the ground in the plot at Jezreel, so that no one will be able to say, "This is Jezebel."'"

Queen Jezebel, whose wickedness was legendary, suddenly ceased to exist. Her evil plots and despicable schemes—what did they come to? Nothing at all. In the end, she and her family perished and every trace of her was completely destroyed.

Indeed, hers is the fate of all wickedness. Allowed to increase for a time and a season, evil is like a mist that suddenly burns up, vanishing in the heat of the Lord's anger, never to be seen again.

So ends the story of the Bible's most wicked queen, an exceptionally devoted woman who discovered, rather too late, that it simply doesn't pay to fight with God.

THE TIMES

Jezebel's story took place during the period 873–841 BC.
Her story is drawn from 1 Kings 16:29–33;
18:1–19:2; 21:1–25; 2 Kings 9.

After Solomon's death, the tribes of Israel became divided into two, with Israel in the north and Judah in the south. Jezebel and Ahab's story unfolds in Israel.

One of the strongest female characters in the Bible, she is also one of the few women who is depicted as entirely evil. As a show of contempt, the biblical writer deliberately distorts her Phoenician name, which means, "The Prince Baal Exists," replacing it with a Hebrew name that conveys a not-so-subtle insult. The Hebrew word means, "Where Is the Excrement (Manure)?"

In addition to slaughtering Israel's prophets, Jezebel actively promoted Baal worship, using her considerable wealth to support 450 prophets of Baal and 400 prophets of Asherah, the female consort of the Canaanite god, El.

In 1964, an ancient seal came to the attention of scholars. Inscribed with her name in Phoenician script, it may have belonged to Jezebel. Though she and Elijah were bitter enemies, the battle on Mount Carmel represented the climax of an ongoing war for supremacy, not between two human beings, but between Yahweh and Baal.

Considered a god of storms and fertility, Baal was widely worshiped throughout the region and was called by various names, like Baal Hadad, Baal Hamon, or Baal Melqart, depending on the location. In a polytheistic society, people believed that the gods operated within a hierarchical structure. Powerful, ruling deities were associated with certain nations while lesser deities were connected to clans and families. Ahab and Jezebel may have been attempting to replace Yahweh with Baal as Israel's national God.

Unlike most of Ahab's prophets, Elijah was not in the employ of the king. As Yahweh's spokesman, he broke ranks with other prophets in the region, whose job it was to flatter the king and legitimize his rule. Instead of paying lip service to Ahab and Jezebel, Elijah repeatedly risked his life to strike at the heart of royal power. He knew that idolatry would destroy his people because they would become like the idols they worshiped rather than like the holy God who had chosen them for his own.

THE TAKEAWAY

1. The root of Jezebel's wickedness was embedded in idolatry, which is a distorted form of worship. Idolatry consists of an excessive admiration or devotion to something false. In what subtle and not-so-subtle ways do you recognize idolatry in contemporary culture, including the Christian community?

2. What does the lopsided battle between Jezebel's 450 prophets and the lone prophet Elijah say about the nature of spiritual power? How have you experienced God's power at work in your own life despite the odds against you?

3. Years passed before Ahab and then Jezebel faced God's promised judgment. In the meantime, Jezebel may have lulled herself into thinking she had defied God without consequences. How is her story a cautionary tale about what happens to those who defy God, whether brazenly or more subtly, as sometimes happens today?

CHAPTER 23

THE STORY OF GOMER

A Prodigal Wife Learns the Meaning of True Love

*For your Maker is your husband—the Lord
Almighty is his name—the Holy One of
Israel is your Redeemer; he is called the God
of all the earth.*

ISAIAH 54:5

She stands outside in the cool, refreshing rain, allowing it to run in rivulets across her cheeks and down her lips. She is like the lily of the valley that spreads its fragrance across the fields or like the lush, abundant grapes that make men glad. Fertility and fruitfulness, celebration and wild abandon—these are the forces that rise and surge within her.

Young, beautiful, and bold, she is always smiling, flashing her big, dark eyes, attracting inevitable attention. God knows how easy it would be to entice her admirers into showering her with gifts of silver and gold. Though she is determined to squeeze every ounce of sweetness from life, that's not all she wants. More than anything, she is looking for someone she can adore.

Suddenly she notices a man hurrying toward her. It is not desire that propels him but pain and hurt. She knows this because she is good at reading people and because it is her husband who draws near.

"Gomer," he says, "come home!"

And so she does, but reluctantly. Hosea is a good man, but goodness can be tiresome. He talks only of God and of faithfulness to the covenant, dampening her high spirits and making her feel ashamed of her sins. But how can it be wrong to dream of having just a little pleasure in this life?

Hosea is distressed by all he sees. The people offer sacrifices at pagan shrines, praising Baal for every harvest. They have forgotten the faith their fathers professed. But she thinks it matters little how people name their gods—whether Baal or Yahweh or Asherah—as long as they acknowledge god by paying homage for the rain and the harvest, the bread and the wine. If Yahweh is so upset, why has the rain been so abundant, the crops so lush, and the peace so prolonged? If everyone is worshiping the wrong god, why have so many people been blessed with so much?

But Hosea insists on pointing out the twistedness in everything—the gap between rich and poor, all the deception and lies, the sleeping around, the killings, and the worship of countless idols. He says God's people have become no different than the Canaanites. Instead of whispering his disapproval, he shouts it, as though he is God's chosen mouthpiece, telling everyone—especially the priests—that they are harlots and whores and that God will surely punish them.

She finds it infuriating and embarrassing to be known as the wife of the prophet Hosea, and her eyes begin to cast about for someone she can truly love.

If Gomer would stop for just one moment and try to read her husband's heart, she would discover that she has broken it more than once. Perhaps she already knows this. But she doesn't know—not yet—how hard it was for Hosea to marry her when he did. She has no inkling that Yahweh, the God of his ancestors and hers, had instructed him, saying, "Go, marry a promiscuous wife and have children with her, like an adulterous wife this land is guilty of unfaithfulness to the LORD." Nor does she realize that her marriage has become a public parable—a story God is telling to his people.

Already she has borne three children. The first was a boy her husband named Jezreel, meaning "God Scatters." Then came a girl he named Lo-Ruhama, meaning "Not Loved," and another girl he named Lo-Ammi, which means "Not My People." Though he hasn't said as much, she knows he doubts the last two babies are his.

Jezreel was where Jehu
assassinated Jezebel, Joram,
and Jezebel's remaining sons,
thereby wiping out the line
of Ahab. Through Hosea,
God declared that he would
punish Jehu's dynasty for their
overzealous brutality and for
their continued tolerance and
promotion of Baal worship. ▪

Yet every time he thunders on about doom and destruction, her prophet-husband can't stop himself from adding a little sliver of hope: "The Israelites will be like the sand on the seashore, which cannot be measured or counted. In the place where it was said to them, 'You are not my people,' they will be called 'children of the living God.' The people will come together; they will appoint one leader and will come up out of the land, for great will be the day of Jezreel."

Gomer knows that Jezreel, which is the name of the large, fertile valley north of Samaria, has more than one meaning. Instead of "God scatters," it can also mean "God sows," signifying that after the coming judgment God will once again provide for his people in this lush and beautiful land.

But she is sick of listening to his dire warnings and so she leaves Hosea and abandons her children. Throwing off every constraint, she begins to lead a life of dissolution. For a while it pleases her. She does what she wants when she wants to do it. Her lovers say nothing disagreeable but only what she longs to hear, that she is the most stunning and exciting woman they have known. She feels enriched by all the gifts they give, silver and gold, wool and linen, wine and oil. But it is not quite enough. Something still is missing.

That something turns out to be someone—a man she meets whose charms are greater than her own. She loves to lean against his chest and feel his strong, encircling arms. A man of influence and quick wit, her lover knows exactly how to please her. As long as he is near, she feels secure. As long as she reveres him, he is glad to stay.

But things begin to turn. He is away more than she likes, and he is not always as attentive as she thinks he should be. Then she begins to cling, to quiz him about where he's been and who he's been with. The more she asks, the less he tells. The more she pursues, the more he backs away until at last he vanishes.

Left alone, she feels her emptiness. Though she tells herself her lover will soon return, her tears reflect the truth—that he is gone forever. As time passes, she begins to realize that loneliness is not her only problem. The world around her has begun to change. For many years, King Jeroboam II presided over Israel. Now the king is dead, and the country is descending into chaos. Life becomes more difficult as one king is murdered and another is quickly crowned.

Gomer is changing too. She is growing older. Many of the men who seek her services seem rough and coarse. When their business is done, they do not linger. In these uncertain times, she has no one to cheer her when she becomes depressed or to care for her when she falls ill. Instead of solid rock beneath her, there is only shifting sand.

Applying layers of makeup, she does her best to conceal the worry that etches itself in tiny lines around her eyes. Fatigue creeps over her like a stubborn fog that will not lift.

By now, her stores of silver and gold have shrunk. She spent freely when she was young but now penuriously because only a few coins are between her and the shelterless streets. On the nights when no one visits, she sits alone, remembering the haunting words her husband spoke the day she left. She can still hear the rage in his voice. She sees the angry tears rolling down his face.

> Rebuke your mother, rebuke her,
>   for she is not my wife,
>   and I am not her husband.

Let her remove the adulterous look from her face
    and the unfaithfulness from between her breasts.
Otherwise I will strip her naked
    and make her as bare as on the day she was born;
I will make her like a desert,
    turn her into a parched land,
    and slay her with thirst.

According to the letter of the law of the day, Hosea could have had Gomer executed for her unfaithfulness, though punishment was rarely carried to that extreme. ▪

Though spoken a lifetime ago, Hosea's words have finally found their mark. She knows what he is talking about. To be abandoned, rejected, cast off like you are nothing. Surely there can be no greater agony.

But then his words turn tender for he speaks of transforming the Valley of Achor (meaning Trouble) into a door of hope. But what kind of magic can turn a person's troubles into hope? This she does not know.

"I will betroth you to me forever," he says.
    "I will betroth you in righteousness and justice,
    in love and compassion.
I will betroth you in faithfulness,
    and you will acknowledge the LORD.

As the words sink in, she feels their sting more than their promise. She has lost too much—thrown it all away. Even though she longs for home and husband and children, she lacks the courage to return. Instead, she spends the last of her treasure and falls into debt. Unable to pay the interest, she sells herself into slavery, and the future stretches out in endless wretchedness.

And then one day, a man comes looking for her. Her man comes looking for her. Hosea has cash in hand, all the money he can scrape together. When he finds he doesn't have enough, he throws some barley into the deal. And she is freed.

But what will she do with her freedom?

Later he tells her what happened. "The LORD came to me," he explains, "and told me to take you as my wife, saying 'Go, show your love to your wife again, though she is loved by another man and is an adulteress. Love her as the LORD loves the Israelites, though they turn to other gods and love the sacred raisin cakes.'[1]

"So I bought you for fifteen shekels of silver and twelve bushels of barley. You are to live with me many days; you must not be a prostitute or be intimate with any man, and I will live with you."

So Gomer, who has lived a dissolute life, returns home to live with Hosea, a husband she does not deserve. But what has become of her children? You will be glad to learn that Lo-Ruhamah is now Ruhamah, meaning "Loved," and Lo-Ammi is called Ammi, meaning "My People."

But what of Israel? Transfixed by the story of the prophet and the prostitute, God's people fail to see how it could possibly apply to them. So they continue on their reckless, wayward course.

After a short while, God allows a king to rise up in the north. Before long, this mighty, pagan king crushes Israel, carrying its people captive. Separated from their own land, the land God gave to them, his people have become as insubstantial as the morning mist or like a bit of smoke escaping through a window. But God, who wastes nothing, uses their hardships to call them to their senses. In time, they will remember the wonderful story of Gomer and Hosea, and the words of the prophet, who said:

Come, let us return to the LORD.
>
> He has torn us to pieces
> but he will heal us;
he has injured us
> but he will bind up our wounds.
After two days he will revive us;
> on the third day he will restore us,
> that we may live in his presence.
Let us acknowledge the LORD;
> let us press on to acknowledge him.
As surely as the sun rises,
> he will appear;
he will come to us like the winter rains,
> like the spring rains that water the earth.

Like Gomer, who suffered greatly for betraying the only man who really loved her, God's people languish in a land that is not their own. But when at last they turn to God, he comes to them just as he said he would—like the winter rains, and like the spring rains that water the earth. He bends down from heaven to bless and provide, betrothing himself to them forever in righteousness and justice, in love and compassion. Only then do they discover how deeply they are loved.

THE TIMES

*Gomer's story took place sometime between 755–722 BC.
Her story is found in Hosea 1–3.*

After Solomon's death, David's kingdom became divided, with Israel in the north and Judah in the south. As one commentator describes the situation, Israel and Judah "were like two cats living in an alley with one tiger named Egypt living at one end and another named Assyria at the other, each scrapping for control over the laneway."[2]

Gomer and Hosea's story unfolded on the northern end of that alley, in the kingdom of Israel. When Hosea first began to prophesy, Israel enjoyed a period of relative affluence and political stability. As life became easier, the nation moved away from God, adopting many of the religious and cultural practices of the Canaanites, including Baal worship.

Since the Israelites depended on rain for a good harvest, the temptations of Baal worship with its stress on the bringing of rain and fertility proved too much for many people to resist. Even though Elijah had dealt a huge blow to Jezebel and the prophets of Baal in the previous century, many people still combined Baal worship with the worship of Yahweh, no doubt considering themselves God's faithful followers even though they were behaving more like followers of Baal.

After the death of Jeroboam II (a descendant of Jehu, the man responsible for Jezebel's death), Israel's prosperity began to decline. Ruled by a succession of weak kings, it became politically unstable at the same time that Assyria was gaining strength in the north.

Throughout their history, God had promised to protect his

people if only they stayed close to him. Sadly, both kingdoms strayed. As a consequence, Israel fell to Assyria in 722 BC and Judah to Babylon in 587 BC.

THE TAKEAWAY

1. Why do you think God asked Hosea to take the radical step of marrying a woman other men would have despised?
2. Why was it so hard for Israel to listen to what God was saying?
3. Even strong marriages can have their difficulties. Comment on the challenges inherent in a marriage between God and his people, between God and you.
4. When God spoke about betrothing himself to his people, he spoke of a relationship that would be characterized by righteousness and justice on the one hand and love and compassion on the other. What does this mean in practical terms?
5. When Gomer's story begins, God's people are behaving like everyone around them. Discuss the similarities and differences between her culture and ours.

CHAPTER 24

THE STORY OF HEROD THE GREAT

How Fear Rules a King

When Herod realized that he had been outwitted by the Magi, he was furious, and he gave orders to kill all the boys in Bethlehem and its vicinity who were two years old and under, in accordance with the time he had learned from the Magi. Then what was said through the prophet Jeremiah was fulfilled:

> *"A voice is heard in Ramah,*
> *weeping and great mourning,*
> *Rachel weeping for her children*
> *and refusing to be comforted,*
> *because they are no more."*

MATTHEW 2:16–18

Herod cannot sleep. His bed is too hard, the air too hot, his head too full of worries that swarm like flies the moment he closes his eyes.

He is staying at Herodium, the impenetrable fortress he has carved from the Judean wilderness. As king of Judea, he has perched his fortress on an artificial mountain he has built on the eastern edge of his kingdom. Adorned with brilliant frescoes, mosaic floors, courtyards, banquet rooms, splashing pools, and terraced gardens, Herod's palace is so lush it makes one think of Eden. It is in this peaceful world of his own creation that he feels most at home. It is also where he plans to be buried.

Though a wily politician and a capable military leader, he will be known as "Herod the Great" not for these or other qualities but because he is one of the ancient world's most gifted and visionary builders.

This morning Herod rises early. From Herodium, he enjoys a clear view in all directions. To the south and east a vast expanse of desert spreads out before him while in the west the Judean hills stand sentry. To the northwest is Bethlehem with Jerusalem only a few miles beyond.

The king stands quietly, meditatively, watching the sun rise over the mountains. Though he is a Jew, he does not begin the day with the customary blessing, thanking God for returning his soul to him in compassion. Nor does he proclaim his smallness in the midst of the Lord's majestic creation.

Instead, he gazes at the blood-red mountains of Moab beyond

the eastern border of his kingdom and thinks only of the color of power. For a man to get what he wants, Herod thinks, he must be willing to pay for it in the currency of other men's blood.

But if power is red, he asks himself, what is the color of fear? Purple—it must be purple—because that is the color of royalty. It is not possible to be king, he thinks, and fearless too. He knows this instinctively and because his father, who had been the real power behind the Jewish throne, was poisoned by a rival.

Herod's first taste of power came at the age of twenty-five, when his father installed him as governor of Galilee. Though his Jewish subjects despise him, his Roman overlords love him. For no one can match the young governor's ability to collect taxes and bring stability to a notoriously unstable region of their empire.

Though religiously Jewish, Herod is racially Arab, the child of an Idumean father and a mother who is the daughter of an Arab sheikh. Handsome and powerfully built, he is considered by those he governs as a half-breed Jew who is also a hammer in the hand of Rome.

To strengthen his claim to the Jewish throne, Herod marries a princess by the name of Mariamne. His beautiful Hasmonean wife is descended from a fierce family of Jews known as the Maccabees, who rebelled against the Seleucid Empire a hundred years earlier.

Herod's ancestors had been forcibly converted to Judaism. His father, Antipater, the founder of the Herodian Dynasty, was an Idumean (Edomite) by birth, and also a devout Jew. ■

Though marrying into the decaying dynasty of the Hasmoneans, Herod has underestimated their thirst for power. His drive for dominance will pit him against many members of his own family, including his wife's mother, Alexandra, who will become his bitter enemy.

When Herod ascends the throne in 37 BC, after insuring that the last of the Hasmonean kings has been killed off by the Romans, he begins his reign by executing forty-five members of the aristocracy, wealthy men whose confiscated riches help fund his kingdom and consolidate his power.

Knowing that the position of high priest is one of immense influence, Herod appoints a man without political ambition. By giving the job to a non-Hasmonean, he has broken with cherished traditions and infuriated Alexandra, who believes this plumb appointment should have been given to her seventeen-year-old son Aristobulus.

Since Alexandra is well connected, she complains to her friend Cleopatra, the Egyptian queen and wife of Marc Antony. Because Antony is Herod's Roman patron, Herod is forced to rescind his initial appointment in favor of his brother-in-law, Aristobulus.

As the young man's popularity surges, Herod's jealousy spikes. Feigning friendship, he invites Aristobulus to cool off in his swimming pool at his palace in Jericho. Conveniently, the high priest is accompanied into the pool by Herod's henchmen, who pretend to play a game with him, holding him beneath the water just long enough for him to drown.

Once again, Alexandra accuses her son-in-law to Marc Antony. Before leaving for Antony's base in Egypt to defend himself against a charge of murder, Herod asks his sister's husband to keep an eye on Mariamne, leaving secret instructions to kill her in the event of his death so the two can enter the afterlife together.

When the king returns to Jerusalem after being cleared of all charges, he hears rumors that Mariamne has taken a lover in his absence. Suspecting that his brother-in-law has watched over her a little too closely, he executes him.

Herod's court swirls with intrigue as family and friends spread rumors in order to leverage the king's paranoia to their advantage. His mother and sister are among the worst of these. Stoking his fear, they finally incite him to execute his beloved Mariamne. In 29 BC, after eight years of marital bliss, the beautiful, young Hasmonean princess is killed by the husband who professes to love her best.

Haunted by his misdeeds, Herod falls into a deep depression, wandering the palace at night plaintively calling her name. When his servants fail to fetch her as he commands them to do, he beats them. Increasingly unstable, he falls seriously ill.

After losing her son and now her daughter to Herod's jealousy, Alexandra plots revenge. Aware of his illness and growing instability, she begins to position herself for the throne. As soon as Herod learns of it, he kills her too.

After murdering his mother-in-law, Herod settles into a period of relative calm, during which time he begins to pursue his passion—which is to construct elaborate buildings and monuments. The king excels at refashioning the natural world to suit his purposes, building an artificial port at Caesarea, diverting water to make the desert bloom, and even erecting and leveling small mountains. He builds cities, palaces, temples, amphitheaters, racecourses, and fortresses, among which are Masada, Antonia, and Herodium. But his crowning achievement, the most brilliant of his architectural feats, with the exception of Caesarea, is the magnificent temple in Jerusalem, which some say he has built to atone for his many sins.

Constructed of gleaming marble, the temple looms over the city like a snowy-white mountain. At its heart is the Holy of Holies, which is covered in gold. Reflecting the rays of the early morning sun, it shines like a blazing fire.

Though Herod has given his people the most beautiful temple in the world, they still despise him. Perhaps it is because he has placed a great Roman eagle at the entrance of the temple, glorifying the very power they find so oppressive.

Over the years, the king has acquired ten wives, who have produced multiple children. Two of his favorite—the sons of Mariamne—stoke his paranoia once again. In 7 BC, worried that they will rise up to avenge their mother's death, he arranges for them to be strangled.

From the beginning to the end of his long reign, Herod is thinking of only one thing. Holding on to power. Like ruthless men in every age, he constantly checks his back. Even at the advanced age of seventy, the old king has a habit of turning his head as though to ward off whatever evil may be trailing him.

The latest threat arrives in the form of wise men who have come to Jerusalem from the east. Making their way through the city, they stir things up by speaking of a newborn king. "Where is the one who has been born king of the Jews?" they ask. "We saw his star in the east and have come to worship him."

When Herod hears of this, he consults the chief priests and teachers of the law, asking, "Where is the Christ to be born?"

"In Bethlehem in Judea," they reply, "for this is what the prophet has written:

> But you, Bethlehem, in the land of Judah,
>> are by no means least among the rulers of Judah;
> For out of you will come a ruler
>> who will be the shepherd of my people Israel.

Summoning the wise men in secret, Herod questions them,

pretending to share their excitement. If he can discover when the star first appeared, he can determine how old the boy king might be.

"Go to Bethlehem," he urges. "Make a careful search. As soon as you find him, report to me, so that I too may go and worship him."

Though the magi have dedicated their lives to the study of the stars, they have not been schooled in the ways of wicked kings. Trusting Herod, they travel to Bethlehem where they discover a child whose name is Jesus. Though he is only a peasant boy, they bow before him, offering gifts of gold, frankincense, and myrrh.

Warned in a dream to avoid returning to Herod, they leave by another route.

As days pass with no sign of the returning magi, Herod grows furious and orders his soldiers to Bethlehem where they massacre every male child under the age of two.

With this wicked act, Herod cements his role as a new pharaoh. Like Pharaoh of old he has both overestimated his power and underestimated the opposition.

For the Lord has already alerted the boy's father in a dream, warning him to flee. "Get up, take the child and his mother and escape to Egypt. Stay there until I tell you, for Herod is going to search for the child to kill him."

Together, Mary, Joseph, and Jesus retrace the steps of their ancestors—of Joseph, Jacob, Judah, and all the rest. Sustained by the gifts of the magi, they will not return home until an angel appears to Joseph with the news of Herod's death.

In one final paranoiac convulsion, five days before his death, Herod executes his eldest son and heir. Gravely ill and knowing that his death will be a cause for universal celebration, he rounds up Judea's leading citizens, imprisoning them in the stadium at Jericho. Then he gives the instruction that they be executed at the moment of his death so that the whole country will be plunged into mourning.

As his soul swings over a great abyss, he is in agony, ravaged by a terrible illness. When he finally succumbs, instead of universal mourning there is great jubilation because the gates of the stadium are opened and the captives are allowed to go free.

Two thousand years will pass before the wicked king's tomb is finally discovered at Herodium. Today it is possible to stand in Bethlehem, the city where Jesus was born, and see the mountain in the distance where Herod the Great was buried.

Two kings. One still alive while the other is merely a ghost whose story reminds us of the haunting question—"And what do you benefit if you gain the whole world but lose your own soul?"

THE TIMES

Herod was governor of Galilee from 47–37 BC
and King of Judea from 37 BC to 4 BC.
His story appears in Matthew 2.

The tale of Herod the Great strains credibility, reading like a royal soap opera. Reliable historical sources paint an even darker picture of a king who would do anything to hold on to power.

The Herodians came to power when the Hasmonean dynasty was in decline and when Syria and Israel were coming under the jurisdiction of Rome. Herod's father Antipater, was an Idumean whom the Romans had appointed to serve as procurator (or governor) of Judea. Though the Hasmoneans were still in the picture, Antipater was the real power behind the throne.

Surprisingly, commentators indicate that Herod the Great may not have been much worse than other kings who ruled in that era and region of the world. ▪

Ten years after Herod was appointed governor of Galilee, he was anointed King of Judea. Five days before his death, he killed his scheming, eldest son, Antipater II. His kingdom was then split between three of his remaining sons: Archelaus, Antipas, and Philip. Matthew's gospel (2:19–23) indicates that Herod Archelaus's reputation for brutality instilled so much fear in Joseph that when he and Mary and Jesus returned from Egypt he decided to settle in Galilee rather than Judea. After Archelaus was deposed, Judea was ruled by a procurator appointed by Rome.

Herod Philip ruled the northeastern part of his father's kingdom while Herod Antipas held sway in Galilee and Perea, two regions in which Jesus and John the Baptist conducted most of their ministry.

Though Herod the Great figures prominently in the early part of Christ's story, it is Herod Antipas who appears most frequently in the pages of the New Testament.

THE TAKEAWAY

1. Briefly reflect on the "bad guys" you have already read about. What characters remind you most of Herod and why? What do their lives imply about God's ability to fulfill his plan for your life, no matter who or what you may be facing?

2. Herod's character is shaped by two things—an unbridled desire for power and paranoia about losing it. Briefly describe your own "territory"—the areas of life over which you have some power or influence. It might include things like your job, how you manage children, your home life, or your volunteer responsibilities. How do you respond when something or someone infringes on what you perceive as your "territory?"

3. Spend a few moments reflecting on the following passage from the prophet Daniel:

   > Praise be to the name of God forever and ever;
   >   wisdom and power are his.
   > He changes times and seasons;
   >   he deposes kings and raises up others.
   > He gives wisdom to the wise
   >   and knowledge to the discerning.
   > He reveals deep and hidden things;
   >   he knows what lies in darkness,
   >   and light dwells with him.
   >
   > DANIEL 2:20–22

4. What parallels do you recognize between Daniel's prayer and the story of Herod and the child Jesus?

CHAPTER 25

THE STORY OF HERODIAS AND SALOME

A Mother and Daughter Wreak Havoc at a Birthday Party

And I saw the dead, small and great, stand before God; and the books were opened: and another book was opened, which is the book of life: and the dead were judged out of those things which were written in the books, according to their works.

REVELATION 20:12

In the moonlight that streams through the window, she can see tiny beads of sweat glistening on her husband's forehead. He is agitated and fitful, disturbed by some nocturnal vision. Even though she knows it's coming, she jumps when his scream tears the silence. And he jumps too, now wide awake. Herod Antipas sits up in bed, recalling the terror he's just lived through.

"It was John," he exclaims. "And real. I saw the slash across his neck, the blood streaming down his beard and clumping in his hair. Suddenly he appeared, out of the darkness, pointing straight at me. Though his mouth was closed, I heard him say: 'You viper! Even now the axe is laid to the root of the trees, and the trees that bear no fruit shall be cut down and cast into the fire.' He kept saying it, over and over, calling me a snake. I grabbed a club to beat him off, but he just stood there staring at me!

"Then I saw them, off to the side—people screaming and in torment, burning but not burning up—and among them there was my face staring back at me!"

The tears are running down his face now. His body shakes. It has been like this off and on since the night of his birthday feast.

Herodias can still smell platters of meat, heaped high with sheep tail, roasted lamb, quail, and veal. She sees the servants weaving in and out of the raucous crowd, carrying trays loaded with grapes, figs, and dates, and delicate dishes made from gazelle meat and bird tongue. There are almonds, olives, pomegranates, and delicious desserts. High officials and military men have gathered to wish Herod well. Wearing garlands on their heads, the leading men of Galilee toast him with endless cups of wine imported from Italy and Cyprus. Paved in beautiful mosaic and bedecked with large, multicolored tapestries, the palace is filled with musicians, dancers, and storytellers whose only purpose is to amuse and delight.

The occasion is Herod's birthday. The location is Machaerus, a palatial stone fortress just east of the Dead Sea. Perched high upon a mountaintop, it is surrounded on three sides by deep ravines and boasts a commanding view of the eastern frontier. From its heights, Jerusalem and Jericho can plainly be seen. Like all fortresses, this one has its share of dungeons. Inside one of them, a man is fastened to the wall in chains. He is Herod's prisoner, a prophet by the name of John.

A wild, unkempt man clad in camel skin and a leather belt, John the Baptizer both fascinates and repels Herod, who brings him out from time to time to hear him preach. The man is so compelling that Herod wonders what it might be like to follow him into the Jordan River so that John can baptize him. But how can he since John has already publicly condemned him, accusing him of committing incest by marrying Herodias, who was both his niece and his half-brother's wife?

Still, Herod's sliver of a conscience tells him it would be a crime to kill a man as good as John. Plus, he knows that murdering the prophet might spark an insurrection. So instead of executing John as he might like to do, he lets him languish in prison for most of a year.

The Jews would have considered Herod's marriage to his niece, who was also his half-brother's wife, to be incestuous (see Leviticus 18:16 and 20:21). ■

But Herodias will not let the matter drop. She hates John for condemning her divorce and remarriage and for doing it so publicly. How dare he threaten and thunder, dragging her name in the dirt, as though he is God? Whenever she speaks of him, Antipas catches a glint of malice in her eye that reminds him of his father of not so blessed memory.

Herod the Great was a man of grand ambitions and abilities. But he was grandly paranoid too. In addition to murdering several of his sons, he put all the baby boys of Bethlehem to death merely on talk of a star and a little child destined to be king.

Herodias herself is the granddaughter of Herod the Great and therefore her husband's niece. Living in the shadow of her grandfather's monstrous paranoia, she is aware that her own father, grandmother, and several of her uncles were among his many victims. With ten wives, he had plenty of children to fear. But Herodias was not one of them. Instead, she was numbered among his favorite grandchildren. Doting on her, he arranged a marriage with one of his surviving sons, her uncle Herod Philip.

But Philip is not ambitious and if Herodias longs for anything, it is for a glittering crown to wear on her head. Thinking Herod Antipas more likely to acquire one, she convinces him to divorce his wife, the daughter of King Aretas IV, a Nabatean ruler with whom Herod Antipas has forged an alliance.

So Herodias abandons one uncle-husband to acquire another. But Herod Antipas is proving something of a disappointment. Merely a tetrarch, who rules over Galilee and Perea—the land beyond the Jordan—he has not yet managed to grace her brow with a crown. As it happens, Antipas's territory is the region in which both John and his cousin Jesus can most frequently be found, preaching, teaching, performing wonders, and stirring up trouble.

Like many of the Herods, Herodias is a schemer. But her first scheme, to use Herod Antipas as a stepping stone to power, had been openly challenged by John, whose insolence quickly ignites her wrath. So she decides to silence him, if not all at once then in measured steps. She begins by pressuring Herod to imprison the popular prophet. Once John is thrown into jail, she waits for an opportune time to finish him off. She pressures Herod, but without results. How is it, she wonders, that even though she is only a woman, she is twice the man her husband is?

Then comes Herod's birthday celebration, the perfect occasion to complete her scheme. She relies on Salome, the daughter she bore to her first husband. Dressing her daughter in a costume of glittering silver, she instructs her to perform her most beguiling dance. Herodias has carefully calculated the scene, counting on Salome's performance to create the perfect moment to advance her plan. And she is not disappointed.

With a sultry smile, Salome spins and twirls, extending her arms in a great, expanding circle as she moves across the floor, inviting every man to imagine what it would be like to become her intimate acquaintance. Finally, when she has exhausted every seductive surprise, she comes to rest like a delicate and fragrant flower at Herod's feet.

"Bravo!" he says and all his guests applaud her.

"Ask me for whatever you want and I'll give it, up to half my kingdom!" he declares.

Excusing herself for just one moment, Salome hurries out to consult her mother. "Ask him," Herodias whispers, "for the head of John the Baptist."

Returning at once, the young girl appears before Herod and says, "I want you to give me right now the head of John the Baptizer on a platter."

The request dismays Herod. He has not seen this coming. The political climate is not conducive for executing such a man. Plus it is a violation of the law to carry out a sentence or to behead a man without first holding a trial. But he has made a public oath and will not shame himself by rescinding it in front of so many powerful men. Immediately he orders John's execution.

In a few minutes' time, while the guests are still murmuring about Salome's extraordinary dance and her shocking request, the executioner returns. He is holding a large platter on which John's head rests. He presents it to Salome, who then presents it to her mother, who accepts it with great pleasure.

On hearing of John's murder, his disciples come and take his body and then lay it gently in a tomb.

When Jesus learns of his cousin's death, he withdraws from the ever-present crowd to be alone and pray. Grieving for John, the best man he has ever known, his own future comes clearly into view.

As the fame of Jesus spreads, people begin to say that he is John the Baptizer risen from the dead. Even Herod, haunted by the possibility, has been overheard, saying, "John, the man I beheaded, has been raised from the dead."

Herodias believes no such nonsense and is haunted by nothing but her continued ambition to one day become queen. But there is more horror to come. In due time, she will accompany Herod to Jerusalem for the Feast of Passover. She will be present on the day that Jesus, the one they call the Christ, appears before him accused of many crimes.[1]

Later, after John and Jesus have both been executed, one by Herod and the other by Pontius Pilate, now Herod's bosom friend, she will watch her husband's armies flee from King Aretas, who is determined to avenge himself on the man who years earlier had divorced his daughter to marry someone else.

Still, Herodias pursues her schemes of greatness, this time

urging Herod Antipas to go to Rome in order to petition Emperor Caligula to bestow on him a royal crown. But her brother Herod Agrippa, Caligula's good friend, is a clever liar, who sends a messenger ahead of them accusing Antipas of sedition. Stripping him of all his lands and goods, Caligula banishes Herod Antipas and Herodias to Gaul, where Herod soon perishes.

Though Herodias lives on, her story fades. Whether her calloused heart led her into more nefarious schemes or whether it was softened by the loss of everything she ever wanted, no one knows. What we do know is that she was guilty of at least one great act of wickedness, choosing to murder the man who through his powerful preaching turned the hearts of many wayward people back to the God who loved them.

THE TIMES

Herodias and Salome's story took place between AD 27 and 29.
Their story can be found in Matthew 14:3–12;
Mark 6:14–29; Luke 3:19–20; 9:7–9.

Herodias's grandfather, Herod the Great, became military governor of Galilee in 47 BC when he was only twenty-five years old. Seven years later, the Roman Senate appointed him king of Judea. When Herod became king, he embarked on massive building projects, including the expansion of the temple in Jerusalem and the construction of the port city of Caesarea Maritima.

Alerted by Magi from the east about a child in Bethlehem who was destined to become King of the Jews, he massacred every boy under the age of two in order to prevent the rise of a contender.

After his death, Herod the Great's territory was divided among three of his sons: Archelaus, Philip, and his youngest son, Antipas. Archelaus proved to be a cruel and incompetent leader. He was banished by the Roman emperor Caligula, and Judea was made a Roman province, which was then governed by a series of prefects, the best known of whom is Pontius Pilate.

Herod the Great's second son, Philip, is not Herodias's first husband, Herod Philip, but Philip the tetrarch, who married Salome, the daughter of Herodias. ■

From the evidence presented in the Gospels, it appears that Herod Antipas was fascinated by both John the Baptist and Jesus. Since his estates were managed by a man named Cuza, whose wife Joanna was a disciple of Jesus, it is possible that Cuza and Joanna spoke to Herod and Herodias about Jesus.

Throughout his rule, Herod Antipas was reviled by his Jewish subjects. As an Idumean, whose family descended from Esau rather than Jacob, and as a Samaritan on his mother's side, he was never trusted by the people he governed.

THE TAKEAWAY

1. Both Herod Antipas and Herodias would have had some exposure to John's preaching with its emphasis on repentance. What has been your own experience of the connection between repentance and new life?
2. What might have prevented Herodias from turning toward God and away from her sins? What prevents you from doing the same?
3. Why is power often such a corrupting force even among good people? How have you handled power, whether on a large or small scale, in your own life?
4. Has God ever called you to speak uncomfortable truths to people of influence? How did you respond? How did they respond?

CHAPTER 26

THE STORY OF HEROD ANTIPAS AND HIS WICKED NEPHEW AGRIPPA

How God Gets the Last Laugh

> *Why do the nations conspire*
> *and the peoples plot in vain?*
> *The kings of the earth rise up*
> *and the rulers band together*
> *against the Lord and against his anointed . . .*

PSALM 2:1–2

Herod's first choice of who would succeed him fell to his sons by his favorite wife Mariamne. But Aristobulus and Alexander were executed in 7 BC. After his eldest son, Antipater was executed in 5 BC for trying to poison him, Herod appointed Antipas as his heir. In 4 BC he changed his mind and drew up a new will that split the kingdom three ways, with Archelaus getting the preeminent share. ▪

Perea was east of the Jordan River. The New Testament refers to it as the "region across the Jordan" or "on the other side of the Jordan." ▪

Joseph decided to settle in Galilee rather than Judea when he and Mary and Jesus returned from Egypt after learning that Archelaus was ruling in Judea. See Matthew 2:22. ▪

Like most rulers, Antipas has enemies. But the worst of these is lying cold as stone in his royal tomb. As Herod the Great's youngest son, Antipas had lived in fear of the brutal side effects of his father's paranoia.

Because of Herod's unfortunate habit of slaughtering family members, the Emperor Augustus once quipped that he would rather be one of Herod's pigs (*hus*) than one of his sons (*huis*). Since Herod adhered to the Jewish dietary laws, pigs had little to fear, though the same could not be said of his sons.

With his father out of the way, Antipas presses his claim to the throne in Rome. But Caesar Augustus splits the kingdom three ways, with Antipas's older brother Archelaus taking the lion's share. While the latter is appointed ethnarch of Idumea, Judea, and Samaria; Antipas holds sway in Galilee and Perea; and their half-brother Philip governs the lands beyond.

Though Antipas and Philip are steady enough, Archelaus inaugurates his reign by killing three thousand people during

Passover. His rule is so heavy handed that it unites two sworn enemies—the Jews and Samaritans. Together they form a delegation to complain to the emperor in Rome. Herod Antipas and Herod Philip also head to Rome to press for their brother's removal.

Since the Emperor Tiberius has no interest in handing over the Jewish throne to yet another scheming member of the Herod family, he deposes Archelaus and converts his territory into a prefecture to be ruled by a governor that Rome will appoint.

Disappointed that he will not be moving his capitol to Jerusalem, Antipas channels his energy into a new city he is building on the western edge of the Sea of Galilee. To curry favor with the emperor, he names it Tiberias. There is only one problem with his beautiful new city. No one wants to live in it because it sits on top of a cemetery, rendering it unclean in the eyes of pious Jews. To overcome the stigma, he is forced to lure prospective residents with promises of free land and homes as well as generous tax exemptions.

On a visit to Rome, Antipas falls in love with his niece Herodias, who happens to be married to one of his half-brothers. Too weak to deny himself whatever he wants, he divorces his wife to marry his niece.

By divorcing his first wife, Herod Antipas has scandalized his Jewish subjects. One man in particular has been stirring things up. A rough looking fellow who subsists on locusts and wild honey, he is revered by the people. John the Baptizer is that rare, pure-hearted man who can neither be pressured nor bribed. John's call for repentance is sweeping. Priests, Pharisees, people low and high—even Herod himself—must admit their sins and return to God. In particular, Herod must forsake his incestuous marriage to his brother's wife.

John voices his criticism so persistently, that Herodias feels his accusation as a slap on the face. How dare he call her out in public? Pressuring her husband to silence John, she is relieved when he arrests him and locks him up in Machaerus, a fortress on the eastern side of the Dead Sea.

Though she urges Herod to execute John, he resists because doing so would be impolitic and dangerous. Since the people are in awe of John, killing him might foment a rebellion. Instead, Herod hides him away, bringing him out when it pleases him, as though John is a trained bear whose primary purpose is to entertain.

After John's death, Herod Antipas begins to hear stories about another pure-hearted man. His name is Jesus and he is John's cousin. In the middle of the night, when rational thought is pushed to the edges of one's consciousness, he wonders if this miracle worker might be John himself come back to haunt him.

Jesus, of course, knows all about Herod. One day, some Pharisees try to run him out of town, saying, "Leave this place and go somewhere else. Herod wants to kill you."

"Go tell that fox," Jesus replies, that 'I will keep on driving out demons and healing people today and tomorrow, and on the third day I will reach my goal.' I must press on today and tomorrow and the next day—for surely no prophet can die outside Jerusalem!"

The man who will one day be known as the Lion of the Tribe of Judah is telling his listeners that he is not afraid of a timid fox like Herod, no matter how clever that fox may be.

It will not be long until Herod and Jesus finally meet up. When they do, it will be obvious to no one which is the fox and which the lion.

It happens like this: Jesus is dragged before Pontius Pilate on a trumped-up charge of sedition. When he discovers that Jesus is a

Galilean, Pilate sends him to Herod Antipas since he is the governor of Galilee.

Though tired of the endless religious quarrels that embroil the region, Herod is eager to meet the man who has captured the hearts of so many. Perhaps Jesus will perform a miracle in his presence.

Holding up his hand to silence the crowd, Herod peppers the prisoner with questions.

Who was your mother? Who was your father?

Is it true what they say about you, that you can turn stones to bread?

Were you one of John's followers?

Your disciples say you are a king. Who do you say you are?

Can you turn water into wine?

Here's a cup of water. Show us what you can do.

But the prisoner makes no reply. His is neither a sullen nor insolent silence but something more unsettling, filled with a meaning Herod cannot grasp.

Though he tries to goad him, Jesus keeps quiet.

"Why do the crowds run after you?" Herod scoffs. "A prophet who can't even talk!

Dressing him in an elaborate robe as though he is a mock king, Antipas sends him back to Pilate as if to say, "He is harmless. Do as you please."

With that, Herod and Pilate, two rulers who had always been enemies, forge a bond of friendship.

In just a few hours, Jesus will be crucified. It matters little to Herod. What is one more man hanging on a Roman cross?

Three years after the death of Jesus, Herod's former father-in-law, the King of Nabatea, attacks his lands and scores so many victories against him that Herod is forced to ask Tiberius to intervene.

None of this endears him to Rome, an empire that prizes stability in its vassal kingdoms. Though Antipas has ruled Galilee and Perea for forty-two years, he is banished to Gaul and his lands are transferred to his brother-in-law Herod Agrippa. When Judea and Samaria are also added to Agrippa's holdings, he becomes king over all the land that was formerly ruled by his grandfather Herod the Great.

A few years after Antipas disappears into Gaul, King Herod Agrippa can be found presiding over a public gathering at Caesarea. Dressed in a splendid robe made of silver, the king glitters in the sun. When people cry out that he is a god and not a man, he glories in their praise. Rather than giving honor to God as a good king should, he soaks up their adulation as though it is the gospel truth. But in the midst of this spectacle, he is struck down by an illness. After suffering severe stomach pains, he dies a gruesome death.

The Jewish historian Flavius Josephus is the source for the story about Herod's silver robe and subsequent death. Though Josephus doesn't mention an angel striking Herod Agrippa down, the New Testament (Acts 12:23) supplies that detail, adding that he was devoured by worms. ■

Like every ruler who builds his house upon the crumbling foundation of human power, the "kingdoms" of Herod Antipas and of his wicked nephew Agrippa quickly pass away. On their own, these horrible Herods would have merited only a footnote in the history books. Because of their association with Jesus and his cousin John, their stories live on.

THE TIMES

Herod Antipas ruled from 4 BC to AD 39 and
Herod Agrippa from AD 39 to 44.
Their stories are told in Mark 6:14–29;
Luke 23:6–16; Acts 12:1–23.

Because several different members of the Herodian dynasty are mentioned in the New Testament, keeping them straight can feel like an impossible task. Here's a quick who's who to indicate where each character appears in the Bible.

The Men

King Herod the Great reigned from 37 BC to 4 BC. Alarmed by reports of a newborn king, he massacred all the males of Bethlehem under the age of two. (Matthew 2:1–19)

Archelaus was the son of Herod the Great and his Samaritan wife Malthrace. He was ethnarch of Judea and Samaria from 4 BC to AD 6. When Joseph heard that he was ruling Judea, he decided to avoid Jerusalem on his return from Egypt. Instead, he and Mary and Jesus settled in Nazareth in Galilee. (Matthew 2:22)

Herod Antipas was the son of Herod the Great and his Samaritan wife Malthrace. Though he was never a king, he ruled as the tetrarch of Galilee and Perea from 4 BC to AD 39. John the Baptist and Jesus conducted most of their ministry in the territory he ruled. He murdered John and mocked Jesus just before his crucifixion. (Matthew 14:1–12; Mark 6:14–29; Luke 3:19–20; 9:7–9; 13:31–33; and 23:6–16; Acts 4:27)

Herod Philip I was a son of Herod the Great, Herodias's first husband, and the father of Salome. (Mark 6:17)

Herod Philip II, also called Philip the tetrarch, was the son of Herod the Great and his fifth wife, Cleopatra of Jerusalem. He ruled the third part of his father's kingdom from 4 BC until his death in AD 34 and was generally liked by his subjects. He married his great niece Salome, the daughter of Herodias and Herod Philip I.

King Herod Agrippa I was the grandson of Herod the Great and the brother of Herodias. He ruled from AD 39 to 44, during which time he executed James the son of Zebedee and imprisoned the apostle Peter. Because he refused to give glory to God, he was struck down by an angel and died a horrible death. (Acts 12:1–23)

King Herod Agrippa II, the son of *Herod Agrippa I,* was the last of the Herods, ruling from AD 50 to 100. The apostle Paul appeared before him when he was imprisoned in Caesarea. (Acts 25:13–26:32)

The Women

Herodias was the granddaughter of Herod the Great. Her first husband was her uncle Herod Philip I and her second was her uncle Herod Antipas. She was also the sister of King Herod Agrippa I. When Herod Antipas was banished to Gaul she went with him voluntarily. (Matthew 14:1–12; Mark 6:17–26)

Salome was the daughter of Herod Philip I and Herodias and the stepdaughter of Herod Antipas. She performed a dance at Herod Antipas's birthday party, after which she asked for John the Baptist's head on a platter. She later married her great uncle Herod Phillip II. (Matthew 14:6–11)

Bernice was the daughter of Herod Agrippa I and the sister of Herod Agrippa II. She and her brother were rumored to have an incestuous relationship. She was with him when Paul appeared before him in Caesarea. (Acts 25:13–26:32)

Drusilla was the youngest daughter of Herod Agrippa I and the sister of Bernice. Married at the age of fourteen, she left her husband to marry Felix, the governor of Judea. They had one son who perished in the eruption of Mount Vesuvius in AD 79. She heard Paul preach when he was imprisoned in Caesarea. (Acts 24:22–26)

THE TAKEAWAY

1. Herod Antipas wanted to see Jesus perform a great miracle. Instead what he saw was a man in shackles, a weakling headed for the cross. How has your own desire to see Jesus act in a certain way shaped your responses to him?

2. Take a few minutes to imagine that you are one of the religious leaders in attendance when Jesus is dragged before Pilate and then hauled across Jerusalem to appear before Herod. It is Passover, which is why both Pilate and Herod are in the city. Try to imagine the atmosphere—the shouting, the smells, the crowds. What feelings and thoughts arise in you as you see Jesus appearing before Herod.

3. John the Baptist and his cousin Jesus were the most spiritually powerful men of their day, and yet they seemed to be no match for the reigning political powers. What do their lives suggest about the nature of authentic spiritual power? About how believers should view the impact of their faith on the world around them?

CHAPTER 27

THE STORY OF THE WOMAN WHO WIPED THE FEET OF JESUS

A Prostitute Lets Her Hair Down, Scandalizing Everyone but Jesus

Blessed are you when people hate you, when they exclude you and insult you and reject your name as evil, because of the Son of Man.

LUKE 6:22

Before Herod's encounter with Jesus just before the crucifixion, the Galilean rabbi had built up a large following of people, some of them drawn from the lowest ranks of society. One of these now sits on the floor with a handful of others, beggars mostly. Unlike the dull-colored robes that help them blend into the wall they lean against, her woven red cloak demands attention. Her hair is swept upward, under a gold-colored head covering, revealing a well-shaped face. Dark eyes find their complement in full, red lips that seem always on the verge of smiling.

Yet Simon passes her by without allowing himself the luxury of a sideways glance. Tonight he has thrown open his doors to one and all, even to women like her. Anyone who wants supper can have it as long as he or she agrees to wait until the honored guests have finished their meal. It is the usual custom, a way to seek God's blessing and display one's generosity to the less fortunate. So they wait—silently, politely, willing their stomachs to be quiet lest they disturb the banquet that will soon commence.

She is glad to be among them, though it's not the feast that has drawn her. She is waiting for someone and in her lap she holds an alabaster jar filled with expensive perfume.

Simon surveys the room, his glance resting not on the riffraff who lean against the wall but on several broad couches arranged in the shape of a *U* that will provide a comfortable place for his honored guests to recline and enjoy their leisurely meal. A table filled with figs, fish, grapes, bread, olives, dates, and roasted goat meat will be set in place once every man has taken his place.

He knows that most of his guests will be eager, as he is, to examine the controversial young rabbi, the one they call Jesus. Many of Simon's fellow Pharisees have their doubts about the man. For one thing, he consorts with tax collectors, Roman stooges who are disguised as Jews. These men grow fat by squeezing money from their own people, taking their cut and then passing the rest on to the Romans. For another, his disciples seem crude and uneducated, rough fellows who are always eating and drinking and never fasting. They have even been spotted picking grain and eating it on the Sabbath. And why, when there are six days a week to work, would Jesus choose to desecrate the seventh day by healing a man with a withered arm as he had recently done?

Still, Jesus attracts ever larger crowds, drawing from the unschooled masses, who are always clamoring for his next miracle. His following has grown so quickly that certain Pharisees have come from Jerusalem for a closer look. Simon has spoken to these men. He shares their concerns.

Lately, another sensational story has been making the rounds. A few days ago, they say, Jesus healed a paralyzed man who was lowered through a rooftop into his presence. Simon has no problem with the idea that a sage could possess healing powers. But Jesus had the audacity to tell the man his sins were forgiven—an obvious blasphemy since only God can forgive sin.

Simon has invited the rabbi to his home to see for himself, to test him and discover what he is made of. Perhaps the tales people tell of him are not all true. Jesus is young. There may still be time to turn him to the right way.

As is customary, Simon honors his guests by welcoming each man with a kiss. He provides water for washing the dust from their feet and olive oil to serve as soap for their hands and anointing oil for their heads.

But what of Jesus? How will Simon greet this popular rabbi when he arrives? Hosting a sage is considered a great honor. But what if the rabbi's teachings are corrupt? Simon has thought long and hard about this and has decided that too warm a welcome could be misconstrued. His other guests might draw the wrong conclusions.

Meanwhile, the young woman continues to wait, sitting quietly in the corner of the room. Simon seems oblivious to her presence. But she notices everything. To pass the time, her mind drifts back to her first encounter with the rabbi. She was one among hundreds, eager to see him perform wonders and hear him preach. In the midst of the enormous crowd, it seemed to her as though he were speaking only to her.

> Blessed are you who are poor,
>> for yours is the kingdom of God.
> Blessed are you who hunger now,
>> for you will be satisfied.
> Blessed are you who weep now,
>> for you will laugh.
> Blessed are you when people hate you,
>> when they exclude you and insult you
>> and reject your name as evil,
>>> because of the Son of Man.

"Do not judge, and you will not be judged. Do not condemn, and you will not be condemned. Forgive, and you will be forgiven."

As she sits on the hillside, the wind carries his voice to her across the crowd and his words fall strong and clear like shafts of light into the darkness of her soul. She begins to pray aloud as many others in the crowd are doing, the tears streaming down their faces.

As she prays she feels a warm, enfolding presence. The Shekinah of God that has descended on her and many others. No longer afraid to face and name her sins, she calls them to mind one by one and then leaves them in the hands of God. There is so much she has to admit and surrender. Rebellion, hurt, rage, unfaithfulness, shame.

Names pass her lips as well, and she sees the faces of the men who paid to share her bed. In this sacred moment she finds the strength to give each man into God's own hands. She has been the object of their lust, and now they will be the object of God's mercy. As she forgives each one, a knot of worthlessness unties itself inside her and is replaced with a sense of peace and freedom.

Shekinah is a Hebrew word that refers to the experienced presence of God dwelling with his people. While it is not a word that occurs in the Bible, the Jews used it to designate the presence of God in Israel's history. ■

She hears the words of Jesus again, "But love your enemies, do good to them, and lend to them without expecting to get anything back. Then your reward will be great, and you will be children of the Most High, because he is kind to the ungrateful and wicked. Be merciful, just as your Father is merciful."

That God loves sinners, this is the message that has drawn her, a wonder that has altered her life. She had hardly imagined that God could feel anything but disgust for her. That he could cherish her and call her his daughter, this upends her world.

Her thoughts are interrupted by Jesus's arrival at Simon's house. Now there is no crowd separating them, only a small group of men conversing with Simon. She watches as he walks into the room. To her surprise, there is no amiable welcome—no kiss, no water for his feet, no oil for his head. Simon merely nods in acknowledgment of his guest and then turns his back, continuing to talk with others.

The insult is obvious. She feels a sudden tension entering the room. Everyone expects the young rabbi to react. Will he explode with anger or shake the dust from his feet and leave the Pharisee's house?

She is used to snubs from men like Simon. Even men who pay for the privilege of abusing her body maintain the pretense of a righteous life by keeping their distance in public places. But she has never seen such treatment of a rabbi. Hospitality is a sacred trust. To treat a guest this way brings shame.

She feels it strongly, as though Jesus has just been slapped in the face and the pain has radiated across the room and landed on her cheek. Her face flushes from the insult.

But Jesus shows no sign of anger. Instead of turning his back on the gathering as one might expect, he merely walks over to a couch and reclines, waiting for the meal to begin.

But this in itself is shocking. For it is always the eldest and wisest who reclines first while the rest of the guests take their places in order of seniority. As one of the youngest men in the room, Jesus has made a remarkable statement.

Missing nothing of what is happening, the woman leaves her place near the wall, concerned by how her beloved rabbi is being treated. She had intended to anoint his hands and head with perfume as a way of thanking him for his gift of forgiveness. But since he is already reclining, she can only reach his feet. Sensing the rejection he must feel, she kneels before him and begins to weep, and then she does the unthinkable. Uncovering her head, she unwinds long, dark strands of hair, using them to wipe the flood of tears that have fallen on his feet. Kissing his feet, she anoints them with the perfume. With this dramatic gesture, too intimate for public display, she shares his humiliation and performs a service his host has deliberately withheld.

"Disgusting!" Simon thinks. "Clearly, my concerns regarding this man are well founded." For he knows that no self-respecting woman would show her hair to her husband until their wedding night. Simon sees her gesture as a declaration of intimacy.

"If he were a prophet," Simon thinks, "he would know who is touching him and what kind of woman she is—that she is a sinner." But instead of rebuking her, Jesus appears to welcome her attention.

"Simon," Jesus says, as though reading his thoughts, "I have something to tell you."

"Tell me, teacher," he replies.

"Two people owed money to a certain moneylender. One owed him five hundred denarii, and the other fifty. Neither of them had the money to pay him back, so he forgave the debts of both. Now which of them will love him more?"

Simon knows that five hundred denarii is a lot of money—two years' wages for a laborer while fifty denarii represents only two months' worth of wages—so he makes the expected reply: "I suppose the one who had the bigger debt forgiven."

"You have judged correctly," Jesus says. And by his tone, Simon catches a hint that the rabbi is also inferring that Simon has not always judged correctly.

Turning toward the woman who has exposed herself to ridicule for his sake, Jesus continues. "Do you see this woman, Simon?"

The question forces Simon to look at the woman, to see her for the first time.

"I came into your house," Jesus continues. "You did not give me any water for my feet, but she wet my feet with her tears and wiped them with her hair. You did not give me a kiss, but this woman, from the time I entered, has not stopped kissing my feet. You did not put oil on my head, but she has poured perfume on my feet. Therefore, I tell you, her many sins have been forgiven—as her great love has shown. But whoever has been forgiven little loves little."

Then Jesus turns his attention to the young woman who is still kneeling before him. "Your sins," he says, "are forgiven. . . . Your faith has saved you; go in peace." And she does.

The guests begin to murmur, saying to each other, "Who is this who even forgives sins?"

Afterward, Simon wonders the same. Though he tells himself he is in the right, he feels off kilter, as though the ground has suddenly shifted beneath his feet. His lips tremble slightly and a small tear runs down his cheek. Working hard to control himself, he can't quite manage it, can't stop asking, "Who is this man who offers to forgive sins? Can he forgive my sins?"[1]

THE TIMES

*This woman's story took place between the years AD 26 and 30.
Her story is told in Luke 7:36–50.*

In the Middle East, hospitality has always been considered a sacred responsibility. To refrain from caring for guests would have been considered a grievous offense.

Mealtimes were often leisurely, especially if guests were being entertained. To eat with someone meant that you enjoyed a good relationship, that there was peace between you. It was the host's responsibility not only to care for his guests but to protect them from harm, even to the point of defending them with his life should that be necessary. This is why so many religious people were scandalized by the meals Jesus shared with notorious sinners.

Instead of sitting down at a table as we do today, people either sat on mats on the floor or reclined on couches. At least one scholar[2] thinks that Jesus and his disciples were reclining on mats or cushions on the floor rather than on elevated couches when they ate their last meal together before his death. For formal dinners, guests sometimes reclined on a *triclinium,* a seating area made up of couches arranged in the form of a *U*. The food would be served on a removable platter that served as the tabletop for a three-legged table. Rather than using silverware, people simply tore off a piece of bread and used it to scoop food from a common bowl.

With this as the backdrop, the story comes into clearer focus. Not only did Simon refrain from offering the usual kiss as Jesus entered his home, but he withheld common courtesies, like providing water and olive oil for Jesus to wash his hands and feet. By not offering these amenities, especially to a rabbi, Simon delivered a stinging, public insult.

But what was a prostitute doing at the house of a Pharisee, a man who would have considered her unfit for his table? To show one's magnanimity, it was common practice to invite outcasts to a formal meal. But these unfortunates were only allowed to eat once all the other guests had completed the meal. Rather than crashing the party, this woman may have humbled herself by identifying with outcasts, thus exposing herself to ridicule because of her desire to thank Jesus for everything he'd done for her.

THE TAKEAWAY

1. Comment on the role reversal that takes place in this story with a "law breaker" becoming the hero while a "law keeper" seems to be the villain.
2. What does this woman's story say about the human tendency to judge others by outward appearances?
3. As you think about the story, take a moment to consider which of the characters you identify with the most. What makes you identify with that person?
4. Have you ever loved someone so much that you didn't care what other people thought? What might your relationship with Christ look like if you loved him that much?
5. Jesus says those who've been forgiven much love much. Take a moment to consider whether there are sins you haven't yet admitted, perhaps even to yourself. Let this woman's story encourage you to tell God everything that is in your heart.

CHAPTER 28

THE STORY OF JUDAS ISCARIOT

The Man Who Lived with the Light but Chose Darkness Instead

"The one I kiss is the man; arrest him."
Going at once to Jesus, Judas said,
"Greetings, Rabbi!" and kissed him.

MATTHEW 26:48–49

Jesus and his disciples are heading south, toward Jerusalem, for what will become his final visit to this holiest, most intractable of cities. Though his disciples crowd him as they walk alongside him on the dusty road, hoping to catch every word, one hangs back.

As far as Judas is concerned, these Galileans are simple men, incapable of an original thought. Like many Judeans, he thinks of these fellow Jews from the north as country hicks. He doesn't realize that the difference between him and the other disciples isn't a matter of intelligence or breeding but simply a matter of love. They are devoted to their rabbi while he is devoted to his ambitions.

Though Jesus hails from Galilee, Judas puts him in a different category entirely. As a rabbi of growing renown, he shows surprising nerve in the face of Pharisees and priests who try to cow people with their knowledge of the law and their so-called piety. This willingness to challenge the religious elites is what first attracted Judas to Jesus. There is also the matter of his miraculous powers, which never fail to attract the crowds.

Surely it was a stroke of luck and a great shock when Jesus invited Judas to become his close disciple. Even better is the delicious irony that he, a petty thief, has been appointed keeper of the common purse. He thinks of his small thefts as little rewards for not running off with the whole purse, a temptation he regularly resists.

Little is known about Judas Iscariot. Some scholars believe *Iscariot* means "man of Kerioth," possibly a village in southern Judea, but the meaning is disputed. If Judas was from Judea he may have looked down on the Galileans, a common prejudice among people who lived in Judea. ■

But why should he run? Jesus is the most popular rabbi in Galilee. Soon he will turn his attention to Jerusalem and then there will be no stopping him. Any man who is his close ally will surely rise with him.

Instead of listening carefully to the rabbi's words as the group walks along the sandy path, Judas is distracted by visions of his glorious future. He sees himself adorned in gold and jewels, ruling as governor over a province or two. Or perhaps he will become the new high priest when Jesus claims the Jewish throne.

Like many ordinary Jews, Judas realizes how adept the chief priests have become at amassing wealth and power under the pretense of piety. What offends him is not their ambition for worldly riches but the fact that this power is granted them by Rome. It comforts him to think that when the Messiah takes up his throne the current power structure will collapse.

Haven't the Scriptures foretold the coming of a great king who would defeat Israel's enemies? The country is feverish with expectation that the Messiah will soon arise to deliver them from their Roman oppressors. Why not Jesus? Why not now?

But there are obstacles. Judas thinks back to that day on the mountaintop when Jesus extolled the meek, the hungry, and the merciful, calling them blessed. He even praised the peacemakers. But why speak of peace when war is inevitable? And why speak of mercy when vengeance is required?

More than once Judas has wondered whether his rabbi has the political spine to claim the throne. Instead of seizing every opportunity to advance his position, Jesus has an annoying habit of disappearing whenever the crowd tries to proclaim him king.

Though ordinary people keep flocking to Jesus, opposition is growing within the ranks of the religious elite—the chief priests,

John's Gospel frequently uses the phrase "the Jews" to designate not ordinary Jews but the corrupt and spiritually blind religious leaders who were opposing Jesus. Most scholars believe that John's audience included Jewish believers who had been kicked out of the synagogues for their faith in Jesus.[1] ▪

Pharisees, and scribes. Ever since that incident in Bethany when Jesus raised a dead man, tensions have escalated.

Jealous of his growing fame, and worried that he and his disciples might spark an uprising, the religious leaders look for some quiet way to stop him. In their concern to hold on to power and protect the nation from the wrath of Rome, they convene a special session of the Sanhedrin, the Jewish governing body, to discuss this very issue.

Because of their animosity, Jesus can no longer move freely in public so he and his disciples withdraw to a small village on the edge of the desert.

Certain that Passover presents the perfect opportunity for Jesus to claim his throne, Judas grows impatient. He knows that hundreds of thousands of Jews will be pouring into Jerusalem to celebrate God's deliverance. During the Passover meal they will commemorate God's mighty deeds when he led the nation out of Egypt.

He knows, too, that it wouldn't be difficult to substitute the word *Rome* for *Egypt* and the name *Jesus* for *Moses*. Indeed many people already believe that Jesus is the new Moses, the one God is calling to deliver his people from Roman oppression.

Judas is not alone among the disciples in his view that if the people rise up as one, acclaiming Jesus as their king, the Romans will be instantly overthrown.

This is exactly what the chief priests and Pharisees fear, though they are not so optimistic about the outcome. They plan to arrest him quietly should he travel to Jerusalem to attend the feast. But first they must find him.

Since timing is everything, Judas hopes Jesus will arrive in Jerusalem before it's too late. He's relieved when they finally head toward Bethany, a village two miles from Jerusalem, just days before Passover. After all, Bethany is the epicenter of Jesus's fame, the place in which he performed his most spectacular miracle. Lazarus, the man he raised from the dead, still lives there, along with his sisters Mary and Martha.

Many eyewitnesses have spread the story of how Lazarus walked out of his tomb still dressed in his grave clothes. With crowds streaming into the city day after day, everyone is talking about the rabbi who has the power to raise the dead.

Meanwhile, Jesus is enjoying a dinner held in his honor in Bethany. Lazarus, Mary, and Martha are also present. While the men recline on couches, enjoying a leisurely meal, Mary does something extraordinary. Holding an alabaster jar full of pure nard, she walks over to the couch where Jesus is reclining. Breaking it open, she pours the precious oil, worth more than a year's wages, over his feet. Then she wipes his feet with her hair.

Though anointing a guest's head with a little bit of oil is common, feet are usually washed with water and then wiped with a towel, never with a woman's hair. Unbinding her hair before anyone but her husband is considered a sign of loose morals. But Mary's love for Jesus is so extravagant that she fails to observe the usual conventions.

Nard is an intensely aromatic, amber-colored oil extracted from a flowering plant that grows in the foothills of the Himalayas in northern India. ∎

Judas is the first to express his indignation. "Why wasn't this perfume sold and the money given to the poor?" he says. Despite the apparent piety of his question, he is thinking not of the poor but of all the money he could have skimmed from the sale.

But Jesus overrides his objection, saying, "Leave her alone. It was intended that she should save this perfume for the day of my burial. You will always have the poor among you, but you will not always have me."

Judas feels it as a double rebuke, first to his greed and then to his dreams. It makes no sense to talk about burial when they should be celebrating the victory to come.

The next day he and the other disciples accompany Jesus as he enters Jerusalem. Riding on a donkey, Jesus is greeted by a huge crowd waving palm branches as though they are hailing a victorious king. Though Judas is delighted by the size of the crowd, he feels uneasy. Why ride a donkey into the city as a sign of peace when what is required is a warhorse?

A little later and the scene shifts. Now Judas is leaning against a wall, once again placing himself a little apart from the others. His face half in shadow and half in light, he is listening as Jesus addresses the twelve. "The hour has come for the Son of Man to be glorified," he says. "I tell you the truth unless a kernel of wheat falls to the ground and dies, it remains only a single seed. But if it dies, it produces many seeds. The man who loves his life will lose it, while the man who hates his life in this world will keep it for eternal life." Looking around at his disciples, his gaze rests upon Judas, as though he is extending an invitation.

But if it is an invitation, Judas declines. He is sick and tired of hearing about death. Nor does he want to be planted in the ground so that other men may flourish. After months of fighting off his doubts about Jesus, he gives in to the worst of these.

As the truth sinks in, Judas realizes that Jesus has no intentions of leading an armed rebellion. There will be no glorious victory. Nor will the men who follow him be elevated to positions of power.[2] Embittered and disillusioned, he moves deeper into the shadows.

It occurs to Judas rather suddenly that perhaps Jesus doesn't love him. Maybe he never has. He remembers how often during the last three years he has felt like an outsider, as though his was the only compromised soul in the bunch. He has tried making something of his life. But now he feels grieved, as though a golden opportunity that will never come again has been taken from him.

Then another thought. If he can't have gold, he will settle for silver.

As the Passover meal commences, Jesus rises from the table. Then he does something that hardens Judas's heart even more. Removing his outer robe, he wraps a towel around his waist. Pouring water into a basin, he kneels down and begins to wash his disciples' feet, drying them with the towel.

This gesture merely increases the contempt Judas feels. Clearly Jesus is either a dreamer or a fraud, but he is no Messiah. For the Messiah would never shame himself by washing another man's feet because wiping a man's dirty feet is a task so menial that even Jewish slaves do not perform it.

Returning to his place at the table, Jesus looks at each of his disciples. "Do you understand what I have done for you?" He asks. "You call me 'Teacher' and 'Lord,' and rightly so, for that is what I am. Now that I, your Lord and Teacher, have washed your feet, you also should wash one another's feet. I have set you an example that you should do as I have done for you. Very truly I tell you, no servant is greater than his master,

The disciples' feet would have been dusty from walking on dirt roads. In some neighborhoods, roads were depositories for trash and human waste making the task of cleaning one's feet both more necessary and repugnant. Foot washing was a task reserved for non-Jewish slaves, the lowest of the low. ∎

nor is a messenger greater than the one who sent him. Now that you know these things, you will be blessed if you do them."

Then he says something that injects a chill into the room. "I am not referring to all of you; I know those I have chosen. But this is to fulfill this passage of Scripture: 'He who shared my bread has turned against me.' Truly I tell you, one of you is going to betray me."

Fearing disclosure, Judas is relieved when Jesus honors him by leaning across the table and offers him a piece of unleavened bread that he has dipped in charoset, a tasty dish that is part of the Passover meal. But as soon as Judas accepts the bread, he feels darkness rush in and take possession of his soul.

"What you are about to do, do quickly," Jesus says.

Finding his way in the dark to the temple, Judas promises the chief priests to deliver Jesus into their power at an opportune time when there are no crowds to witness his arrest. In return they promise to reward him with thirty pieces of silver. It is less than he had hoped for but at least it's enough to keep him going for a few months, since he no longer has a job.

After the meal, Jesus and his disciples leave the city and make their way to the Garden of Gethsemane to pray. This is a place Judas knows well. Leading a crowd of men armed with swords and clubs he approaches Jesus and then kisses him on the cheek. This is the pre-arranged signal, so that the soldiers will know whom to arrest.

Rather than trying to escape, Jesus steps forward and asks who they're looking for.

"Jesus of Nazareth," they say.

"I am he," Jesus replies.

Stepping back, Judas watches the soldiers as they move toward Jesus. Suddenly, they pull back, collapsing on the ground. Too much power is emanating from their would-be captive for them to advance.

Once again, Jesus asks, "Who is it you want."

When they say "Jesus of Nazareth," he replies, "I told you that I am he. If you are looking for me, then let these men go." He speaks now of his disciples.

Unwilling to run, Simon Peter suddenly pulls out his sword and strikes the high priest's servant, cutting off his right ear.

Fearing one of the disciples will attack him next, Judas thinks about making his escape. Before he can leave, Jesus intervenes, saying, "Put your sword away! Shall I not drink the cup the Father has given me?"

Thrown into confusion, Peter and the other disciples flee.

The next morning, Judas is seized with remorse. Wave after wave of shame washes over him in an endless, nauseating stream. In a vain effort to distance himself from the judicial murder that is now taking place, he heads to the temple to confess his sin. "I have betrayed innocent blood," he cries. But the chief priests and elders ignore him. Why should they care about Judas and his pangs of conscience? A disciple who betrays his rabbi is worth less than dirt. "What is that to us?" they reply. "That's your responsibility."

Throwing the coins onto the floor of the temple, Judas runs out.

Retrieving the thirty pieces of silver, the priests talk about how to dispose of the money. They must preserve their purity by not spending it on themselves or the temple. Instead they purchase a field that will become a cemetery for foreigners, thus fulfilling the words of the prophet Jeremiah who said, "They took the thirty silver coins, the price set on him by the people of Israel, and they used them to buy the potter's field."

Few men were as privileged as Judas Iscariot and none as cursed—a man who lived with the light but chose darkness instead.

THE TIMES

Judas's story took place about AD 27–31.
*His story is told in Matthew 26–27; Mark
14; Luke 22; John 12–13; 18:1–14.*

In the run-up to the first century, some men became known for their devotion to studying and teaching the Torah, the first five books of the Bible. These were ordinary working people—farmers, blacksmiths, carpenters—who told parables and explained the Scriptures. Some worked at their trade for part of the year and then traveled from synagogue to synagogue teaching.

In Jesus's day, such men were addressed as "my master," which in Hebrew is *rabbi* (pronounced *rah-BEE*). It wasn't until after AD 70 that "rabbi," became a formal title used for scribes or theologians who were trained in the Law.

During the first century it was common for a rabbi to take disciples, who after several years of studying with him would in turn become rabbis. Jesus broke with tradition by not apprenticing himself to a rabbi. Instead, he simply laid down his carpenter tools and selected twelve undistinguished men to follow him. That too broke precedent, as would-be disciples would normally petition a rabbi, asking him to take them on as his students.

Teaching sessions were frequently conducted near the marketplace, on the side of the road or in a field. Rabbis were never paid but relied on the hospitality of others.

The task of a disciple was not merely to listen to his rabbi's teaching but to "read the book of his life." In other words, a disciple was expected to observe his teacher closely to imitate the way he responded to people and life circumstances.

Many disciples lived and traveled with their rabbi, just as Jesus's disciples did. To express their respect and love for him, they were to treat him with the honor they would give a father. They were also expected to serve his personal needs, much as a slave would serve a master.

The goal of disciples was to learn from the rabbi how to understand and apply God's word to their own lives. By studying both the Scripture and the text of the rabbi's life, disciples hoped to acquire, not only their master's grasp of the Torah but also the depth of his moral character. Understanding how intimate the bond was between rabbi and disciples helps us to understand how scandalous Judas's betrayal of Jesus was.[3]

THE TAKEAWAY

1. Imagine yourself as one of the characters in Judas's story. Are you Mary of Bethany, anointing the feet of Jesus with precious oil, Lazarus who has been raised from the dead, a member of the crowd waving branches as Jesus enters Jerusalem, or one of the chief priests complicit in his arrest? From the perspective of that character, how would you describe your relationship with Judas or your view of him?

2. What does Judas's story suggest about the condition of the human heart? In what ways does this aspect of his story challenge you?

3. When God revealed himself to Moses in the Hebrew Scriptures he used the mysterious phrase, "I AM WHO I AM" (Exodus 3:14). Why do you think the soldiers fell down when Jesus said, "I am he," when they tried to arrest him in the Garden of Gethsemane (John 18:5–6)?

4. Jesus's disciples would have become fearful, confused, and disheartened when they realized that he wasn't going to be the Messiah they wanted him to be. In what ways, if any, do you relate to the disciples in this regard?

CHAPTER 29

THE STORY OF PONTIUS PILATE

How a Terrible Dream Came True

> *When Pilate saw that he was getting nowhere, but that instead an uproar was starting, he took water and washed his hands in front of the crowd. "I am innocent of this man's blood," he said. "It is your responsibility!"*
>
> MATTHEW 27:24

His head throbs as though a tiny hammer is swinging to a steady beat inside his skull. The headaches have become a regular feature of his day. He thinks of them as the cost of doing business as a Roman governor in a backwater region of the empire.

Sitting on the edge of his bed, Pontius Pilate looks over at the sleeping figure of his wife. It is rare for an official's wife to follow her husband to an assignment in a far-flung region of the empire. Loving her for it, he rises without disturbing her.

Remembering how restless she had seemed a few hours ago, he wonders if a dream may have troubled her sleep. He has learned to respect the wisdom of her night visions.

Six years earlier, Pilate's friend Sejanus, a confidant of the Emperor Tiberius, had helped him secure his position as prefect of Judea. But Sejanus's execution on suspicion of treason has undermined Pilate's standing in Rome. Like a man who has hoisted his sail on treacherous seas, he feels vulnerable to every political wind.

Though Pilate usually resides at Caesarea Maritima, the magnificent Roman city Herod the Great had built on the eastern edge of the Mediterranean, he stays in Jerusalem during times of unrest or whenever the feasts are observed. In addition to collecting taxes and adjudicating criminal trials, his solemn duty as governor of Judea is to maintain the peace.

Lest a display of Roman power provoke the anger of his intransigent subjects, he does his best to keep a low profile whenever he is in Jerusalem, especially during the feast of Passover. He leaves the daily governance of the city to the Sanhedrin, the Jewish court presided over by the high priest.

Pilate has not always been so sensitive to the customs of those he governs. His first foray into Jerusalem nearly provoked an insurrection. Ignoring the policy of previous Roman governors, he and his soldiers had entered the city carrying military standards that his Jewish subjects considered idolatrous. Too stubborn to admit his mistake, he tried stonewalling. After five days of mounting protests, he attempted to bully his way out of the crisis by ordering the execution of anyone who continued to agitate.

But the Jews continued to resist, and in the face of their stubborn defiance, his bluff collapsed, and he was forced to remove the offensive insignia.

But this morning, Pilate is not thinking about past mistakes, if he even thinks they were mistakes. As daylight steals across Jerusalem, he is greeted by members of the Sanhedrin who have brought a prisoner for judgment.

Last night, while the rest of the city slept, the religious leaders arrested this man, roughed him up, and then drew up charges against him. Since Jewish law prohibits the court from handing down judgments beneath the cover of darkness,[1] this surprises Pilate. He wonders what kind of prisoner could provoke them to act with such haste and secrecy.

Aware that the Jewish leaders cannot enter his residence without rendering themselves ritually unclean, he goes out to meet them. From the *bema* (the judgment seat) constructed on a raised platform, he listens to their complaints.

Roman governors usually heard cases from daybreak until 11:00 a.m. ▪

The precise timing of Jesus's civil trials before Pilate and Herod cannot be established, though they likely occurred between 6:00 and 9:00 a.m. ▪

"What charges are you bringing against this man?" he asks.

"If he were not a criminal, we would not have handed him over to you," they say.

Their defensive tone tells him there is more to the story.

"Take him yourselves and judge him by your own law," he says.

"But we have no right to execute anyone," the religious leaders object.

Ah . . . so this is the game. They want me to handle their dirty work.

"We have found this man subverting our nation," they continue. "He opposes payment of taxes to Caesar and claims to be Christ, a king."

The allegations are serious. Urging people to withhold taxes is itself a capital crime, and of course there can be no king but Caesar. But Pilate suspects the charges may have been trumped up to cover a religious dispute. This would not be the first time such a tactic was used.

Stepping down from the *bema* and walking into the Praetorium, Pilate summons the prisoner in order to question him privately.

"Are you the king of the Jews?" he asks.

"Is that your own idea or did others talk to you about me?" Jesus replies.

"Am I a Jew?" Pilate scoffs. "It was your own people and your chief priests who handed you over to me. What have you done?"

He expects the prisoner to mount an energetic defense.

But Jesus merely replies, "My kingdom

Though Pilate is the only one with absolute power over life and death, the Romans sometimes tolerated local executions, as in the case of Stephen in Acts 7. ■

———

The Praetorium is Pilate's headquarters in Jerusalem, located in the former palace of Herod the Great. ■

is not of this world. If it were, my servants would fight to prevent my arrest by the religious leaders. But now my kingdom is from another place."

"Ah, you are a king then," Pilate says, looking at Jesus with an inquisitive eye.

"You are right in saying I am a king," Jesus replies. "In fact for this reason I was born, and for this I came into the world, to testify to the truth. Everyone on the side of truth listens to me."

"What is truth?" Pilate asks, rubbing his forehead to relieve the mounting pressure in his skull. How he hates these miserable headaches!

Satisfied that his prisoner is not a criminal but merely a Jewish sage who has aroused the envy of the religious elite, he returns to the *bema*, announcing to the chief priests and the crowd, "I find no basis for a charge against this man."

"He stirs up the people all over Judea by his teaching," they shout. "He started in Galilee and has come all the way here."

So, the man is from Galilee! Perhaps there's an easier way to defuse the situation. Since Herod Antipas is staying in the city for Passover, Pilate decides to send Jesus to him. Maybe that old fox will find a way to calm things down.

In a matter of minutes, Jesus is transported to the other side of the city. Since Herod finds nothing with which to charge him, the prisoner is back in Pilate's custody by 7:00 a.m. Once again, Pilate questions Jesus, expecting him to defend himself.

"Aren't you going to answer? See how many things they are accusing you of."

Surely the man is aware that Roman law requires him to pronounce against him if he fails to defend himself.[2]

But Jesus says nothing.

Returning to the *bema*, Pilate addresses the crowd. "I find no basis for a charge against him. But it is your custom for me to release to you one prisoner at the time of the Passover. Do you want me to release 'the king of the Jews'?"

While he is speaking, a soldier arrives with an urgent message from his wife. "Don't have anything to do with that innocent man," it says, "for I have suffered a great deal today in a dream because of him."

Her words pierce him. For a split second he feels as though he is entering a different dimension, a dream of his own. The noise of the boisterous crowd recedes while the steady pounding in his head grows worse. Sitting on the judgment seat, he looks into the eyes of Jesus. For a moment, it seems to him as if he and his prisoner are the only two people in the city. Who, he wonders, is the captive and who the judge?

Then he hears the voice of his wife, as though she is standing right beside him: "Have nothing to do with this innocent man."

Closing his eyes for a moment, he remembers Barabbas—an insurrectionist and murderer who is locked up in the Praetorium. Surely the religious leaders will not want to see that fanatic released. Perhaps he can strike a deal.

"Which one do you want me to release to you: Barabbas, or Jesus who is called Christ?" he asks the crowd. He does not realize they are all stooges of the chief priests.

"No, not Jesus! Give us Barabbas!" they shout in unison.

"What shall I do, then, with Jesus who is called Christ?" asks Pilate.

"Crucify him!"

"Why, what crime has he committed?"

But they shout louder, "Crucify him."

Pilate then orders Jesus to be flogged. The punishment will be delivered by a multi-stranded leather whip, each strap of which is embedded with pieces of bone and lead. Unlike the Jews, who limit the number of lashes, the Romans have no such rule. At times they flog their prisoners to death.

The soldiers drag Jesus into the Praetorium, strip him and then dress him up as a bogus king. Fastening a soldier's cloak around his shoulders, they twist branches into a crown of thorns and then mash it onto his head. Shoving a staff into his hand to serve as a scepter, they kneel before him and say, "Hail, king of the Jews!" Then they strike him on the face.

This is one of their favorite entertainments, the way they love to treat pretenders.

After they finish with him, Pilate addresses the crowd. "Look, I am bringing the prisoner out to you to let you know that I find no basis for a charge against him. Here is the man!"

As soon as the chief priests and officials catch sight of Jesus's bloodied face, they yell, "Crucify him! Crucify him!"

"You take him and crucify him," Pilate says. "As for me, I find no basis for a charge against him."

Soldiers of that era liked to play a cruel game with insurrectionists. Dressing the prisoner in a scarlet robe, the outer cloak of a Roman soldier, they dressed him up as a king, made fun of him, threw dice, and then moved him around like a pawn on a game board that was etched into the floor.[3] ▪

"We have a law," they object, "and according to that law he must die, because he claimed to be the Son of God."

When Pilate hears this, his grows even more afraid. "Where do you come from?" he asks Jesus.

But his prisoner is silent.

"Come on, man! Why do you refuse to speak to me? Don't you realize I have power either to free you or crucify you?"

"You would have no power over me," Jesus says, "if it were not given to you from above."

Though Pilate wants to free Jesus, the religious leaders keep shouting, "If you let this man go, you are no friend of Caesar. Anyone who claims to be a king opposes Caesar."

Hearing this, the governor realizes he has lost the fight. Despite his strong desire to heed the warning of his wife's dream, his standing in Rome is so precarious that he cannot risk a complaint reaching the emperor. His opponents know this and have leveraged his fear against him.

Dipping his hands into a bowl of water, Pilate washes them in front of the crowd, saying, "I am innocent of this man's blood. It is your responsibility."

"Let his blood be on us and on our children," they shout.

Then he releases Barabbas and hands Jesus over for crucifixion. It is 8:00 a.m.

At 9:00 a.m. Pilate's soldiers hammer Jesus to a cross.

Above the head of the crucified man is a plaque that reads: JESUS OF NAZARETH, THE KING OF THE JEWS.

The timing in the account in John's Gospel differs from that in Mark's Gospel. John indicates that Jesus was condemned to death at the sixth hour, which would have been 12:00 noon. It may be that John was using Roman time, which would account for the differences. ∎

When Pilate finally steps down from the *bema* that day, his head feels as if it will explode. The trees are filled with screeching birds and the air feels thick and suddenly warm.

Hearing an ominous rumble, he feels the ground begin to quake. Suddenly, everything goes dark.

Those who are in the temple fall down as they hear a great tearing noise—it is the curtain separating the Holy Place from the Most Holy Place ripping in two from the pressure of the earthquake.

Because of the man on the cross, the world as Pilate knows it—indeed as everyone knows it—will never be the same.

THE TIMES

*Pontius Pilate was the Roman gover-
nor of Judea from AD 26 to 36.
His story is found in Matthew 27:1–31; Mark
15:1–20; Luke 23; and John 18:28–19:16.*

Roman governors generally relied on local authorities to police the public. However, the aristocratic priesthood that governed Jerusalem frequently abused its power, particularly when dealing with people it considered a threat to its control.

The Jewish high court, called the Sanhedrin, was dominated by the party of the Sadducees, which was comprised of members of the priesthood and aristocracy. During the New Testament period, its seventy-one members, who were frequently at odds with each other, were drawn from the Sadducees, Pharisees, and members of the aristocracy.

Because Jesus was tried in the middle of the night in the home of the leading judge rather than during the day in the meeting hall near the temple, his trial would have been considered unethical. It is likely that many members of the Sanhedrin were absent from the special session that was convened to condemn Jesus because it was held in the middle of the night during a festival.

The high priest, an appointee of the Roman governor at this stage in history, served as both the president of the Sanhedrin and the supreme priest of the temple. Under him were the chief priests, the temple treasurer and the remainder of the priests and Levites. In the first century AD there were several thousand priests, most of whom lived at home and took turns serving in the temple for a period of one week.

As governor, Pilate had the ultimate authority. But his power was mitigated by political realities, one of which was that his Roman patron, Sejanus, had come under suspicion and was executed in 31 BC. In AD 36 Pilate was forced to step down as governor because of how he handled an incident in Samaria. Nothing is known about his death.

THE TAKEAWAY

1. Pilate appears to have been deeply conflicted about condemning Jesus. Briefly review the various factors and events that pulled Pilate in different directions.

2. Ultimately, Pilate did what was politically expedient rather than what was right. Much like Judas, who threw the thirty silver pieces into the temple, Pilate tried to distance himself from his own regrettable decision. If you were to defend Pilate's position, what arguments would you make on his behalf? Similarly, what arguments would you make against Pilate's position?

3. Describing the human condition, the apostle Paul wrote, "There is no one righteous, not even one" (Romans 3:10). It is easy to see how this applies to those who were complicit in Jesus's death. But how does it apply to the rest of us?

4. Take a moment to consider what Jesus must have suffered as he was dragged between Pilate and Herod and tortured by their troops. More than once, Jesus makes it clear that he is not a victim. "You would have no power over me," he says to Pilate, "if it were not given to you from above" (John 19:11). And earlier he had said to the disciples, "No one can take my life from me. I sacrifice it voluntarily. For

I have the authority to lay it down when I want to and also to take it up again" (John 10:18 NLT). Why is it important to understand that Jesus isn't a victim—that he makes the choice to die from a position of power and authority?

5. Jesus loved you so much that he willingly chose to take your place beneath the judgment seat. What comes to mind as you reflect on the depth of his love and his sacrifice for you? If you find it helpful, use one for more of the following sentence starters as part of your response:

> Because of your love, I . . .
> Your sacrifice for me means . . .
> *I praise you for loving me by* . . .

CHAPTER 30

THE STORY OF MARY MAGDALENE

A Demon-Possessed Woman Becomes a Devoted Disciple

News about him spread all over Syria, and people brought to him all who were ill with various diseases, those suffering severe pain, the demon-possessed, those having seizures, and the paralyzed; and he healed them.

MATTHEW 4:24

He is close enough to smell her unwashed body and to see the caked-on dirt that lines her fingernails. Greasy strands of hair straggle from beneath her scarf, framing a face that looks far older than it is. She is sitting in shadows, rocking back and forth and looking straight through him, as though he doesn't exist. He watches as she clutches her throat as if she is trying to throttle the voices that come unbidden.

Her fits arrive like sudden tempests. Gales of shrieking laughter, followed by loud wailing, and then a long spell of muttering, as though she is conversing with ghosts that no one else can see. He listens to their changing pitch as one follows another in quick succession. One is low and threatening, the next high and wheedling. They snarl, quarrel, and bite each other, this tangle of demons that lives inside her.

The people of Magdala are used to Mary's fits. She is mad, they say, hopeless and beyond help. Surely she has committed terrible sins to deserve such torment. Unable to understand her, people simply ignore her. All except the children, who cringe and keep their distance. The mean ones taunt her, calling out "Devil Girl!" or "Witch!" whenever she passes by.

But she is no witch. Only a tortured soul whose mind has already descended into hell while her body lives on earth.

Jesus knows this. That's why he's come. To save her. As he steps closer, she grabs a fistful of stones from the mound of rocks heaped beside her feet. Before she can launch the first, she hears him saying something sharp and clear: "Come out!"

His voice is so commanding that it shakes her to the core. She feels the ground begin to shake too. But instead of swallowing her whole and dragging her down to the grave, as she thinks it must, it is something deep inside that shatters, a locked place filled with fear. Then, with a shudder, she feels them leave. Before she can make sense of what has happened, she hears screams of mingled rage and terror. But they are not hers. Disembodied now, the demons howl and fade away.

A great weight of anguish has been lifted, and she is herself again. How long has she been trapped beneath the darkness that took possession of her soul? She cannot say. She only knows her chains are broken. She feels so light she thinks that she will float away.

"Mary," Jesus says, calling her back to herself. His voice is tender and familiar, as though he has known her all her life. When she takes his outstretched hands in hers, she sees in his expression only love and mercy, but so deep and wide she cannot measure it. Tears roll softly down her cheeks and a smile lights her face—the first in many years.

Months later, she has become a kind of celebrity. "There she is!" People point and jostle for a closer look as a group of Jesus's disciples pass by. They cannot imagine how such a stately woman, tall and self-possessed, could have lost herself in so much darkness. But many have heard the story from eyewitnesses, friends and family members who were present when the miracle occurred.

Now Mary of Magdala travels freely with those who number themselves among Jesus's close disciples. Joanna, Susanna, and several other female disciples pay for Jesus's expenses out of their own purses.[1] Wherever they go, they are the topic of conversation. To see a band of men and women roaming from town to town as they follow their rabbi is surprising if not shocking, a matter of outrage to some who see it as yet another mark against this controversial rabbi. For women normally travel in the company of unrelated men only when they are able to spend the night with relatives.

Though the gospels don't comment on whether anyone was scandalized by the fact that female disciples traveled with Jesus and his male disciples, it is likely that the social scene presented in the gospel would have been extraordinary.[2] ■

But Mary cares nothing for convention or about where she will rest her head at the end of the day. She simply wants to be with Jesus. To love and serve him and to learn from him and follow him. So she is there on the mountaintop when he multiplies bread to feed thousands and there when he astonishes the poor and the rich by declaring that the first will be last and the last will be first.

She watches as he opens the eyes of the blind and enables the lame to walk. Whenever Jesus drives out demons, she is the first to share her story and pray with those who've been set free. A leader among the women, she buoys everyone by her faith.

Mary has been traveling the length and breadth of Galilee and Judea with Jesus and the other disciples. Now they are heading into Jerusalem for the feast of Passover. The city has become a cauldron of political and religious fervor. Accompanied by a great crush of people, they walk down the Mount of Olives beside Jesus who is riding on a donkey—a symbol of humility, indicating that he will ascend his throne through peaceful rather than violent means. Voices in the crowd acclaim him, shouting:

"Hosanna to the Son of David!"

"Blessed is he who comes in the name of the Lord!"

"Hosanna in the highest heaven."

She feels a thrill at his triumphant entry into Jerusalem, as he rides over the cloaks and palm branches people have strewn across the road. Despite the fact that he has encountered stubborn opposition from the religious elite, ordinary people want to make him king. She wonders what the next few days will hold and what wondrous work God will do to put Jesus on the throne.

Though Mary is aware of the political risks, she is certain that nothing is impossible for God. Haven't the prophets spoken of this day? Hasn't God provided miracles and wonders pointing to the fact that Jesus is the Messiah they've all been waiting for?

In the midst of her jubilation, Mary cannot imagine that in just a few days she will become part of another crowd, a great throng of people who will accompany Jesus again. But this time he will be on his way out of the city and up to the place of execution.

Joining thousands of other pilgrims, Mary stays in Jerusalem to celebrate the great feast of Passover. Like the rest of her people, she will commemorate God's deliverance by recalling the wonderful deeds he did for them in Egypt, delivering them from the hand of their oppressors and leading them toward the land of promise. It is a time of feasting and celebration that will last late into the night.

When Mary finally awakens it is not to rumors of glory but to unthinkable disaster. She hears that the Lord has been arrested, tried, whipped, and sentenced to death!

The gospels indicate that Jesus was crucified at Golgotha, or "the place of the skull." Though we don't know its exact location, the Church of the Holy Sepulcher, which was built in the fourth century, marks the likely spot today. At the time of Jesus, this may have been an oval-shaped abandoned quarry where there were both tombs and gardens.[3]

———

Both Roman and Jewish law mandated that crucifixions take place outside the city walls. The Romans usually planted crosses along heavily trafficked roads so that this gruesome form of execution would serve as a deterrent to would-be criminals and rabble-rousers.

Even now he is being marched to the quarry outside the city walls where criminals are crucified.

She hurries to join the swelling crowd, praying the rumors are false. As she makes her way through the mob she looks for Jesus's disciples. But the twelve are nowhere to be seen.[4] Then she catches sight of her friends—Mary the mother of Jesus, Salome, and Mary the mother of James and Joseph. They are clinging to each other, inconsolable. Jesus is lying on the ground a few feet away. A heavy beam has just fallen across his shoulders, and his tunic is soaked with blood. On his head he wears a crown of thorns.

"Get up!" the soldiers yell, grabbing his arm and pulling him to his feet. As he staggers forward, the women try to break through the crowd to reach him. But the soldiers push back and their anguished cries are drowned by the deafening roar of the mob.

Now Mary is holding on to Salome's hand as the two stumble forward, toward the place of crucifixion. She watches as Jesus is stripped and nailed to the crossbeam, which is then fastened to a tall upright beam that's already fixed in the ground. Soldiers press his legs to either side of the wood, driving long nails into his ankles in order to fasten him to the cross.

The scene is so gruesome that many who see it double over, unable to control their stomachs. Though Mary has seen crucified people lining the road before, she has never been this close. Unwilling to leave Jesus, she stays with her friends who keep

Though victims were often crucified without clothing, the Romans were aware of Jewish scruples about nakedness and would probably have left Jesus with a loincloth.[5] ■

Wood was scarce, so crossbeams may have been used more than once. They were carried by the condemned person to the place of execution and then affixed to upright beams or trees that were already in place. ■

Crosses could be shaped like an X, Y, I, or T.[6] ■

vigil together, watching and waiting. As people pass in and out of the city along the busy road that skirts the quarry, some stop and shake their heads, shouting at Jesus, "You who are going to destroy the temple and build it in three days, save yourself! Come down from the cross, if you are the Son of God."[7]

The priests and the elders join the mocking, saying, "He saved others, but he can't save himself! He trusts in God. Let God rescue him."

Mary wants to slap them, to scream in their faces, and tell them the truth, that of all the fools who ever walked upon the earth they are the worst. But before she can make a move, darkness descends over the entire area. With it comes the weight of a sorrow too deep to voice. Despite the burden of her grief, she will not leave the Lord. How can she abandon her deliverer when there is no one to deliver him?

After a long while, she hears Jesus crying out in a loud voice, *"Eli, Eli, lama sabachthani?"* which means, "My God, my God, why have you forsaken me?"

She feels it now, the agony she tried to keep her heart from knowing. The question she cannot stop herself from asking breaks out. *Where is Abba? How can he abandon his beloved Son to this tortured death?*

Through the shadows she sees men moving. They are lifting up a sponge soaked in wine and fastened to a stick, offering it to Jesus to ease his suffering. But he will not take it. Then she hears him cry out again in a loud voice: "Father, into your hands I commit my spirit."

Before Mary and the other women can voice their grief, the earth begins to shake and rumble. Huge rocks split apart. Crevices open in the earth. Those who had been mocking Jesus moments earlier now cower in the blackness that surrounds them.

When the earth finally settles, they slink away, one by one. Now only the women and a contingent of Roman soldiers are left. By evening, a secret disciple of Jesus, a wealthy man by the name of Joseph of Arimathea, arrives. He has obtained permission to remove the broken body from the cross and carry it to a tomb that's been freshly carved in a section of the quarry. At least Jesus will not suffer the disgrace of a shameful burial, his body flung into a common pit along with executed criminals.

Sitting opposite the tomb, Mary watches as Jesus is laid to rest. Loaded down with spices, Joseph and Nicodemus, a member of the Jewish ruling council and a secret follower of Jesus, crouch low to enter the tomb. Packing the body, they wrap it in linen strips as is the custom. Once they finish, they seal the tomb by rolling a large stone across the entrance, preventing animals from entering.

John 19:39 indicates that Nicodemus brought with him about seventy-five pounds of myrrh and aloes, an astonishing amount in line with what would have been used for royal burials.[8] ▪

That night Mary barely sleeps. Passing in and out of dreams, she listens as the shrill voices of her old tormenters batter her heart. Taunting and triumphant, they tell her they have won and that they will soon return and never leave. No one can help her now.

But the love of God creates a barrier they cannot pass.

On Sunday, Mary rises early, before daybreak, and hurries to Jesus's grave along with two other women—Salome and Mary the mother of James. It is the only thing she can think to do. She and the other women carry spices they will use to anoint his body. Leaving soon after sunrise, they remember the large stone that bars the entry to the tomb. Who will roll it away so they can enter?

But there is no need to worry, because the stone has already been removed. Peering inside, Mary realizes that Jesus's body is gone. Someone has stolen it! Rushing into the city, she finds Peter and John, telling them, "They've taken the Lord and we don't know where they've put him!"

Running to the grave, Peter enters first. He sees strips of linen lying on the ground and the burial cloth that had been around Jesus's head now neatly folded and set aside.

After Peter and John return to the city, Mary remains at the tomb, weeping. Bending over to look inside, she is startled by two angels in brilliant white, seated on the ledge where Jesus's body had been.

"Woman, why are you crying?" they ask.

"They've taken my Lord away, and I don't know where they've put him."

Then from behind her, another voice, inquires: "Why are you weeping? Who is it you are looking for?"

Turning around she sees a man she thinks must be the gardener. Pleading with him, she says, "Sir, if you have carried him away, tell me where you have put him, and I will get him." Though Mary had been powerless to prevent Jesus's shameful death, she will do anything to ensure he is treated reverently in death.

Then a single word disarms her. "Mary," the man says, and the tenderness in his voice is unmistakable.

"Rabboni!" she exclaims.

Before she can reach out and touch him, Jesus says, "Do not hold on to me, for I have not yet returned to the Father. Go instead to my brothers and tell them, 'I am ascending to my Father and your Father, to my God and your God.'"

Suddenly the darkness that has been stalking Mary for the last three days lifts and an explosion of joy fills her soul. Jesus is alive! Death has been defeated! Anything is possible now!

So Mary Magdalene, from whom Jesus had expelled seven demons, is chosen by God to be present at the moment the greatest story in the history of the world reaches its stunning climax. Loving Jesus to the bitterest of bitter ends, she is the first person to be given the honor of sharing the good news of his resurrection from the dead, telling others, "I have seen the Lord!"

THE TIMES

Mary Magdalene's story probably took
place between AD 27 and 30.
*Her story is told in Matthew 27:56, 61; Mark 15:40,
47; 16:1–11; Luke 8:2; 24:10; John 19:25; 20:1–18.*

In the ancient Near East, belief in demons and in the power
of magical incantations and amulets to control them was common.
By contrast, the Bible discouraged people from the use of magic or
from trying to make contact with spirits. Both the Old and New
Testaments make it clear that only God has complete power over
evil spirits. Notably, when Jesus delivered Mary and others from
evil spirits, he did so based on his authority and not on the use of
magical incantations or objects.

Throughout the centuries, many writers have mistakenly
portrayed Mary Magdalene as a harlot, confusing her with the
woman who lived a sinful life and who washed Jesus's feet with
her tears. But the gospels merely identify her as a woman suffering
from demonic possession. After her deliverance, Mary became a
devoted disciple of Jesus, traveling with him along with other of
his followers. Some scholars believe she may have been a leader in
the early church. Her name is preserved in all four gospels, and
she is also mentioned first in the list of women disciples presented
in Luke 8:1–3 and first among the women mentioned in Mark
16:1.

Mary Magdalene was also the most prominent witness of Jesus's
death, burial, and resurrection. Since women were not considered
reliable witnesses in early first-century Israel, many scholars see this
as more evidence of the veracity of the New Testament. They point

out that no writer of that period would have willingly included such information unless it were true.

Though most of the disciples fled when Jesus was arrested, Mary and many other women were with him at the crucifixion. As a woman who remained faithful to Jesus throughout his crucifixion, death, burial, and resurrection, she is a model of what it means to follow Jesus.

When the Romans crucified insurrectionists or criminals, they usually left their decaying bodies hanging on the cross to serve as a mark of shame and a crude warning to other malcontents. But it was Jewish practice to bury bodies on the day of death.

Ordinary people were buried in shallow pits while the wealthy were buried in family tombs carved from the rock. Generally these consisted of underground chambers accessed through a low entry-way and sealed by a stone to keep animals out. The body was laid on a bench cut into the rock, anointed with oil and spices, and then wrapped in linen strips. The jaw may have been held in place by a separate piece of cloth that wrapped around the head, and the entire body may then have been wrapped in a shroud.

Among the Jews, as with many people, burial practices were extremely important. For a body to be left in the open rather than being honorably buried was considered shameful and tragic.

THE TAKEAWAY

1. Mary's experience of Jesus presents a dramatic "before and after" story. How have your own encounters with Jesus changed your life? Comment on other "before and after" stories of people you know who have encountered Christ in a deep way.

2. What compelled Mary and the other women to stay at the cross? Do you think you would have had the strength to do the same?

3. When tragedy or difficulty strikes, we might be tempted to think that darkness is stronger than light. How have you experienced God in times of personal darkness?

4. Imagine that Jesus has just spoken your name as you stand weeping outside of his empty tomb. What does that feel like? How does this experience impact your understanding of who he is? Of who you are in relationship to him?

ACKNOWLEDGMENTS

As always, it takes—if not a village—at least a good sized crowd to publish a book and then launch it with any degree of success. I am grateful to David Morris, Zondervan's trade publisher, and to associate publisher Sandy Vander Zicht, both of whom enthusiastically supported the idea for this book. Along with Alicia Kasen, senior marketing director of Zondervan trade books, and Sue Smith, manager of Baker Book House, a stellar bookstore right in my own backyard (or perhaps I am in theirs), they formed a team of experts who advised me as I explored how to focus and shape the book.

As with many of my previous books, Sandy Vander Zicht was able to bring her considerable editorial skill and experience to the project, providing guidance that has helped improve it in countless ways. I am thankful for her role as friend, encourager, and devil's advocate, a part that every good editor must play. As I think of her contributions to the book, I am reminded of how Erik Larson acknowledged his editor at Crown Publishers, saying, "She proved a master at the art of offering praise, while at the same time shoving tiny knives under each of my fingernails . . . ."[1] Thank you, Sandy, for being generous with the praise while sparing most of my fingernails, at least for the time being.

Thanks also to Christine Anderson and John Sloan, both of whom supplied wonderful encouragement and many insightful suggestions for how the manuscript could be improved. I am very grateful to Bob Hudson for his careful editorial hand as he guided the project to its conclusion and am also indebted to the late Verlyn Verbrugge for the considerable help he rendered not just for this book, but for many of the books I have published over the course of my writing career.

On the marketing side, I am grateful to Alicia Kasen and her team—for their unflagging work ethic and their constant creative efforts to spread the word about this book.

Gratitude also goes to my agent, Sealy Yates, for his wise counsel, which I have come to rely on over the course of many years. Thanks also to Karen Yates, who provided critical help when it came time to title the book.

I'm also grateful to my friend Chris Meyer, who suggested I read Leon Kass's fascinating book *The Beginning of Wisdom: Reading Genesis*. Kass's insights into the first book of the Bible were immensely helpful as I wrestled with how to retell the foundational stories of Judaism.

The *Zondervan Illustrated Bible Backgrounds Commentary* was another rich resource for understanding the ancient biblical world and the stories that help bring it to life.

Whatever the book's deficiencies may be, I hope readers will be able to overlook them and that they will share my enthusiasm for the ancient stories that have shaped our civilization and for the rich insights they inevitably yield to those who spend time reflecting on them.

NOTES

Introduction

1. Quoted in Cornelius Plantinga Jr., *Engaging God's World* (Grand Rapids: Eerdmans, 2002), 49.

Chapter 1: The Story of Adam

1. Lois Tverberg, "Together Again," Engedi Resource Center, posted on http://www.egrc.net/articles/Rock/Jesus'_Jewish_Teachings/TogetherAgain.html.
2. Ibid.

Chapter 2: The Story of Eve

1. For an insightful commentary on Genesis and for more on why the garden of Eden might be considered part of God's residence in Eden, see John H. Walton, "Genesis," *Zondervan Illustrated Bible Backgrounds Commentary on the Old Testament*, ed. John H. Walton (Grand Rapids: Zondervan, 2009), 1:10–38.

Chapter 3: The Story of Cain

1. Though the NIV translates Genesis 4:1 as "With the help of the LORD I have brought forth a man," Leon Kass points out that this conventional rendering is an interpretative interpolation and that

the context favors, "I have gotten [*or* created] a man [equally] with God." See Leon R. Kass, *The Beginning of Wisdom: Reading Genesis* (Chicago: The University of Chicago Press, 2003), 126.

2. See John H. Walton, "Genesis," *Zondervan Illustrated Bible Backgrounds Commentary on the Old Testament*, ed. John H. Walton (Grand Rapids: Zondervan, 2009), 1:38.

Chapter 4: The Story of Sarah

1. See John H. Walton, "Genesis," *Zondervan Illustrated Bible Backgrounds Commentary on the Old Testament*, ed. John H. Walton (Grand Rapids: Zondervan, 2009), 1:73–74.

2. See John H. Walton, "Genesis," 1:91.

Chapter 5: The Story of Jacob and Esau

1. Many commentators criticize Rebekah for her duplicity. But what if Rebekah is the heroine of this family drama? What if she, unlike her elderly husband, has come to realize that of her two sons, only one is fit to take over the leadership of the clan, thus carrying the covenant forward? For a fascinating discussion of this story, see Leon R. Kass, *The Beginning of Wisdom: Reading Genesis* (Chicago: The University of Chicago Press, 2003), 376–403.

2. See the note to Genesis 30:25, *NIV Cultural Backgrounds Study Bible*, ed. John H. Walton and Craig S. Keener (Grand Rapids, Zondervan, 2016), 70.

3. See John H. Walton, "Genesis," *Zondervan Illustrated Bible Backgrounds Commentary on the Old Testament*, ed. John H. Walton (Grand Rapids: Zondervan, 2009), 1:115.

4. The location of Rachel's tomb is contested though the traditional site is just outside of Bethlehem.

5. According to Genesis 46:15, Jacob had additional daughters, whose names are not mentioned.

Chapter 6: The Story of Shechem

1. The text doesn't say how old Dinah was but she was a young girl, probably about twelve or thirteen years old.
2. I am indebted to Leon Kass's interpretation of this ancient story. For more details see Leon R. Kass, *The Beginning of Wisdom: Reading Genesis* (Chicago: The University of Chicago Press, 2003), 476–499.
3. Leon R. Kass, *The Beginning of Wisdom: Reading Genesis* (Chicago: The University of Chicago Press, 2003), 313.
4. Ibid., 314.

Chapter 7: The Story of Tamar

1. While many translations of the story seem to indicate that Tamar was functioning as a shrine prostitute, that is, as a woman who engaged in fertility rites, scholars now think that this may be a mistranslation and that the Hebrew word may simply mean "prostitute." So it seems unlikely that Tamar and Judah were engaging in some kind of pagan fertility rite.
2. Despite the fact that this Hittite law was recorded long after the period in which this story takes place, it captures the law as it may have been practiced at the time of Judah and Tamar. Quoted in John H. Walton, "Genesis," *Zondervan Illustrated Bible Backgrounds Commentary on the Old Testament*, ed. John H. Walton (Grand Rapids: Zondervan, 2009), 1:126.

Chapter 8: The Story of Judah and His Terrible Brothers

1. For an in-depth consideration of how Judah has grown into a man capable of leading his unruly family, see Leon R. Kass, *The Beginning of Wisdom: Reading Genesis* (Chicago: The University of Chicago Press, 2003), 509–648.

2. For a fascinating but critical look at Joseph see Leon R. Kass, *The Beginning of Wisdom: Reading Genesis* (Chicago: The University of Chicago Press, 2003), 509–526, 538–659.

Chapter 9: The Story of Miriam

1. Also known as Mount Sinai.

2. See "The Egyptian Priests and Their Snakes," in *The Archeological Study Bible*, ed. Walter C. Kaiser Jr. (Grand Rapids: Zondervan, 2005), 96.

3. Though the biblical text translates the scene as though Miriam is playing a tambourine, scholars indicate that the tambourine had not yet been invented. More probably the text is referring to a hand drum of some kind. See Miriam Feinberg Vamosh, *Women at the Time of the Bible* (Nashville: Abingdon, 2007), 66.

4. Moses married a Cushite woman before returning to Egypt to deliver his people from slavery.

Chapter 10: The Story of Pharaoh, King of Egypt

1. See Leon R. Kass, *The Beginning of Wisdom: Reading Genesis* (Chicago: The University of Chicago Press, 2003), 654.

2. For an explanation on how this Hebrew word came to be mistranslated as "Jehovah," see my book, *Praying the Names of God* (Grand Rapids: Zondervan, 2004), 74–78.

Chapter 11: The Story of Rahab

1. Quoted in Richard S. Hess, "Joshua," *Zondervan Illustrated Bible Backgrounds Commentary on the Old Testament*, ed. John H. Walton (Grand Rapids: Zondervan, 2009), 2:19.

Chapter 14: The Story of Hannah and Peninnah

1. See Mary's prayer, which is often called "The Magnificat," in Luke 1:46–55.
2. For a more complete explanation of sacrifice at this time, see William K. Gilders, "Sacrifice in Ancient Israel," *Teaching the Bible: An E-Newsletter for Public School Teachers by Society of Biblical Literature*, http://www.sbl-site.org/assets/pdfs/TBv2i5_Gilders2.pdf.

Chapter 15: The Story of Saul

1. See "Introduction to 1 Samuel," in *The Archaeological Study Bible*, ed. Walter C. Kaiser Jr. (Grand Rapids: Zondervan, 2005), 396.

Chapter 16: The Story of the Medium of Endor

1. Though the Bible doesn't say she was a widow, the medium of Endor is pictured alone. Since widows had little power to provide for themselves, it is conceivable that one might turn to the practice of sorcery to stay alive despite the dangers.
2. See "Akkadian Divination," in *The Archeological Study Bible*, ed. Walter C. Kaiser Jr. (Grand Rapids: Zondervan, 2005), 277.

Chapter 17: The Story of Michal

1. Though the poetry quoted here was not written by David but is part of the Song of Songs (4:1, 3, 5–7), David was a poet/musician and might well have composed a love song for Michal.
2. Most scholars believe that Michal placed a household idol on the bed.

Chapter 18: The Story of David

1. Quoted in V. Philips Long, "2 Samuel," *Zondervan Illustrated Bible Backgrounds Commentary on the Old Testament*, ed. John H. Walton (Grand Rapids: Zondervan, 2009), 2:416.

2. See V. Philips Long, "2 Samuel," *Zondervan Illustrated Bible Backgrounds Commentary on the Old Testament*, ed. John H. Walton (Grand Rapids: Zondervan, 2009), 2:457.

3. In 2 Samuel 11:3, Bathsheba is identified as the daughter of Eliam. If this is the same Eliam mentioned in 2 Samuel 23:34, he would have been one of David's best soldiers. Eliam's father was Ahithophel, a close advisor to the king. These associations would have made David's sin all the worse in the eyes of his contemporaries.

4. Commentators disagree on whether Bathsheba bears any responsibility for what happened. Kenneth Bailey makes the case that Bathsheba knew what she was doing when she bathed in clear sight of the palace. (See Kenneth E. Bailey, *Jesus through Middle Eastern Eyes* [Downers Grove, IL: InterVarsity, 2008], 40–41). Others cast her as an innocent victim. If the latter is true, David's sins would have been even more grievous.

5. Though Uriah was a foreign mercenary, he was a worshiper of the Lord. He is numbered as one of David's mighty men (2 Samuel 23:39; 1 Chronicles 11:41).

6. The Bible indicates that David wrote this psalm (Psalm 51) after he was confronted by Nathan for his adultery with Bathsheba.

7. See V. Philips Long, "2 Samuel," *Zondervan Illustrated Bible Backgrounds Commentary on the Old Testament*, ed. John H. Walton (Grand Rapids: Zondervan, 2009), 2:461.

8. See Phillip Keller, *A Shepherd Looks at Psalm 23* (Grand Rapids: Zondervan, 1997), 97.

Chapter 19: The Story of Bathsheba

1. For a different interpretation of Bathsheba's role in the story, read Ann Spangler and Jean Syswerda, *Women of the Bible* (Grand Rapids: Zondervan, 2007), 176–84.

Chapter 20: The Story of David's Sons—Amnon, Absalom, and Adonijah

1. The Bible does not explicitly state that David did nothing. But its silence on the point combined with subsequent events would seem to indicate that he did nothing to insure that his daughter received justice.

2. See V. Philips Long, "1 Samuel," *Zondervan Illustrated Bible Backgrounds Commentary on the Old Testament*, ed. John H. Walton (Grand Rapids: Zondervan, 2009), 2:370.

3. David's second son, whom he had with his wife Abigail, was Kiliab. It may be that he had previously died as there is no mention of him in this story.

4. In 2 Samuel 14:2, she is called a "wise woman." In this instance, she is probably characterized as "wise" because of her shrewdness and her ability to persuade others.

5. In addition to serving as part of a city's defensive structure, city gates were places where markets were held and legal proceedings conducted. Prophets sometimes delivered messages at the city gates, and kings frequently held audiences in which the public could bring up matters requiring the king's decision.

6. In 2 Samuel 11:3, Eliam is identified as Bathsheba's father. If this is the same Eliam mentioned as the son of Ahithophel in 2 Samuel 23:34, Ahithophel would have been Bathsheba's grandfather.

7. Princes and kings usually rode on mules. The rich symbolism of Absalom's demise is spelled out in the note to 2 Samuel 18:9 in *The*

Archaeological Study Bible, ed. Walter C. Kaiser Jr. (Grand Rapids: Zondervan, 2005), 2:466.

8. *Zondervan Illustrated Bible Backgrounds Commentary on the Old Testament*, ed. John H. Walton (Grand Rapids: Zondervan, 2009), 2:469.

9. See D. Freedman, "Kingly Chronologies: Then and Later," *Eretz-Israel* 24 (1993): 41*-65* as cited in John Monson, "1 Kings," *Zondervan Illustrated Bible Backgrounds Commentary on the Old Testament*, ed. John H. Walton (Grand Rapids: Zondervan, 2009), 3:98.

10. Even though the text does not indicate that Bathsheba realized what Adonijah was asking for, she would have remembered how Absalom slept with David's concubines to advance his own claim to the throne. It is possible that she purposely repeated Adonijah's request to get her son to eliminate his rival.

11. "The Middle Assyrian Laws," *The Archaeological Study Bible*, ed. Walter C. Kaiser Jr. (Grand Rapids: Zondervan, 2005), 179.

Chapter 21: The Story of Jonah

1. See H. L. Ellison, "Jonah," in Kenneth L. Barker and John R. Kohlenberger III, ed., *Zondervan NIV Bible Commentary* (Grand Rapids: Zondervan, 1994) 1:1464.

2. See H. L. Ellison, "Jonah," in Kenneth L. Barker and John R. Kohlenberger III, ed., *Zondervan NIV Bible Commentary*, (Grand Rapids: Zondervan, 1994) 1:1463.

Chapter 23: The Story of Gomer

1. Hosea 3:1; note that people offered raisin cakes to Baal in thanksgiving for a good harvest.

2. J. Glen Taylor, "Hosea," *Zondervan Illustrated Bible Backgrounds on the Old Testament*, ed. John H. Walton (Grand Rapids: Zondervan, 2009), 5:6.

Chapter 25: The Story of Herodias and Salome

1. Though the gospel does not say this, it is a reasonable assumption that Herodias would have traveled to Jerusalem with her husband at that time.

Chapter 27: The Story of the Woman Who Wiped the Feet of Jesus

1. I am indebted to Kenneth E. Bailey for his fascinating interpretation of this story in his book *Jesus through Middle Eastern Eyes* (Downers Grove, IL: InterVarsity Press, 2008), 239–60. Though Bailey does not speculate on whether Simon showed signs of repentance as I have done in this story, he does make it clear that the story Jesus tells Simon speaks of forgiveness that is extended to both people, the one with the large debt and the one with the small one, implying that Simon is the person with the smaller debt.

2. Dr. Steven Notley as mentioned in Ann Spangler and Lois Tverberg, *Sitting at the Feet of Rabbi Jesus* (Grand Rapids: Zondervan, 2018), 217.

Chapter 28: The Story of Judas Iscariot

1. See "The 'Jews' and 'Jewish Leaders'" in *NIV Cultural Backgrounds Study Bible*, ed. John H. Walton and Craig S. Keener (Grand Rapids, Zondervan, 2016), 1810.

2. The Bible doesn't indicate whether Judas drew this conclusion, but it is a plausible explanation for his decision to betray Jesus. Like everyone else, the disciples were expecting a Messiah who would be a great military leader who would overthrow Rome.

3. For more on the rabbi-disciple relationship in the first century, see Ann Spangler and Lois Tverberg, *Sitting at the Feet of Rabbi Jesus*

(Grand Rapids: Zondervan, 2018) and my book *Praying the Names of Jesus* (Grand Rapids: Zondervan, 2006), 134–37.

Chapter 29: The Story of Pontius Pilate

1. See Luke 22:66, which seems to indicate that a second session of the Sanhedrin was held shortly after sunrise in order to give the appearance of legitimacy.
2. See note on Mark 15:4, *The Archaeological Study Bible*, ed. Walter C. Kaiser Jr. (Grand Rapids: Zondervan, 2005), 1659.
3. See note on Matthew 27:28–31, *The Archaeological Study Bible*, ed. Walter C. Kaiser Jr. (Grand Rapids: Zondervan, 2005), 1614.

Chapter 30: The Story of Mary Magdalene

1. That Jesus had female disciples is attested to in Matthew 12:48–50; Luke 8:1–3; 10:38; and Acts 9:36.
2. See Kenneth E. Bailey, *Jesus through Middle Eastern Eyes* (Downers Grove, IL: InterVarsity, 2008), 192–93.
3. See David E. Garland, "Mark," *Zondervan Illustrated Bible Backgrounds Commentary*, ed. Clinton E. Arnold (Grand Rapids: Zondervan, 2002), 1:298–99.
4. John's gospel is the only one of the four gospels to indicate that any of Jesus's twelve disciples were present (John 19:27).
5. See David E. Garland, "Mark," 1:301.
6. See note on John 19:17, *Archaeological Study Bible*, ed. Walter C. Kaiser Jr. (Grand Rapids: Zondervan, 2005), 1758.
7. Matthew 27:40.
8. See note on John 19:39, *Archaeological Study Bible*, 1760.

Acknowledgments

1. Erik Larson, *Dead Wake* (New York: Crown Publishers, 2015), 358.

Sitting at the Feet of Rabbi Jesus

How the Jewishness of Jesus Can Transform Your Faith

Ann Spangler and Lois Tverberg

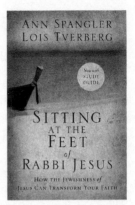

A rare chance to know Jesus as his first disciples knew him.

What would it be like to journey back to the first century and sit at the feet of Rabbi Jesus as one of his Jewish disciples? How would your understanding of the gospel have been shaped by the customs, beliefs, and traditions of the Jewish culture in which you lived?

Sitting at the Feet of Rabbi Jesus takes you on a fascinating tour of the Jewish world of Jesus, offering inspirational insights that can transform your faith. Ann Spangler and Lois Tverberg paint powerful scenes from Jesus' ministry, immersing you in the prayers, feasts, history, culture, and customs that shaped Jesus and those who followed him. You will hear the parables as they must have sounded to first-century Jews, powerful and surprising. You will join the conversations that were already going on among the rabbis of his day. You will watch with new understanding as the events of his life unfold. And you will emerge with new excitement about the roots of your own Christian faith.

Sitting at the Feet of Rabbi Jesus will change the way you read Scripture and deepen your understanding of the life of Jesus. It will also help you to adapt the rich prayers and customs you learn about to your own life, in ways that both respect and enrich your Christian faith. By looking at the Jewishness of Jesus, Ann Spangler and Lois Tverberg take you on a captivating journey into the heart of Judaism, one that is both balanced and insightful, helping you to better understand and appreciate your own faith.

This newly expanded softcover edition includes a discussion guide for both individuals and groups, and instructions for a simple home Passover Seder celebration.

Praying the Names of God

Ann Spangler, Bestselling Author

A twenty-six-week devotional study by the bestselling coauthor of *Women of the Bible*. Names in the ancient world did more than simply distinguish one person from another, they often conveyed the essential nature and character of a person. This is especially true when it comes to the names of God recorded in the Bible.

Praying the Names of God explores the primary names and titles of God in the Old Testament to reveal the deeper meanings behind them. El Shaddai, Elohim, Adonai, Abba, El Elyon—God Almighty, Mighty Creator, Lord, Father, God Most High—these are just a few of the names and titles of God that yield rich insights into his nature and character.

Praying the Names of God shows readers how to study and pray God's names by focusing each week on one of the primary names or titles of God:

- Monday—readers study a portion of Scripture that reveals the name.
- Tuesday-Thursday—readers pray specific Scripture passages related to the name.
- Friday—readers pray Scripture promises connected to the name.

By incorporating the divine names and titles into their prayers—and learning about the biblical context in which the name was revealed—readers will gain a more intimate understanding of who God is and how he can be relied on in every circumstance of their lives. *Praying the Names of God* is a unique devotional, one that offers a rich program of daily prayer and study designed to lead people into fresh encounters with the living God.

Available in stores and online!

ZONDERVAN®
.com

Praying the Names of Jesus

Ann Spangler, Bestselling Author

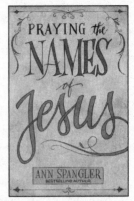

Joy, peace, and power—these are only some of the gifts promised to those who trust in the name of the Lord.

Praying the Names of Jesus will lead readers into a richer and more rewarding relationship with Christ by helping them to understand and pray his names on a daily basis. By understanding the biblical context in which these names and titles were revealed, readers will gain a more intimate knowledge of Jesus and his plan for their lives. They will also begin to see how each of his names holds within it a promise: to be our Teacher, Healer, Friend, and Lord—to be God with Us no matter the circumstances. Prince of Peace, Lamb of God, Bread of Life, Yeshua . . . through his names and titles, we come to understand more fully how Jesus reveals God's heart to us.

Praying the Names of Jesus focuses on twenty-six of his most prominent names and titles to provide six-months of devotions. Each week provides a unique devotional program designed for personal prayer and study or for use in small groups. *Praying the Names of Jesus* is the companion volume to the bestselling *Praying the Names of God*. In ways both surprising and profound, it reveals a rich portrait of Jesus that will move readers toward a deeper experience of his love and mercy.

Available in stores and online!

Women of the Bible

A One-Year Devotional Study

Ann Spangler and Jean E. Syswerda

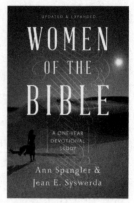

Bestselling, updated, and expanded devotional study, *Women of the Bible*, by Ann Spangler and Jean E. Syswerda, focuses on fifty-two remarkable women in Scripture—women whose struggles to live with faith and courage are not unlike your own.

Special features in *Women of the Bible* include:

- A list of all the women of the Bible
- Timeline of the women of the Bible
- A list of women in Jesus' family tree
- A list of women in Jesus' life and ministry

Vital and deeply human, the women in this book encourage you through their failures as well as their successes. You'll see how God acted in surprising and wonderful ways to draw them—and you—to himself.

This year-long devotional offers a unique method to help you slow down and savor the story of God's unrelenting love for his people, offering a fresh perspective that will nourish and strengthen your personal relationship with him.

Men of the Bible

A One-Year Devotional Study of Men in Scripture

Ann Spangler and Robert Wolgemuth

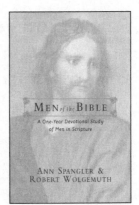

Men of the Bible offers both men and women a fresh way to read and understand the Bible— through the eyes and hearts of the men whose stories unfold in its pages.

This unique book takes a close-up look at fifty-two men in Scripture— complex flesh-and-blood characters whose strengths and weaknesses will seem strangely similar to your own. Heroes and villains, sinners and prophets, commoners and kings ... their dramatic life stories provide you with a fresh perspective on the unfolding story of redemption.

Though our culture differs vastly from theirs, the fundamental issues we face in relation to God and the world remain the same. We still reach for great dreams and selfish ambitions. We wrestle with fear and indecision, struggle with sexual temptation, and experience the ache of loneliness and the devastation of betrayal. And, like many of these men, we long to walk more closely with the God who calls us into an intimate relationship with himself and who enables us to fulfill his purpose for our lives.

Men of the Bible offers men and women today a unique devotional experience that combines five elements. Each week becomes a personal retreat focused on the life of a particular man:

MONDAY: His Story—a narrative retelling of the biblical story
TUESDAY: A Look at the Man—focusing on the heart of the man and how his story connects with your own life
WEDNESDAY: His Legacy in Scripture—a Bible study on principles revealed through the life of the man
THURSDAY: His Legacy of Promise—Bible promises that apply to his life and yours
FRIDAY: His Legacy of Prayer—praying in light of his story

Designed for personal prayer and study or for use in small groups, *Men of the Bible* will help you make Bible reading a daily habit. Whether you dip into portions or read every page, this book will help you grow in character, wisdom, and obedience as a person after God's own heart.

Peace God Promises

Closing the Gap Between What You Experience and What You Long For

Ann Spangler

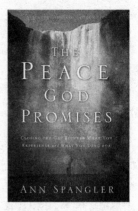

If God has promised to give us the "peace that passes understanding," why do we sometimes feel so anxious? What are we so afraid of? Are there ways of living that lead to peace? Conversely, are there ways of thinking and acting that lead to anxiety and a conflicted life? How does Jesus embody peace and where did his peace come from?

The Peace God Promises sets our longings for peace beside God's promise to provide it.

In her desire to experience greater peace, bestselling author Ann Spangler probes these and other questions. Exploring the stories that shape us, the memories that define us, and the relationships that connect us, she looks for ways to help us become more peaceful.

What can we learn from Scripture, from Jewish tradition, from the Amish and others about rest, simplicity, healing, and peace?

The stories she shares and the answers she discovers may surprise you. If you put them into practice, they may even transform you, enabling you to experience the peace God wants you to have.

Tender Words of God
A Daily Guide

Ann Spangler

This unique devotional is the result of a personal quest. In order to let the truth sink in—that God is love—Ann Spangler began hunting through the Bible for the words that every person longs to hear—words of peace, protection, and mercy. Realizing her tendency to absorb the harsher words of the Bible more easily than its encouraging words, she devoted several months to reading and reflecting only on God's tender words. The result is a series of morning and evening readings designed to cut away our unbelief so that we can hear the truth about love from God himself. Each week contains morning and evening readings, enough for ninety days—passages to soak in and call to mind when one is tempted to doubt. While the core of the book is Scripture, each reading is framed with personal reflections related to the week's theme, making this devotional read equally well as a thought-provoking message for those who want to know God better.

Available in stores and online!